The Great Civil War

CARLISLE

NEWCASTLE

SCARBOROUGH

Marston Moor ✗   ⊙ YORK

Adwalton   ⊙ LEEDS   HULL
PRESTON ⊙   *Moor* ✗

LIVERPOOL   *Gainsboro* ✗   R. Trent

⊙ LINCOLN

CHESTER

Rowton Heath ✗   NEWARK ⊙   *Winceby* ✗
✗   NOTTINGHAM ⊙
Nantwich   ✗
Hopton Heath ✗   *Grantham*

SHREWSBURY   LEICESTER ⊙

✗ *Naseby*

Edge
WORCESTER ⊙   *-hill* ✗
Powick Bridge ✗   *Ripple*
✗ *Field*
R. Severn   OXFORD
GLOUCESTER   ✗ *Chalgrove Field*
R. Thame
Lansdown ✗   READING
BRISTOL ⊙   *Roundway* ✗
Down   ✗ *Newbury*   LONDON
DOVER ⊙
Basing House ✗ *Alton*
✗ *Langport*   ✗ *Cheriton*
✗ *Torrington*   ⊙ SHERBORNE
Stratton   EXETER ⊙   LYME REGIS   POOLE
✗ *Launceston*   PORTSMOUTH
Braddock Down ✗   PLYMOUTH
Lostwithiel   WEYMOUTH
DARTMOUTH

ENGLAND, SHOWING THE SCENES OF THE CIVIL WAR

The Great Civil War

A MILITARY HISTORY OF
THE FIRST CIVIL WAR
1642–1646

Lieut.-Colonel Alfred H. Burne
D.S.O., F.R.HIST.S.

&

Lieut.-Colonel Peter Young
D.S.O., M.C., M.A.

EYRE & SPOTTISWOODE
15 BEDFORD STREET · LONDON WC2

Catalogue No. 6/2375
Printed in Great Britain
by Billing and Sons Ltd., Guildford

Contents

Maps

Preface

To write the history of the Civil War is not a simple matter. At first sight it appears to be quite devoid of form or pattern; a disjointed series of battles, sieges, and skirmishes – several taking place simultaneously in separate corners of the country. There is no county that did not witness the tramp of armed men: few altogether escaped the ravages of war. Yet there was a certain pattern to the campaigns, and it is one of the main objects of this book to disclose it, and, while omitting disconnected actions and insignificant details – however picturesque or thrilling – to trace the main stream of events. Much has had to be omitted so as to keep the book within its planned limits, and for this reason little has been said of the famous sieges of the war, or of contemporary operations in Scotland.

Considering the importance of the Great Civil War in the history of England and of the English-speaking peoples there have been surprisingly few accounts of the struggle. Between the publication of Lord Clarendon's famous but extremely unmilitary work, and that of Dr S. R. Gardiner over two hundred years later no general history of the war appeared, though Miss Veronica Wedgwood's work is now in course of publication. It is still more suprising that the purely military side of the war has been strangely neglected: no soldier has so far written a commentary on the war, the nearest approach being Colonel T. S. Baldock's *Cromwell as a Soldier*, published over half a century ago. The present book is an attempt to repair the omission. It is true that we have in *Cromwell's Army* much valuable detail, which we do not propose to repeat here, of the military administration of the day, particularly of the New Model Army, but there is no modern history of the war as a whole. There are a number of histories, varying in value, of the war in particular regions and counties, but, while recognizing the intense local feeling of the period, it must be admitted that this is an unsatisfactory treatment from a military point of view. Campaigns cannot be confined within the borders of a single county. The war can conveniently be treated by regions, West, North, and Centre, and indeed we have followed this method, but the county is generally too small a unit, and the treatment by counties has led to an exaggeration of the view that the war was nothing more than a disconnected series of petty local struggles.

The war, like any civil war, impinged upon every aspect of the national life, political, religious, economic, and social. All these aspects have been fully dealt with by Miss Wedgwood. In this work we have endeavoured to limit ourselves to the purely military aspects of the first Civil War, for while we do not for one moment believe that the war can be understood without consideration of its social and economic background, we have only treated such questions in so far as is necessary to make the course of military events intelligible.

Though assessments and judgments of events and persons are by their nature matters of mere opinion and even speculation the authors have not shrunk from expressing their views and opinions, sometimes in downright terms, even though they run counter to previously accepted views. The authors can, however, make the somewhat surprising claim that there has been no serious divergence of view between them throughout the book.

In assessing the military merits of the leading figures in the war it should be borne in mind that these assessments refer to the actual period of the First Civil War; the reader should not be influenced by the knowledge of what happened in the later military careers of the chief actors. No men are born leaders, and it is easy, and tempting, to descry in their early actions signs of brilliance that may not have been there.

One must beware of judging the armies and the commanders of the Civil War by modern standards. In the first place it is obvious that the practice of war has moved forward enormously since the days of Edgehill. In the second place the great majority of the combatants were amateurs. One may argue as to the time it takes to turn a recruit into a trained soldier, given good officers, but nobody can deny that the great majority of the men who fought at Edgehill were raw recruits.

The modern officer, however small his aptitude for his profession, and however lacking in originality he may be has but to turn to the manuals and drill-books, memoirs and official histories dealing with every aspect of war. In the Civil Wars it was different. It is true that there were drill-books in plenty, from which one could master the rudiments of infantry and cavalry drill at the regimental level; but there was little indeed to guide the senior officers. Amateurs frequently found themselves commanding brigades, even armies; but there was no manual from which they could learn the Principles of War, or how to give out orders in a clear and logical sequence. By reading such works as *The Commentaries of Sir Francis Vere* the seventeenth century officer might hope to discover some practical methods of conducting operations, but in truth the high commanders had little to depend on but their own genius and the analysis of their own experiences. As time went by a number of efficient tacticians emerged, men who could command in actual combat. Strategists, men with the vision to conceive and control a whole campaign, were then – as ever – rare indeed.

The accounts of nine of the more important battles are based on chapters in *Battlefields of England* and *More Battlefields of England*, both by Lieut.-Colonel A. H. Burne, but all have been thoroughly revised and to some extent rewritten. Thanks are due to Messrs. Methuen and Co. for permission to make use of these passages, as also certain of the maps. Thanks are also due to the Ven. R. V. H. Burne for reading the book in typescript, and for giving much sage advice; to Mr Christopher Hill of Balliol College, Oxford, for his efforts to keep us 'on the rails' where the political aspect of the war is concerned; to Brigadier O. F. G. Hogg for helping with his unrivalled knowledge of ancient ordnance; to Mr H. G. Tibbutt, who has placed unpublished papers of Sir Samuel Luke at our disposal; to Mr P. Whitmore who has drawn several of the maps, and last (but perhaps it should be first) to Mrs Peter Young for typing out not only the whole book several times but also her husband's voluminous correspondence with his colleague.

A. H. B.

September 1958.   P. Y.

The Great Civil War

CHAPTER I

Introduction

Preliminaries

O N 3 NOVEMBER 1640 King Charles I opened his fifth and last parliament – known, for good reason, as the Long Parliament. From the outset there was dissension between the two. This was hardly suprising for King and Parliament held fundamentally different views on the status of the sovereign. Charles held, in the words of the Vicar of Bray, that 'Kings are by God appointed', whereas Parliament – more precisely, a majority of the Commons – maintained that a greater ultimate power should reside in the People. The King wanted money wherewith to maintain his army in the North, for a Scottish army had crossed the Border and had advanced practically unopposed as far as Durham. In addition, he needed money to pay the Scots army who had made this demand an essential preliminary to peace, in order to force Charles to call a Parliament. But Parliament was more intent on the redress of grievances, and the punishment of ministers who were obnoxious to it. Pym, the leader of the opposition, was in secret communication with the invaders and the King was tempted to arrest him for high treason.

The Scots, moreover, had brought with them a crusade for presbyterianism, and a considerable portion of the Commons had been affected by it, whereas the King, as Defender of the Faith, felt it to be a sacred duty to maintain the established church of the land. This caused yet further estrangement between the two parties. The die was cast on 3 January 1642 when Charles with some 300 armed followers went down to the House of Commons and attempted to arrest the five members. Warned of the impending *coup d'état* Pym and his colleagues had, however, taken refuge in the City. The breach was now wide open and amid the howls of the mob the King quitted his capital, never to return as a free man.

Making his way to the North Charles spent the next few months taking measures to form an army, while Parliament did the same in London. On 22 August 1642 the King set up his military standard on a hillock at Nottingham. It was blown down a few days later, to the consternation of the superstitious and faint-hearted. This Setting up of the Standard was the old signal for assembling of retainers and feudatories for military service. It was in effect a declaration of war — civil war.

While the rival hosts are assembling we must take stock of the means and resources at the disposal of each side, on the eve of the first great campaign, which began in October 1642. The first thing to note is that there had been no fighting in England for nearly a century, and knowledge of the military art was at a low ebb. Numerous officers had served on the Continent in the Thirty Years War and in the North during the Bishops' Wars, and a few German and Dutch instructors had been hastily summoned by the Roundheads, as the rebels had been called since the previous winter; nevertheless we must look upon both hosts as armies of amateurs. Every civilian of military age thus became a potential soldier, and in order to compare relative resources it would be a question of counting heads — who were for the King, and who against. Here the historian is in a difficulty, for, as Sir Winston Churchill has put it, it became a 'tragic conflict of loyalties and ideals', with the result that there was no clear cut territorial delineation. It is indeed difficult to find any region, however Royalist or Roundhead in complexion, where there was not an important minority supporting the other party.

Though the great majority of the nobility sided with the King and most of the towns were against him, this was no class war. Educated men enlisted on each side according to the dictates of conscience, though one cannot ignore the great number of tenants who followed their landlord into the field, almost as in feudal times.

The ramifications of county alliances made it difficult for any gentleman to take the field without the risk of crossing swords with some near relative. In Parliament itself the great majority of the Lords and perhaps forty per cent of the Commons may be accounted Royalists. It would be misleading to suggest that M.P.s can be neatly divided into two parties as from the beginning of the Long Parliament. In the course of 1641 and 1642 men's political allegiances became more clearly defined, but, once hostilities had begun, other con-

siderations came to bear – for example, whether a man's estates were
in a Royalist or a Parliamentarian area.

Turning now to physical and material factors, it is first to be noted
that London, the capital, was in the hands of the Roundheads throughout the war. This was a very great asset for with it went its men,
money, port and the Tower armoury, where most of the heavy
ordnance of the country was stored. London sent forth the regiments
of Lord Brooke and Denzil Holles to fight in the first campaign and
in addition there were the 6,000 men of the London Trained Bands;
by 1643 there were no less than 15 regiments of them, 16,000 strong.
These Trained Bands were unique in that they alone could on
occasion be induced to operate away from home. Money was if anything more important even than manpower. The resources of the City
were bound in the long run to outweigh the voluntary contributions
of the King's supporters whose wealth, consisting for the most part of
land, timber, and mines could neither be realized speedily nor at their
real value. This financial strength meant that from the outset the Parliamentary armies were better paid and equipped than their opponents.

Besides the capital, the Roundheads also had the other principal
ports – Bristol, Plymouth, and Hull. This was particularly unfortunate
for the King since the main arsenals in the country were in the hands
of his enemies, and all ordnance stores ordered from abroad had therefore to run the blockade. Most of the other large towns were also in
the possession of Parliament; indeed Oxford was one of the few towns
of importance that Charles could implicitly and continuously rely
upon; others were Chester, Worcester, and Newark.[1]

The economically advanced areas – including the rural clothing
areas – were strongly anti-Royalist. As the war dragged on the
resources of the Home Counties and East Anglia, predominantly
anti-Royalist, weighed heavy in the scales. Once an efficient system of
taxation had been evolved, and once a national army – the New
Model – had replaced the local militias, the ultimate victory of the
Parliament was inevitable. John Pym and Sir Harry Vane had far
greater financial reserves than the King; drawing heavily on the City
companies for administrative personnel, they had a far better organizational potential. The eventual superiority of their artillery, for example,
may be regarded simply as an organizational achievement.

Strategically Parliament enjoyed the advantages of interior lines

[1] A detailed examination of the distribution of the adherents of the two
sides is given in the Appendix to this chapter.

and command of the sea. London was a magnet which attracted the trade of all England. Charles was to try in vain to develop Bristol as a centre for the export of cloth, for merchants behind the Royalist lines in the south-west still preferred the hazards of sending their cloth to the capital, rather than export it via Bristol. Political loyalty to the Parliamentary party may sometimes have prompted men to run the gauntlet of Donnington Castle and the other Royalist fortresses guarding the roads to the West. It is more likely that long-established trading connections account for the risks run. Ties of this sort gave enormous strength to the side that controlled London, quite apart from the capital's resources in men, money, and skilled administrative personnel.

The fleet, with the exception of a few officers, had declared for Parliament in July 1642, and though small it was to prove of great value. For the Summer Guard there were 16 men-of-war in the Downs and two in Irish waters, besides 24 armed merchant ships. Ironically enough it was due to Ship Money, for which they had the King to thank, that they were in good order. Though insufficient to cut off all communication between the Cavaliers and the Continent and Ireland, this fleet was able, when necessary, to relieve Roundhead ports in Cavalier territory, a factor of the first importance. The Roundheads rarely used their command of the sea to assist their land forces by true amphibious operations, but, nevertheless, they exploited it to good effect. On the other hand it is not generally realized that the Cavaliers, particularly those of Cornwall, managed by stupendous efforts to improvise their own navy, and by normal trading and by privateering helped to provide for their armies in the field. At the beginning of the war they had no ports, save Newcastle, Chester, and Falmouth; but in the Channel Islands Castle Cornet in Guernsey and Castle Elizabeth in Jersey ensured their communications with France.

The arms, equipment, and transport of the Royalist armies came in the main from six sources. They were: foreign purchases, captures, improvisation, the magazines of the trained bands, the resources of cities, towns, and universities and private armouries and stables. It is difficult to assess the relative importance of these six sources of supply.

Purchases on the continent were made mainly in Holland, Denmark and France – the former being by far the most important thanks to the influence of the Stadtholder. There was a liberal provision of small-arms from Holland. The Northern Royalist armies would have been very poorly armed had it not been for Frederick Henry of Orange. Aid from Denmark and France was useful but scarcely vital.

Early victories gave the Cavaliers a rich haul of captures in horses as well as arms, ammunition, and ordnance. It was their Western Army which profited most from this source. It is difficult to see how it could have kept the field at all without the windfalls received from the Parliamentarians both by land and sea. The rich spoils of Bristol – shared by the armies of the Centre and the West – were the most important individual prize.

Both sides endeavoured to secure the magazines of the county trained bands, and although it may be that the Parliamentarians secured as many as the Royalists, they were of no special importance to the former, since they could draw on the far better provided armouries of the Tower and of Hull. To the King with no similar fortresses in his hands the munitions of the county trained bands were of great importance. The infantry who accompanied him from York were volunteers from the county trained bands, armed with their ordinary weapons, to which they were already accustomed. As he advanced Charles mustered the trained bands, enrolled those who were ready to fight for him, and disarming the remainder, distributed their arms among such of his supporters as had come out with no better weapon than a scythe, pitchfork, or stout cudgel. In the West the Cornish trained bands, thanks to the influence and loyalty of their colonels, took the field as a well-armed body. They were sufficient to maintain the control until volunteer regiments could be raised from men ready to venture 'abroad' – into Devonshire.

The arms of cities, towns, and universities were a strange assortment. Necessity made the Cavaliers great improvisors. Oxford, their capital, became a veritable arsenal. A powder-mill was set up in the ruins of Osney Abbey and a sword factory at Wolvercot; in the Schools a host of tailors busied themselves with the making of uniforms for the foot. The spoils of the Gloucestershire cloth trade provided coats, breeches, stockings and montero caps for Charles' infantry. The magazine was established in the little cloister of New College, admirably suitable for the purpose being difficult of access. In Magdalen College Grove the train of artillery was parked.

Similar activities went on in the other Royalist centres. York had its press, Newark and Exeter their mints – though the former merely stamped diamond shaped pieces of plate. Shrewsbury had its powder-mill during the period when it was Rupert's headquarters.

The resources of private armouries and stables were of great value. The gentleman who did not have one or more horses was poor indeed. It was the exception rather than the rule for the gentry to go unarmed, and though few may have possessed pistols many could provide fowling pieces. These last were much better made than the ordinary military musket of the time, and served to arm the dragoons. Defensive armour was not easy to come by, and much of it dated from an earlier period[1] some no doubt from as far back as Bosworth and Towton. Nevertheless it was the offensive weapons and the horses that were important.

At first the Cavaliers were unable to give their troopers the normal armour of a seventeenth century 'harquebusier' – back, breast, and pot. Richard Atkyns, for example, tells us that in his troop of 80 men – 20 being gentlemen – only some 30 were fully equipped, two being cuirassiers. Mr John Dutton, one of the richest men in Gloucestershire, if not in the Kingdom, had generously given him nearly all this equipment.

Infantry weapons were also forthcoming though some were obsolescent bills or country-made halberts.

The importance of these private arsenals will be readily appreciated when it is said that noblemen like Lord Paulet and Lord Mohun were able to provide small field-guns.

The Armies

'The history of the Civil War is the history of the evolution of an efficient army out of chaos.' Thus runs the opening sentence of Sir Charles Firth's invaluable *Cromwell's Army*. It follows that any attempt to give a brief description of the two armies can only be the purest generalization, for both were constantly changing. Moreover, both were what may be called amateur organizations, far removed from any 'sealed pattern'. All we can do, therefore, is to present a bald outline of the armies as they were constituted at the outset, ignoring the many exceptions and the abnormal and only glancing at the administrative side. Important changes and developments will be noted in their context as the narrative proceeds.

The High Command

The Royalists enjoyed an indisputable advantage where the High Command was concerned, for there was a single and unchallenged

---

[1] The helmet of one Phillipson – 'Robin the Devil' – is still preserved in Kendall Church. It is evidently an Elizabethan morion.

supreme commander, who combined in his person the political command also. Parliament, on the other hand, attempted to conduct the war by committee – the Committee of Lords and Commons for the Safety of the Kingdom, of which Pym was the unchallenged head and Harry Vane was the most conspicuous member. Neither Pym nor Vane possessed any military experience.

King Charles conducted military affairs through a Council of War, consisting of a variable number of members, senior generals forming the majority. When possible he presided over this Council personally. Lieut.-General Patrick Ruthven, Earl of Forth, a Scotsman who had served in the Swedish army, was virtually the chief of staff of the Royalist armies.

On the Parliamentary side the Captain-General or Commander-in-Chief, the Earl of Essex, exercised a nominal power and control over the subordinate army commanders in the North, East Anglia, and the West, but in practice they seldom sought or regarded his infrequent directions. The King also decentralized to the extent of forming a Council of the West, in 1645, which sat regularly and, in default of specific orders from Oxford, carried on according to their own volition.

In the field, it was customary on both sides to make decisions on major matters of strategy and tactics only on the advice of a war council which consisted of the senior officers, and it required a strong commander such as Prince Rupert to ignore or override them in the presence of the enemy.

Cavalry

In the Civil War the cavalry might well claim to be called the Queen of the Battlefield. Indeed, in the Royalist army it consisted largely of gentry, their tenants, and yeoman farmers. Naturally they were at the outset better mounted than their opponents and better horsemen.

Their armour consisted of 'back and breast' plates and a pot helmet. Their weapons were the sword and a pair of pistols. (Lances were used only in the Scottish army.)

They were organized in regiments (maximum strength 500), each regiment having six troops, two or more troops constituting a 'division'. (Modern squadron.)

Cavalry usually formed the wings of an army drawn up in battle order, the Royalists in three ranks, the Parliamentarians generally in six ranks. In battle they concentrated on the charge, but in the open their function differed but little from that of modern horsed cavalry. The normal procedure in the charge was to advance at a trot to within pistol range of the enemy, halt, discharge pistols and then close, and exchange sword-thrusts until the enemy gave ground. But Prince Rupert changed all this in the Royalist army. He taught his troopers to charge at full gallop, not to pull up or to discharge pistols, but to reserve them for in-fighting after penetrating the hostile ranks. In this matter of three deep and of the galloping charge Rupert was following the example set by Gustavus Adolphus, the Swedish king, whose military reforms were largely adopted in England.

Dragoons

Dragoons were, in effect, mounted infantry, and rode small horses or cobs. They wore no armour. They carried sword and carbine (or sometimes fowling-pieces). They paraded with the cavalry and worked under the orders of the cavalry commander. They were raised as regiments but their organization was a loose one, and they are usually described merely by their numbers. Their main function was to cover the approaches to the position and watch the flanks. To carry out this function their favourite method was to line convenient hedges and ditches in the vicinity. They worked dismounted, a small number being detailed as horseholders to the remainder. On rare occasions they were known to make a mounted charge.

Infantry

The infantry were rightly considered the backbone of the defence in battle. Whereas the majority of the cavalry were volunteers the infantry of both armies were mainly conscripted.

Though similar in type of clothing worn – coat, breeches, stockings, and cap – there was a deal of variety in dress and colour, due to the influence of the regimental colonel, who in many cases had raised the regiment himself. In order to distinguish one side from the other, both armies took to wearing 'field signs' in their head-dress – sprigs of foliage, coloured bands, and so on. Some troops were lucky enough to possess corselets, worn over the coat, and many pikemen wore helmets. Otherwise they usually wore no armour.

Their weapons consisted of musket, or pike and sword. The musket was a matchlock – dangerous near open powder barrels, and useless in the rain which would extinguish the quick match. The few firelocks present in each army were normally employed as escort for the guns.

The range of the musket was about 400 yards, and its rate of fire one round per three minutes. The pike was up to 18 feet in length. When standing to resist a charge it would be grounded, placed against the right foot and held by the left hand, whilst the right hand wielded the sword.

As the musketeer carried but 12 cartridges per man, and replenishment in battle was doubtful, he easily became a prey to cavalry attack. In such cases he was reduced to using the butt of his musket as a personal weapon. The pikeman was not so vulnerable, but he formed an easy target for the hostile artillery.

The organization of the infantry was simple; it revolved round the regiment, whose nominal strength was 1,200 (though that figure was seldom attained), divided into a varying number of companies. A few regiments in large armies would be brigaded together under the senior colonel; but this organization could be freely broken up.

In battle the pikemen were placed in the centre, the musketeers on the wings. The formation was in six ranks, in place of the Swedish ten ranks. The number of ranks was governed by the time taken to reload the musket. The front-rank man, after firing, stepped to the rear, his place being taken by the second rank man, and so on. When the first man worked his way to the front rank again it was calculated that he should just have finished re-loading. Thus a 'rolling fire' could be kept up so long as the ammunition held out.

Whether both armies advanced or only one, they each employed musketry fire during the advance, and when they got within pike-reach of the enemy it became what was called 'push of pike'. In moments of danger the musketeers were placed in the intervals of the pikemen in order to give them protection against cavalry charges.

Artillery

Sir Charles Firth claimed that the skilful use of artillery 'exerted considerable influence in deciding the fortunes of campaigns and battles'. As far as battles are concerned it seems difficult to justify this claim, but there can be no doubt that it was often the most important factor in the reduction of defended towns and fortified places.

The various 'pieces of ordnance' were generally designated by names, more rarely by the weight of shot they fired. For all practical purposes they can be grouped in three classes. *Siege:* cannons (64 pdr.), demi-cannon (32 pdr.), and Culverins (16 pdr.). *Heavy Field:* Demi-Culverins (9 pdr.). *Light Field:* A large variety of ordnance of which the biggest were the 5-pdr. Sakers. The name Drake seems to have been applied to all or any of the lighter pieces – Minions, Falcons, Falconets, Robinets. The term is not used by the artillery writers of the period. The name sprang from a few light pieces which were purchased abroad in 1625. The so-called 'Leather' guns (seldom used) consisted of a metal tube with a leather jacket or covering. These were one-pounders drawn by a single horse, and were a relic of the Middle Ages.

The rate of fire is given by a contemporary writer as 10–12 rounds per hour. He was presumably referring to the heavy guns; the remainder must have been capable of more rapid fire than that. There are no exact data regarding extreme ranges attainable by guns, the difficulty of assessment being that by merely digging a hole for the trail very long ranges could be obtained – over 3,000 yards – but that at these extreme ranges the projectile lost its man-killing power besides being hopelessly inaccurate. In practice heavy field guns would seldom fire at over 1,000 yards, and light guns at over 600 yards. In a siege on the other hand the gunners liked to get as close up to their target as possible, so long as they kept out of musket range, in order to obtain the greatest possible breaching power.

Artillery was normally horse-drawn, but the bigger guns were sometimes drawn by oxen. Whether with horse or ox transport, the artillery could not keep up with the infantry.

Ammunition was solid iron shot, but guns of all calibres occasionally fired cannister or case-shot (small pieces of metal or shot, enclosed in a can or case), and fired at point-blank range.

In a large army the artillery had its own commander, working directly under the army commander. For administrative purposes the guns came under the Lieut.-General of the Ordnance.

In battle, the light field guns were posted – usually in pairs – in the intervals between regiments. Heavy field guns were placed further back, and overhead fire – to use a modern term – must often have been employed.

In the Royalist army galloping guns, small brass pieces, mounted on light carriages were employed with the cavalry, and may be regarded as the earliest form of horse artillery, for the gunners did not march but rode beside them on horseback.

In addition the Train of Artillery included engineers, miners, drivers, artificers, fireworkers, pioneers, and surgeons: in short, everyone who came under the Ordnance department.

Transport

Wagons and carts were generally hired or requisitioned from civilian sources and were controlled by a Wagon-Master General. They were employed in the carriage of wounded, victuals, and ammunition. In the Royalist army good use was made of barges on the Thames between Oxford and Reading. The Roundheads made use of their general command of the sea to transport guns and stores to their outposts, Hull, Plymouth, and Milford Haven, for example. Horse-litters were sometimes used to carry the wounded, and noblemen occasionally provided their coaches for the same purpose.

Pay

The basic rates of pay seem to have been much the same on both sides. In 1644 a Royalist infantry soldier's pay was 4s. a week: in 1645 when the New Model was formed the Roundhead foot soldier received 8d. per diem — much the same as an agricultural labourer — while the dragoon and the cavalry trooper were paid 1s. 6d. and 2s. respectively.[1]

The King had the greatest difficulty in providing pay for his soldiers; officers were fortunate if they received half-pay and the cavalry were usually given free quarters in lieu of pay: many of the troopers were able to subsist only because their families maintained them, and provided them with horses and arms. The Parliament, despite its greater resources, was not a good paymaster. In the early years of the war all was confusion, though mounting money was provided so that troop commanders could buy horses, saddlery, and distinguishing scarves for their men. Even the pay of the New Model army was frequently in arrears.

Numbers

It was at first the practice to exclude officers when describing the size of a force and so most Civil War authorities are inclined to understate by a fairly substantial amount the numbers of the armies engaged. Persons who would now be classed as non-commissioned officers or musicians were counted as officers. As the war progressed the size of regiments tended to diminish. A few wealthy or successful commanders on each side managed to keep up the strength of their regiments either by good pay or by *esprit de corps*, but they were exceptions; notable examples were Prince Rupert, Oliver Cromwell, and the Marquis of Worcester, the last-named because he constantly paid his men from his

[1] The average price of a quarter of wheat was 35s. at this time.

own purse; the first two because they were able to inspire their men with their own tireless energy and devotion to the cause they served.

Throughout the war a strength of 5,000 constituted a respectable army, 12,000 was an exceptional size. It is doubtful whether the King ever commanded as many as 20,000 at any one time.

Miscellaneous

The seventeenth century general's art was greatly hampered by his poor equipment. The *telescope* or 'perspective glass' had been in use since the turn of the century though it was by no means in common use; few generals and even fewer colonels can have enjoyed its aid. *Watches* were probably rather more common, but not sufficiently widely used to secure the synchronization of the movements of separate formations.

Maps too were inadequate. John Speed's survey of 1610 covered the entire country, county by county, but the information given as to roads and rivers was inadequate, while the high ground is shown in a most misleading way.

Foreign Aid

Parliament received little military assistance from the Continent beyond that of individual officers, such as Colonel Johan Rosworm, the German, who was employed by the citizens to direct the defence of Manchester, which he did for six years at a salary of £60 per annum. The Roundheads had the sympathy of the States of Holland. The Cavaliers on the other hand had the active support of Frederick Henry of Orange, for in 1641 his son William had married King Charles' daughter Mary. Though Queen Henrietta Maria was the daughter of Henry of Navarre it was not in France but in Holland that she was able to raise money and buy arms. It is true that French officers joined her two regiments, but their number was not very great. There were three English regiments in the French service, but while Cardinal Richelieu was in power France was not going to intervene even by sending them to join King Charles. After Richelieu's death in 1643 the Cavaliers seem to have received rather more help from France, and in 1646 there was a French brigade serving in the West country. Parliament, however, received some aid from Huguenot immigrants.

The King of Denmark, who was sympathetic to Charles, sent him arms and money in 1642, but his contribution, welcome though it was, was not sufficient to turn the scales. Frederick Henry's efforts were of an altogether different order. There were four English infantry regiments and several troops of horse in the Dutch service. Any English officer who wished to go home had first to obtain the Prince's permission, for he was Captain-General; it was always forthcoming for those who wished to fight for the King. When Rupert and Maurice sailed in August 1642 they took with them 100 officers; Goring later joined Newcastle with 200, nor were these all that went. In armies composed of raw militia such numbers of trained officers were certainly significant.

On 1 November 1642 the States General by proclamation forbade the export of arms to either side. Nevertheless, despite the scruples of Dutch officials, the Prince sold guns from his country's arsenals to the Cavaliers, and provided Dutch warships to transport them. Moreover, he gave letters of marque to Dunkirk privateers employed against the Parliament.

Still more important, he borrowed 800,000 guilders for the Queen, and negotiated the pawning of the Crown Jewels, which would have been impossible without his assistance. This transaction, done in his name, raised a further 1,265,300 guilders, and led the Republic to the brink of war with the Roundheads. It may be said that not even the Marquis of Worcester or the Earl of Newcastle rendered Charles comparable services.

The intervention of Ireland was less important. After the armistice of 1643 Charles brought over a number of English regiments, which had been employed there in putting down the rebellion that had broken out in 1641. The Roundheads who had the press on their side, except for *Mercurius Aulicus* the Court's weekly newspaper, made good propaganda of this, alleging that Charles was using Irish papists to massacre his English subjects. Not long after they called in the Scots, whose intervention was naturally a big factor in turning the scales against the King.

APPENDIX

Distribution of Adherents

At the opening of the war the King's adherents in the North and West had already levied considerable forces. In the four northern counties the Earl of Newcastle, despite the opposition of the tenants of the Earl of Northumberland and Lord Grey, was busy raising an army. In Yorkshire the Royalists had been weakened by the King's departure. In the West Riding the Fairfaxes with the backing of the clothing towns overawed their Royalist neighbours; in the East Riding Hull held out for the Parliament. In the North Riding Scarborough was yet another Roundhead stronghold.

In Lancashire the Roundheads of Manchester were successfully defying Lord Strange,[1] who later sent two regiments to the main army at Shrewsbury, so that the balance of power in the county was left fairly even. This indeed was the case in many regions. In Nottinghamshire, for example, the Cavaliers of Newark served throughout the war to counterbalance the Parliamentary garrison of Nottingham.

Wales, poor in money if not in men, was almost entirely Royalist. The eastern and home counties, for the most part wealthy and populous, inclined to the Parliament; Kent and Surrey, because they were overawed by the Roundheads' possession of London; Buckinghamshire, Essex, and East Anglia partly because of their longstanding religious and political radical tradition. In addition the influence of the local Parliamentary grandees, John Hampden and Arthur Goodwin in Buckinghamshire; Warwick in Essex; Lord Saye in Oxfordshire, should not be underestimated. Bedfordshire produced very few Cavaliers; but they included Lord Cleveland who was to command a brigade; his son Lord Wentworth, a major-general, and several colonels.

In North Oxfordshire, the influence of the Earl of Northampton went far to balance that of his neighbours Lord Brooke and Lord Saye. Everywhere the influence of the local leaders, Sir Bevill Grenvile in Cornwall, the Marquis of Worcester in Monmouthshire, Oliver Cromwell in Huntingdonshire, was of the utmost importance. The case of Shropshire illustrates this point forcibly. Basically a Royalist county, its lack of a commander of the first rank or of dynamic character condemned the Cavaliers, though strong in loyalty and in numbers, to a painful struggle to make head against their Parliamentary neighbours. Even in Cornwall, the county which seems to have produced more Cavaliers than any other, there was a tough nucleus of Roundheads. Regionalism, and the influence of county families, was in those days of an importance which we living in the twentieth century can scarcely comprehend.

On the whole the towns seem to have been Roundhead in sympathy, with the exception of the university and cathedral cities.

Minor factors worth noting must include such things as the possession by the Roundheads of the Sussex ironworks, and by the Cavaliers of the Cornish tin and the Durham coal mines.

[1] He became the Earl of Derby in September 1642.

CHAPTER 2

The Campaign of Edgehill

LTHOUGH, AS WE have seen, the King raised his Standard at Nottingham on 22 August, it was not until 9 September that Essex left London for Northampton, where his army, some 15,000 strong, had been concentrating since early in the previous month.

Charles was as yet unready to take the field, for his army was still only a few thousand strong and his train of artillery was incomplete. Indeed Sir Jacob Astley, the veteran Sergeant-Major-General of the army, said that he could not give any assurance against His Majesty being taken out of his bed if the rebels should make a brisk attempt. From a purely military point of view the Roundheads certainly missed a great opportunity by not taking the offensive while the Cavaliers lay at Nottingham. In the south-west fighting had already broken out. It is described in the next chapter. In the south the Cavaliers were losing ground. Colonel George Goring had surrendered Portsmouth to Sir William Waller on 7 September; Sir John Byron had withdrawn from Oxford on 10 September and that city was occupied by Roundheads two days later. At Sherborne the Marquis of Hertford found himself in such a precarious position that on 19 September he withdrew to Minehead, whence he crossed into Wales.

For Charles the inviting strategy was an advance on London, but since Essex barred his road with fully twice his strength, this was clearly impossible. In order to increase his numbers he marched on 13 September for Shrewsbury, gathering reinforcements on the way, and arriving there on the 20th.

Essex, too, moved westwards, uncertain whether the King would march directly on London or whether he would push down the Severn valley. Robert Devereux, third Earl of Essex, was 51 years of age. Though phlegmatic and indolent by nature he was a soldier of some experience. He had seen service as a company commander in the Palatinate in 1620, and later had fought in the Low Countries. In

1625 he had been Vice-Admiral in the Cadiz expedition, and in 1639 he had been second in command of the army raised for the war against the Scots. He now marched slowly towards Worcester, which city Byron, escorting the plate of the University of Oxford with his regiment of horse, had reached on 19 September. The King was not without hope of holding the town, which throughout the war was to show conspicuous loyalty, and he sent Prince Rupert with eight troops of horse and 10 companies of dragoons, to join hands with Byron and the Worcestershire Cavaliers.

The Prince was one of the most remarkable men of his age. 'Il était toujours soldat', says Sir Philip Warwick, meaning that he was never a courtier. Tact, most overrated of the virtues, Rupert did not possess. At 23 he was already a veteran, for he and his brother Maurice had distinguished themselves at the Siege of Breda, and later at Lemgo, where Rupert, already colonel of a cavalry regiment at the age of 16, had been taken prisoner by the Imperialists. Three long years of imprisonment he had whiled away in studying the theoretical side of his chosen profession, so that although young he was already well versed in the art of war. It is easy to say that he was merely a successful cavalry brigadier, but that is a partisan view. He was also a master of siege warfare; it was he who first introduced mining at Lichfield in 1643, and he was also the pioneer of horse artillery. He was later to demonstrate his versatility not only as an Admiral but, curiously enough, as an artist. Rupert, tall, handsome, and 'sparkish' in his dress, an adept with sword and pistol, a fearless horseman, was the very man to inspire the Cavaliers, who now flocked to his uncle's standard, and who asked nothing more than a definite lead. It was the Prince's misfortune that, unlike Newcastle and Hopton, he had no private fortune to draw upon to pay and clothe his men.

The Prince reached Worcester on 23 September, and finding no ammunition and all things in great disorder, ordered a withdrawal. While the necessary preparations were being made he rode out to Powick Bridge, a mile and a half to the south, and took up a covering position. He dismounted his troopers in a slight fold in the ground just north of the river Teme, posting his dragoons in the hedges between them and the bridge. Removing such defensive armour as they possessed, the Cavaliers lay down to snatch a few hours sleep and to refresh themselves before the night march that lay ahead. The force at Rupert's disposal probably numbered at most 1,000 men, half of them being dragoons.

Meanwhile, a Roundhead force under Colonel John Brown, a professional soldier commanding a dragoon regiment, had approached the city from the south. Leaving Essex at Alcester on 22 September they had come via Upton-upon-Severn, making a tedious march of 27 miles, mostly by night.

The main object of this operation was probably to get in contact with a force of Gloucestershire Roundheads which was advancing on Worcester via Tewkesbury, where it had in fact halted to await orders from Essex. Brown's force numbered no more than 10 troops of horse and five companies of dragoons, 800 to 1,000 men in all.

Before dawn broke the Roundhead force had reached Powick Ham, the meadows south of the bridge, not without argument between Brown and his troop commanders, three of whom, Captains Edward Wingate, Nathaniel and John Fiennes, were Members of Parliament. Brown was supported by Colonel Edwin Sandys, the next senior officer who was evidently a 'fire-eater'. On arrival they kept their tired men on horseback for the rest of the night, which according to one of Fiennes' troopers only served 'to sore them'.

Brown sent nobody across the bridge, even when it got light, but he did put his dragoons on the low ridge which runs along from Ham Hill to Powick Church. They failed to observe Rupert's approach which a sentry on the tower certainly ought to have seen.

The day passed quietly until at about 4 p.m. a messenger arrived from Sir William Balfour, Lieut.-General of the horse, to say that Essex's main body was now nearing Worcester, although the artillery had not kept up. On hearing this Brown and Sandys decided to march at once. Thereupon the debating society got to work again. Captain Wingate desired that they should go on with a little more consideration, to which Sandys replied: 'Those that will may follow. Those that will not may stand and look on!' Wingate prayed him not to mistake the troop commanders' affection to the service, merely insisting that they desired to proceed advisedly. Once more Sandys had his way, being 'so extreme earnest to march, that the Captains condescended', only staying to sing a psalm before they moved off.

Nathaniel Fiennes now suggested sending some commanded men ahead to get intelligence, while Colonel Brown was bringing down his dragoons. Sandys consented, and two men were selected from each troop. Before they could be drawn out the Colonel crossed the bridge, where only four could go abreast, and moved on up the lane: there he halted, almost within musket shot of Rupert's dragoons, and called for

c

the commanded men to go on in front. No sooner had they passed than Sandys pressed on again into the field, in the upper part of which the Cavaliers were 'placed in battalia', in such a way that the Roundheads could not discover them till they came to the top of the hill.

Meanwhile, Rupert, surrounded by his principal officers including his younger brother Prince Maurice, had been resting under a haw-thorn tree.

As Sandys came on Rupert's dragoons opened fire, shooting point-blank at the Roundhead horsemen in the lane, and though their fire was insufficient to stop Sandys, the sound of their musketry warned the Cavaliers of his approach. There was not a moment to lose, barely time for the officers to mount and join their troops. Nor was there time to consult as to what to do, but Rupert was not the type of commander who will do nothing without a Council of War: as soon as the Round-heads came in sight he declared that he would charge. Then Prince Maurice, Lord Digby, Wilmot, Byron, and the officers and gentlemen around him fell in about the Prince while their weary troops came on in order behind them.

Sandys was moving so fast that the troops in rear had to gallop to keep closed up. Once in the field the Roundhead commanders made all possible speed to deploy and put their men in order, but before the first five troops were through the gate and before those that were in the field could draw up their divisions Rupert charged them.

Sir Lewis Dyve's troop advanced a little ahead of the other Cavaliers and charged Nathaniel Fiennes' troop, the men firing their pistols as they came on, in the continental style. Fiennes' men let them come up until their horses' noses were almost touching before they opened fire with their carbines. Then sword in hand they fell upon Dyve's men who were 'pretty well shattered' with the volley they had just received. But suddenly Fiennes' men found all the Roundhead troops on both flanks had melted away, and that their rear had been carried away with them, and in the end Nathaniel Fiennes found himself surrounded by Cavalier troopers, while some of his men were jostled into his brother's troop, which was on his left. He managed to hack his way back to the gate, and with his cornet and four or five men rode for the bridge and got across.

Colonel Sandys' troop, somewhat discouraged by the fire of the Royalist dragoons, seeing their leader fall, ran without charging home. Some of the Parliamentary troops fought bravely but they were soon carried away in the rout, and the Cavaliers swept down to the banks of the Teme driving the broken Roundheads before them, but they did not cross the river. Brown with some of his dragoons held the bridge, trying to cover the retreat of his men, some of whom galloped down the steep and slippery bank into the river. When the Cavaliers, doubtless in some disorder, appeared at the north end of the bridge the Roundhead dragoons emptied a few saddles and checked any further pursuit.

Here Nathaniel Fiennes tried in vain to make some of the cavalry stand but many of the officers had fallen and the troopers were not stopping for anyone. After a time Brown fell back to Upton Bridge where he made another stand, and where 40 or 50 of his men caught up.

Essex's Lifeguard marched into Pershore just as the runaways appeared from Powick, riding very hard with drawn swords and many of them hatless. Edmund Ludlow, one of the troop, describes how they learned of the defeat 'not without improvement by reason of the fear with which they were possessed', and when their lieutenant, trying to deploy them so that they could charge if necessary, gave the command 'wheel about', the gentlemen of the troop 'not well under-standing the difference between wheeling about, and shifting for themselves', and imagining the Cavaliers to be hot on their heels rode, loose rein and bloody spur, back to the army!

The Cavaliers meanwhile had rounded up 50 or 80 prisoners and retired into Worcester, marching that night to Tenbury. The wounded Roundhead officers were left in the city, Prince Rupert giving orders that they should be carefully looked after. Richard Crane, the com-mander of the Prince's Lifeguard from 1642 to 1645, an officer who had fought under him at Breda and Lemgo, took the despatch and six or seven captured cornets to the King, whom he found at Chester. Charles knighted Crane, whose news no doubt came as a good omen to the Cheshire Cavaliers, then actively engaged in levying soldiers.

The casualties in this action were few in number: 28 men were buried, some of them Cavaliers; in addition a number of Roundheads were drowned. In all Brown's casualties may have totalled between 100 and 150, including at least 15 out of some 60 commissioned officers.

The Cavaliers lost few killed, and none of name, though Prince Maurice, Wilmot, Dyve, Sir Charles Lucas and one of the Byrons were among the wounded.

The results of the first action of any campaign are moral rather than physical. An engagement where not more than 2,000 men were involved would warrant little attention in the later stages of the war. There were many such, and some must pass altogether unnoticed in these pages. But at Powick, the first serious clash between the main armies of Charles and Essex, the Cavaliers drew first blood, setting the tone of much that was to follow. In Clarendon's opinion the action was of 'unspeakable advantage' to the King; 'it gave his troops great courage, and rendered the name of Prince Rupert very terrible'.

Charles had so far met with scant success in military affairs. In Scotland and before Hull he had found only humiliation. But now his favourite nephew, whom in a happy moment he had made General of his Horse, had shown himself to be a real soldier. At last the King, who often found it difficult to make up his mind, or to trust his own better judgment, had discovered someone whom he could trust, someone of definite views and downright character. Until the Queen herself, now in Holland, stepped once more upon the stage, nobody in Charles' Councils was to have more sway than Rupert.

By mid October Charles' army had grown enormously, and although regiments were still coming in, the King determined to advance on London without further delay. The campaigning season was already far spent; in a few weeks he would be compelled to put his army into winter quarters.

On 12 October the King set out from Shrewsbury to march on London. Essex allowed himself to be out-manoeuvred, and instead of keeping his army between the King and the capital, hung on to Worcester too long, thus letting Charles slip past him. Thus on the evening of 22 October, while Essex was at Kineton, 10 miles south of Warwick, Charles was at Edgecott some four miles to the south-east.

The problem before the King was: should he continue on his way or turn and shake off his opponent first? Inspired by Prince Rupert, Charles decided on the latter course, and orders were sent out to occupy the high ridge of Edgehill five miles south-east of Kineton on the following morning.

Now, had Essex advanced at dawn on 23 October, he could have engaged or turned the Royalist position before the King had time to complete its occupation, for his quarters were scattered. But Essex lost this opportunity, probably because some of his foot and the greater part of his artillery had not yet come up. Thus by the time he had advanced and drawn up his army on the low ground to the north of Edgehill, the Cavalier army was ranged along the brow of the hill. The positions had become reversed; instead of Essex being between the King and the capital, it was the King who was between Essex and his base.

Edgehill is a conspicuous ridge, rising 300 feet out of the plain, three miles long, facing north-west – that is, square to the road to London. The slope is steep, reaching a gradient of 1 in 4. Though now fringed with a belt of trees, it was open ground at the time of the battle except for one small clump. The plain between the hill and Kineton was fairly open in the centre, though there was some scrub and furze, and a single hedge ran between what are now Thistle and Battle Farms. This hedge still exists, a track running alongside it. On the Cavalier right wing there were five or six hedges between the two armies, but the other wing was very enclosed on the Kineton side with a number of small fields and orchards. What makes the battlefield difficult to locate with precision nowadays is that some copses that were present at the time of the battle have been cut down, and others have been planted since that time. The chief of these are shown on the sketch map – Battle Holt, the Oaks, and the two small copses in the exact centre of the field, the triangular one being Graveyard Coppice, and the other unnamed.

In point of numbers the rival armies were very evenly matched. The Cavaliers had 2,500 horse, 1,000 dragoons, and 10,000 foot, a total of 13,500. The Roundhead army also numbered about 13,000 of which not less than 2,500 were cavalry. The Earl of Essex may not have been a heaven-born general, but at least his sway was undisputed, whereas in the opposing camp there were divided councils and almost divided command: while the Earl of Lindsey was the titular commander, Prince Rupert was independent of him. It is not surprising that old Lindsey refused to put up with such a nonsensical arrangement and resigned the command on the eve of the battle. At this period the King, as Generalissimo, held a vague 'watching-brief' over the whole. As he grew more experienced in military affairs he took the conduct of operations more and more upon himself.

The two armies probably spotted one another simultaneously. 'A worthy divine' on the Roundhead side claims to have first discovered the Cavaliers on the top of Edgehill through his 'perspective glass', and to have reported it to Essex. Meanwhile the King himself was also engaged with a perspective glass from Knowle End, the right-hand edge of the ridge. Essex was then slowly marching out of Kineton and marshalling his host in line of battle about two miles outside the town. It was past noon before this operation was completed, and meanwhile the Cavaliers, having completed their own dispositions, stood still. A pause – typical of civil war engagements, where neither side is anxious to strike the first blow – ensued. It looked for the moment as if no fight would take place. Essex was clearly unwilling to assault such a strong position, and the King eventually realized that if there was to be a battle that day he must take the initiative in the matter. An incident that may have decided him then occurred. A gunner in the Roundhead army spotted the King, still stationed on Knowle Hill, and laid a cannon at him. The ball was fired, but fell short, landing in a field below him (still called Bullet Hill).[1] Charles was roused to action. He ordered the whole army to advance in line down the hill and engage. The steepness of the slope made the descent difficult for the cannon and the horses had to be taken out and harnessed to the traces or drag-ropes in the rear.

It was one o'clock. Both armies were now drawn up a few hundred yards apart, somewhere between Kineton and the little village of Radway, the Roundheads being about 200 yards south of the above mentioned hedge.

Both had the infantry in the centre, winged by cavalry with dragoons in the hedges and bushes on the extreme flanks. Essex had three brigades of foot: Meldrum's on the right supported by two regiments of cavalry under Stapleton and Balfour; Charles Essex's on the left supported by Ballard's brigade of foot in reserve behind it. Feilding's regiment of horse was on the right and Sir James Ramsey had 24 troops of horse on the left wing.

The Cavalier foot were drawn up according to the system known as the Swedish brigade. It was too complicated a formation for inexperienced troops, hence the quarrel between Lindsey and Rupert. The former – quite rightly – would have preferred the simpler formations in vogue in the Dutch service. Another serious defect in the Cavalier dispositions was the lack of any true reserve. Their army drew up in two lines, but there was no compact body of horse and foot which could be flung in to take advantage of any opportunity which might occur once the main bodies had joined battle.

The guns in each army were for the most part placed in the inter-

---

1 A copse in the shape of a crown was later planted to mark the spot where the King stood.

vals between the infantry regiments. But the heaviest guns were some way further in the rear. In the case of the Cavaliers this would be near the road for convenience, and about Battleton Holt.

The extent of the Roundhead position is nowhere recorded. All we know for certain is that it was in two lines. Thirteen thousand men in six deep formation would hardly have occupied more than two miles at the outside. Thus, if the centre rested on the Kineton-Radway road – a reasonable assumption – it could hardly have extended further to its left than the Kineton-Knowle End road, while its right would rest near the present Oaks plantation. When the Cavalier army advanced, doubtless it conformed, in the accommodating way customary in those days, to its opponent's position and frontage.

The battle opened with a rather feeble and ineffective artillery duel. Simultaneously the Cavalier's dragoons cleared the hedges on the flanks of each army. These preliminaries were followed by the advance of Prince Rupert's cavalry.

Rupert, having descended the hill in column along the Knowle End-Kineton road, extended his line to his left, abreast of King's Leys Barn. His regiments in two lines then trotted forward about one mile down the gentle descent to the brook which, being very narrow, they took in their stride. On the slight ridge opposite them they could see Ramsey's horse drawn up. Breaking into a canter, then a gallop, they headed straight for the Roundhead cavalry. The sight of this formidable onslaught was altogether too much for the half-trained Roundhead horsemen whose left was outflanked. Shaken at the moment of contact by the defection of Sir Faithfull Fortescue's troop, they fired, turned, and fled. Rupert's men quickened their pace in pursuit, and between the ridge and the town of Kineton they jumped five or six hedges. The ground was now almost level, and the broad pastures must have presented much the same appearance as they do today.

Not only the Roundhead cavalry but the neighbouring infantry were swept away by this onslaught, and Lord Wharton declared, in a moment of candour only a few days later, that four regiments of foot, including his own, took to flight. This disposed of the brigade of Colonel Charles Essex, the left of the Roundhead front line. He and some of his officers did not run but joined Meldrum's brigade, where he himself died fighting.

Rupert's Cavaliers swept on into Kineton, where some of them stopped to plunder; the remainder continued their impetuous charge

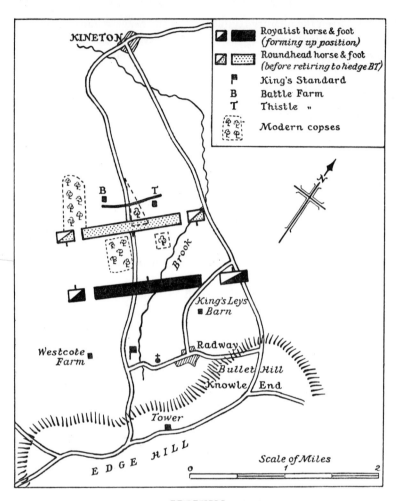

KINETON

Royalist horse & foot
(forming up position)
Roundhead horse & foot
(before retiring to hedge BT)
King's Standard
B   Battle Farm
T   Thistle   „
Modern copses

B   T

Brook

King's Leys
Barn

Westcote
Farm

Radway

Bullet Hill

Knowle End

Tower

EDGE HILL

Scale of Miles
0   1   2

EDGEHILL

up the Warwick road for close on two miles, till they encountered Colonel John Hampden with Roundhead reinforcements at a place since known as Rupert's Headland, and their pursuit was checked. Fugitives were collected and gradually some sort of a line of Parliamentary troops brought the Cavalier horse to a standstill.

While Rupert was charging, Sir Jacob Astley led forward the Royalist infantry. Initially forming five brigades in two lines the rear brigades came up into the intervals, forming a continuous front as they advanced to the attack. Crossing the little brook and marching slowly up the gentle slope, they encountered the Roundheads on the ridge-top. What then happened is described in detail by only one eyewitness, and his account has been ignored by most writers. That eyewitness was none other than the future King James II. He was then a boy of 9, and together with his elder brother Charles he witnessed the early stages of the fight at close quarters. Later the two lads were hurried away to safety on the top of Edgehill. James relates that the Cavaliers fired their muskets while they were advancing. On the top of the ridge they came to 'push of pike', and though James does not mention it, the Roundheads gave some ground, falling back at least in places to the hedge, which they lined with musketeers. To continue James' account: 'Each, as if by mutual consent, retired some few paces and stuck down their colours, continuing to fire at one another even until night.' The fighting in the centre of the field thus became static and featureless.

Not so on the flanks. Rupert's action on the right flank was shortly followed by a similar action by the smaller body of cavalry under Lord Wilmot on the left. For some way the ground over which they charged was as open as on the other flank, and the charge was almost as successful. Feilding's regiment of horse was swept away and Wilmot's men penetrated right behind the hostile foot. Dismayed by this charge, Sir William Constable's regiment of foot took to its heels. But two things altered the complexion of affairs in this quarter: the enclosed nature of the ground previously referred to impeded and disorganized the Cavaliers, and in the course of their charge they had ridden too wide to take in two enemy cavalry regiments – those of Balfour and Stapleton, drawn up behind the foot of the front line. These two regiments now played a big if somewhat confusing part in the battle. It is significant that of these two regiments only one troop, that of Nathaniel Fiennes, had been at Powick Bridge. The rest of the runaways were with the unfortunate Ramsey.

Accounts of cavalry actions are generally confusing. Events happen so fast, and when the terrain is at all enclosed it is difficult for any one eyewitness to take in all that is happening, and to remember events in their right order afterwards. So it is not suprising that the records at this stage become fragmentary and somewhat contradictory. Out of it all we can, however, distinguish two separate charges by the Round-head cavalry under Balfour. His regiment was stationed behind the centre of the line near Battle Farm and advanced through the intervals between the Roundhead front-line regiments and made a frontal charge on Feilding's – the centre brigade. The horsemen broke right through it, capturing Feilding and two of his colonels, Stradling and Lunsford, and pursuing the fleeing Cavaliers to their heavy guns, which were some hundreds of yards in rear, in the neighbourhood of what is now Battleton Holt. Here many of the fugitives threw down their arms and surrendered, as the pursuing Roundheads, flushed with victory, surged round the battery. The gunners, cowering under their guns, were sabred, and Balfour shouted excitedly: 'Nails! Nails!' These were required for the purpose of 'nailing up' or 'spiking' the guns. But nails were, as might be supposed, not immediately forthcoming. Balfour was therefore reduced to cutting the ropes so that the guns could not be dragged away. He then returned to his own lines. In so doing he was mistaken for the enemy and fired on by his own guns. Thus the upshot was disappointing. But it taught him the necessity of co-ordinating such attacks with his own foot.

Profiting by this lesson he now mounted a second attack, in which he obtained the promise of the foot regiments on the right flank to co-operate. This was the first sign on any part of the front, in either army, of the least attempt to co-ordinate the two arms in attack. The result was a deserved success. While the cavalry swept round once more, the infantry, leaving the protection of the hedge, advanced with the Kineton-Radway road as axis. While the foot attacked the opposing infantry in front, the horse struck into their flank. This was the end of a phase; the Cavalier infantry reeled and recoiled, first on their left flank, but the movement gradually extended in lesser degree all along the line. Thus the retrograde movement partook of a partial wheel, till the line reached and crossed the brook.

This retreat exposed the King's standard, borne in the ranks of his Foot Lifeguard, to danger. A homeric struggle ensued; the standard-bearer, Sir Edmund Verney, was killed and the standard captured. Sir Nicholas Byron's brigade suffered very heavily. The Earl of

Lindsey had fallen mortally wounded at the head of his regiment. His son, Lord Willoughby d'Eresby, Colonel of the redcoats of the Lifeguard, after laying low two Roundhead officers with his half-pike, had been captured trying to rescue his father. The guns were by some unrecorded means withdrawn, and some sort of new line was taken up.

It was a critical moment for the Royalist cause. The least additional pressure and the whole line might crumble and fly. But three things combined to prevent this catastrophe: the exhaustion and shortage of ammunition of their enemies, the reappearance of their own victorious cavalry on the field, and their own heavy guns.

If Wilmot followed the chase too recklessly there were some among his followers who realized that they had other work to do. One of these was Captain John Smith, of Lord Grandison's regiment. Among the horse pursuing the flying Roundheads he saw some who he knew should be acting as a reserve to assist the Cavalier foot. He sought out his own Colonel, and Lieut.-Colonel Sir Charles Lucas, and advised them to return speedily to the help of their infantry. They soon rallied about 200 horse. After three charges in which Smith took a colour of Lord Wharton's regiment he found that only one man remained with him.

Moving back towards the King's army Smith observed six horsemen, guarding a seventh on foot, who was carrying what appeared to be a colour of the King's Foot Lifeguards. A boy called to him: 'Captain Smith! Captain Smith, they are carrying away the Standard!' and with some difficulty convinced him that the trophy really was the great Banner Royal. 'They shall have me with it, if they carry it away!' quoth Smith, and charged in with his rapier shouting, 'Traitor deliver the Standard!' In the melée that followed the Captain was wounded, but he injured one of the Roundheads and killed another whereupon the rest fled, leaving the Standard in his possession. This exploit won him a knighthood.[1]

Prince Rupert has been unrestrainedly condemned by practically every writer for his impetuosity. Gardiner even asserts that: 'Little recked Rupert how the battle fared behind him.' Such criticism betrays a lack of appreciation of the difficulties of controlling a cavalry charge. Unless the commander rides ahead of the whole line he cannot control

---

[1] Godfrey Davies has pointed out that this is the likeliest account of Smith's exploit; only one source, and that Roundhead, claims that the Standard was rescued by a stratagem.

or direct the charge once it has been launched. The leading ranks can neither see nor hear him; and if he spurs his horse forward in order to get to their head, the ranks he is trying to pass will merely quicken their pace; no horse likes being overtaken by another. It would be more logical to blame Sir John Byron, who commanded the second line and who instead of following Rupert ought to have swung left and charged Ballard's brigade, the Roundhead reserve of foot.

There is the further difficulty that, when the charge has spent itself and come to a natural standstill, the troopers are so scattered and disordered, and their horses are so blown and weary that any further concerted movement of an offensive nature is for the time being out of the question. It would have required a large, well-mounted and well-trained staff, which Rupert did not possess, to restore order and cohesion to a body of horse that was in a few brief moments scattered over several square miles of country. It looks so obvious and easy for the 'armchair critic' to see what ought to be done by Rupert, but it is so difficult to do it. No one has recorded Rupert's own motions and acts during the period when his horse were absent from the battle-field, but there is no reason to suppose that he did not strive vigorously (and as unsuccessfully) as Prince Edward under similar circumstances at the battle of Lewes. Clarendon draws this apt comparison between the two Princes.

Be that as it may, dusk was falling when at length he reappeared on the battlefield with a substantial proportion of his cavalry.[1] Lord Falkland urged him to engage the enemy once more, but Rupert, though he would have liked to accede, did not do so. His men were either still in no condition, or in no mood, for a further fight; they were dead-beat – the reaction of inertia that overtakes most of the actors on the battlefield at the close of a hard-fought day was too much for them. The martial flame was now only flickering in their breasts and their bodies called out for repose.

Nor was this flame burning with a brighter light in the ranks of the Roundheads. The truth is that both sides were utterly exhausted. Silence descended with the dusk upon the scene. Both sides, alike new to warfare, had had their fill; they were licking their wounds. It is even probable that soldiers from each army stole down to the brook and tacitly shared its thirst-quenching water – just as did our men and the French at the brook of Talavera. The stout-hearted King was urged

---

[1] It is significant of the confusion and dispersion that some of them, on return via the left flank, had ridden right round the hostile army.

to abandon the position in the night, but declined to do so. Indeed, he himself spent the night at the foot of the hill at what is now called King's Leys Barn, only a few hundred yards behind his front line.

The battle was, in fact, over, and history has rejected the claims of both sides to victory, declaring it a drawn battle. We challenge this judgment. When two armies engage in battle each has an object in view. When one of them achieves its object while the other fails in it, there can be no doubt which side can claim the victory.

What was the King's object? To shake off the pursuit of the Roundhead army. What was Essex's object? To prevent the Cavalier army getting to London. Now the upshot of this battle was that Essex so far from holding his opponents from London, retired 12 miles in the opposite direction to Warwick, leaving seven of his guns and many colours in the hands of the Cavaliers. On the other hand, the King, having held his ground next day in case his opponents should desire to renew the battle (they had received 4,000 reinforcements and guns) resumed his march on London unmolested, and a week later entered Oxford in triumph. The battle of Edgehill was a victory for the King – and by the King. For there is little doubt that his bold decision to spend the night himself on the actual battlefield and to offer battle next morning was the deciding factor.

The Cavaliers' advance had caused great agitation in London and on the same day that Charles entered Oxford some members of the House of Lords proposed to reopen peace negotiations. There was a Peace-party not only in the City but in the Commons. Had the King at this juncture strained every nerve to appear with his army in the outskirts of the capital, it may well be that his cause would have triumphed. It may be argued that the Cavalier armies did not reach the height of their powers until the summer of 1643. On the other hand it may well be that it was already a case of 'now or never'. With London untaken the Roundheads must win in the long run; in November 1642 the Cavaliers had their best chance to end the war with one swift stroke.

But while the Earl of Essex wound his way slowly back to London moving round the north-eastern flank of the Cavalier army, Charles lingered at Oxford. It was not until 4 November that he reached Reading, but he was still slightly ahead of Essex who by this time had fallen back to Woburn in Bedfordshire (42 miles N.E. of Reading). The stages of his march are not stated, but a study of the map suggests that joining Watling Street (A5) at Weedon, he marched via Tow-cester and Stony Stratford and won the race for London.

While negotiations proceeded the Houses prepared for the coming struggle, levying new forces and voting money for the remnants of Essex's Edgehill army.

On 7 November Rupert summoned Windsor Castle, only to meet with a firm defiance. On the 9th Charles was at Colnbrook, but on this day Essex, who was now back in the capital, was ordered to take the field once more. The Cavaliers had already lost their best oppor-tunity when on the night of the 11th the King gave orders for an attack on Brentford, an operation which was to be a preliminary to his further advance on the capital.

The Action at Brentford, 12th Nov. 1642

Rupert advanced by night and attacked at dawn under cover of the heavy mist which hung over the Thames valley. Holles' regiment, which had fought stoutly at Edgehill, bore the brunt of the onslaught. After an obstinate struggle it was driven back onto Lord Brooke's regi-ment, which was quartered in the town. The two regiments held out for some time, but were eventually overwhelmed; many were killed or captured and many, seeking to escape by swimming the river, were drowned. Essex was slow to intervene and when at length Hampden came up with reinforcements he was only in time to rally the survivors of Brooke's men. Holles' regiment was annihilated. Five hundred prisoners, 15 guns and 11 colours fell into the hands of the victors.

So far the operation had gone well for the Cavaliers, but they made no further progress that day, being fully occupied in sacking Brentford. The Roundheads, now thoroughly alarmed, poured out of London in force, and mustered in Chelsea Fields. The west road must have presented a striking spectacle on that winter evening as the City Trained Bands, their bright arms touched by the sinking sun, marched out to face their King. At their head was Major-General Philip Skippon, a veteran of the Dutch service in which he had risen from the ranks by sheer merit; few generals on either side were to earn a higher reputation for skill, courage, and leadership. Under such a commander the London Trained Bands, well drilled if inexperienced, were bound to give a good account of themselves. Moreover, they had numbers on their side, for by the morning of 13 November an army estimated at 24,000 men was drawn up on the common at Turnham Green. Three thousand more under Sir James Ramsey held the passage of the

Thames at Kingston, the first bridge above old London Bridge. In order to be able to operate on either side of the river Essex very sensibly used his pontoon train to throw a bridge of boats across the Thames at Putney. This done he decided to withdraw Ramsey's force to London Bridge so as to cover the City from the south. It was strange strategy to abandon so important a post as Kingston before the place was even threatened, the more so since Essex certainly outnumbered the King by at least 10,000 men. This move may have been prompted by a minor disaster on the previous day when a curious, if not unique, encounter had taken place on the Thames opposite Kew.

The Cavaliers had occupied Sion House, on the north bank, with a body of musketeers and some cannon. Some 600 of Ramsey's men in about 14 barges with 13 cannon and some ammunition attempted to slip past going down river. But the Cavaliers were on the alert and when the barges came opposite Sion House an artillery duel broke out. Since the barges were on the move the guns on each side had to fire at moving targets – a most unusual thing at that period. The range must have been about 500 yards. The Cavaliers gained the upper hand with the result that four or five of the barges were sunk and the rest captured.

The battle of Turnham Green was never fought. Not without reason Professor Gardiner called it the Valmy of the Civil War. Charles, impressed by the broad array of Roundheads facing him – far more than he had met at Edgehill – fell back to Hounslow during the night, keeping his army embattled on the heath until the dawn. As the Cavaliers fell back Essex advanced his host to recapture Brentford. Old Astley, another veteran of the Dutch service, conducted the Cavalier rearguard with his usual skill, while Rupert stood his horse in the river encouraging the men to keep order, and fire steadily. But there was hope for Charles yet, for Kingston was now entered by his forces: it was still possible to advance south of the river and join hands with the Kentish Cavaliers. Essex's army, though formidable in numbers, was unhandy in manoeuvre, and the King with his superior cavalry and a more homogeneous force might still by a bold stroke have spread panic among the Peace Party and brought about the collapse of the Roundhead cause. Nothing venture, nothing win. Unhappily for Charles, prudence, so often the enemy of good strategy, prevailed. He lingered at Oatlands for some days and then fell back to Reading, which he re-entered on 19 November. The campaign of Edgehill was over.

Both sides now sent their main armies into winter quarters. Essex, with his advanced post at Windsor, disposed his forces to cover the western approaches to the capital, while on 9 December the King's Council of War at Oxford had settled their winter quarters over a wide area in Oxfordshire, Buckinghamshire, and Berkshire. Sir Arthur Aston, Colonel-General of dragoons, a testy and imperious veteran who had served in the Russian and Swedish armies, was fortifying Reading. He had six regiments of foot and two of horse. His communications with Oxford were secured by strong garrisons at Wallingford and Abingdon. Oxford itself was held by four regiments of foot. A circle of garrisons girdled the King's temporary capital; Banbury, Brill, Wallingford, Abingdon, Faringdon, and Burford formed an outer ring. Oxford was entirely covered by rivers – Thames and Cherwell – except on the north side, which was doubly protected for in that direction there was a second line of regiments quartered at Enstone, Woodstock, and Islip. Fortifications, the plan of which has been carefully preserved for us by de Gomme, were put in hand and first and last cost over £30,000. The mediaeval walls of Oxford were not used. On the north side the line ran east and west through the sites now occupied by the University Museum and Keble College, St. Giles Church being just inside the line.

The campaign ended, Essex was quite prepared to hibernate. Many of his followers, Cromwell and Ireton to name but two, returned to their own districts to defend their homes and levy new forces. On the King's side the same thing happened. Richard Bagot, who had fought the campaign as a captain in Bolle's regiment, returned to Staffordshire and rose to be Governor of Lichfield; Gervase Holles, the antiquarian, who had been major to Sir Lewis Dyve, returned as a colonel to his native Grimsby. Both the main armies were seriously weakened by this process, a by-product of the intense regionalism of those days.

But if Essex was only too happy to live a quiet life, the Cavaliers were more active, and during the winter they began to clear their communications with the West. Wilmot stormed Marlborough on 5 December and on 2 February 1643 Rupert assaulted Cirencester. On the Parliamentary side only Sir William Waller displayed any activity. He destroyed two regiments of Cavaliers at Winchester on 12 December, adding to the reputation he had already begun to make by his capture of Portsmouth.

APPENDIX

Cromwell at Edgehill

What part did Cromwell play at Edgehill? He was only a captain at the time, and the question would not be worth asking, were it not that he rose to the rank of lieutenant-general in the next two years.

The meagre authorities for his actions at Edgehill are fully discussed by Professor Abbott,[1] so we need only summarize.

Essex's quarters were widely dispersed and Cromwell's troop did not come up until the battle had already begun. The Royalist Sir William Dugdale asserts that climbing a steeple Cromwell tried with the aid of a 'perspective glass' to find out what was going on, and seeing that the two wings of Roundhead horse had been utterly routed made such haste to be gone that instead of descending the stairs he swung down by the bell-rope! Nathaniel Fiennes tells us that Oliver's troop joined John Fiennes and others and marched towards Kineton, at length joining Hampden's brigade, and advancing with it to the army. But although his share in the battle was slight there is no evidence to support Colonel Denzil Holles' charge of cowardice, which was made several years later, and is purely malicious.

Nevertheless, after Edgehill Cromwell told Hampden, 'You must get men of a spirit . . . that is likely to go on as far as gentlemen will go, or else I am sure you will be beaten still'. The little he had seen of the battle showed him that much, and since for his own part he took pains to raise just such men we may regard Edgehill as an important stage in his development as an officer.

[1] Wilbur Cortez Abbott: *Writings and Speeches of Oliver Cromwell.* Vol. I. p. 203.

D

CHAPTER 3

The War in the West — I

THE EARLY PHASES of the War in the West saw three distinct campaigns; one in Somerset and two in Devon and Cornwall, these last two being divided by a forty-day truce.

While the two main armies were marshalling and marching sporadic fighting was already taking place in the West – the first clash took place in Somerset where despite tactical successes at Marshall's Elm, near Somerton (4 August 1642), at Sherborne (2–6 September) and Babylon Hill, near Yeovil (7 September) – all fought before the battle of Edgehill – the Royalists under the Marquis of Hertford were driven out of the county and split up.

The Parliament, alarmed by the rout at Marshall's Elm, had sent down the Earl of Bedford who, towards the end of August, had concentrated 7,000 men at Wells. To oppose this army Hertford could not muster more than perhaps 1,500 men, and with them he retreated to Minehead, which he reached on 22 September. Here the Cavaliers divided; the Marquis with the foot and guns took passage in coal-boats to South Wales, joining the King in time for Edgehill, while Hopton and 160 mounted men rode through North Devon into Cornwall.

Bedford, satisfied that the Roundheads of Devon and Cornwall could easily deal with so small a body, rejoined Essex with most of the forces he had led into the West, and he also fought, as General of the Horse at Edgehill. But he was leaving his work half done.

The Royalist commander for his part had achieved very little. William Seymour, first Marquis of Hertford, was a loyal, wealthy, and indolent grandee, 54 years of age. He was entirely without military experience, yet he had been made lieutenant-general of the six western counties. It is interesting to speculate as to what might have happened had he secured Bristol or relieved Portsmouth – both of which were in his territory – but he attempted neither of these operations.

His second in command, Sir Ralph Hopton, K.B., was a man of very different mettle. At this time he was 44 years old. He was no longer a professional soldier, though he had served on the continent during the early years of the Thirty Years' War, fighting for the Elector Palatine and reaching, in 1624, the rank of lieutenant-colonel. At the beginning of the Civil War Hopton owed his position as one of the Cavaliers' leaders to his wealth and social standing, for his previous military experience, though valuable, was by no means remarkable. His reputation was yet to be made.

Hopton arrived in Cornwall on 25 September. His coming tipped the balance in favour of the Cornish Cavaliers, who up to that time had succeeded in levying but few soldiers. In Cornwall men doubted the legality alike of the Parliament's Militia Ordinance and of the King's Commission of Array. Both sides were anxious for a truce until the harvest was gathered in, and when, on 17 August, the Cavaliers had called for a general muster on Bodmin race course, no more than 180 men had appeared, and the majority of these were Sir Bevill Grenvile's servants and tenants.

A strange episode marked Hopton's arrival in Cornwall. He was arraigned at Truro Assizes for bringing armed forces into the Duchy. The jury not only acquitted him, but thanked him for coming to their aid. The trained bands came out for the King, and the mayor agreed to let them have the town arms. When on 4 October Hopton reviewed the Posse Comitatus on Moilesbarrow Down he found himself at the head of 3,000 well-armed men, besides a number of others armed with cudgels. They were for the most part ill-trained peasantry, but Sir Richard Buller, the Roundhead leader, had only succeeded in assembling 700 of the same sort. Advancing Hopton was able to occupy Launceston unopposed, and to secure the line of the Tamar. Buller fled into Devonshire.

Recognizing the difficulty of persuading the trained bands to leave their own county Hopton and the Cornish Cavaliers now began to raise an army consisting of five full-strength infantry regiments, all volunteers, and upwards of 500 mounted men. The Royal fortresses, Pendennis and St. Mawes,[1] opposite Falmouth, were secured by their Cavalier governors, Sir Nicholas Slanning and Lieutenant Hannibal Bonython. The former organized a fleet of privateers which, despite Warwick's warships, preyed upon the merchant shipping in the

---

[1] These were two 'modern' fortresses – built by Henry VIII to guard the mouth of the river Fal.

Channel, and brought munitions into Falmouth, St. Ives, and Penzance.

The Committee of Public Safety, despite its preoccupation with the defence of London spared a thought for Plymouth and the West. Early in October it authorized the Deputy-Lieutenant of Cornwall to raise 1,000 men and ordered two troops of horse to join this army. It also commanded the Committee in Devon to provide 500 dragoons. Later in the month it again sent down the Earl of Bedford with seven more troops of horse and 1,000 foot.

All this was not sufficient to prevent Hopton's cavalry raiding across the Tamar, but it was not until early December that he cut off Plymouth's water supply. The Committee now gave Lord Robartes command, and ordered that three regiments of volunteers and 1,000 dragoons should be raised for the relief of the town. Arms and money were forwarded by sea.

In December the Cavaliers decided to close in on Plymouth. Their first move was to occupy Mount Edgcumbe House and Millbrook and secure the Cornish side of the Sound. Their second, to cross into Devonshire and drive the Roundhead General Ruthin, a Scots officer, from his quarters at Plympton.

The first move provoked the Roundheads to attempt two amphibious raids on Millbrook.[1] On the first occasion they landed and captured some dragoons, but Major Walter Slingsby held out until relieved by Hopton in person. On the second raid the Roundheads landed by night, evidently in some force. Slingsby beat them from his half-completed works forcing them to a disorderly retreat.

The Cornish army proved insufficient to blockade Plymouth and so the Cavaliers attempted to raise the Posse Comitatus at Modbury on 6 December. The Devonshire men were not as warlike as their neighbours and Hopton was disappointed to find the gathering 'rather like a great fair than a Posse'. During the night Ruthin surprised this gathering. The High Sheriff and many of the Devonshire gentry were taken and the Posse dispersed while Hopton and Slanning had a narrow escape.

At the end of the month the Cavaliers summoned Exeter, but once more Ruthin foiled them, for advancing swiftly he slipped through the Cornish lines and reinforced the garrison. The end of the year found the Royalists back in Cornwall.

---

[1] Oddly enough in country constantly used for Commando training in the summer of 1940.

Ruthin now attempted to force the passage of the Tamar at Saltash. Planting his artillery on the Devon side, he brought three warships into the river, and battered the town for about a week with their guns, which are said to have numbered no less than 80. Under cover of this supporting fire he attempted to land his infantry from boats, but his bombardment had done little damage and he was everywhere repulsed. The element of surprise was lacking and without it his river crossing operation had little chance of success.

This check was not serious to the Roundheads for reinforcements from Somerset and Dorset now managed to cross the Tamar. The Cavaliers were compelled to abandon the line of the river, but they had foreseen this and some days previously had summoned the Posse to join them at Bodmin. Ruthin concentrated at Liskeard eager to add to his successes before the Earl of Stamford, who was approaching with yet another Roundhead contingent, should supersede him.

Meanwhile the Cavaliers had a windfall. On 17 January 1643 a fierce storm drove three Parliamentarian warships, well furnished with arms and money, into the Royalist port of Falmouth. It was a re-organized Cornish army that met once more on Moilesbarrow Down, rearmed, and with a fortnight's advance of pay in its pockets. Morale was high when, without artillery or baggage, they advanced and quartered in Lord Mohun's park at Boconnoc, two and a half miles east of Lostwithiel. There they held a Council of War and decided to attack next day whether they found Ruthin in the field or at Liskeard. By the King's commission the western army was commanded jointly by Lord Mohun, Hopton, Berkeley, and Colonel William Ashburnham, or any two of them. This strange arrangement they now set aside, inviting Hopton to act as commander-in-chief.

The Battle of Braddock Down. 19 January 1643

Next morning the Cavaliers marched out and at about noon came in full view of Ruthin's army drawn up upon a fair heath between Boconnoc and Braddock Church. Information about the positions adopted is rather scanty. The Roundheads according to Colonel Sir Bevill Grenvile 'were possessed of a pretty rising ground which was in the way towards Liskerd [sic], and we [Cavaliers] planted ourselves upon such another against them within musket shot'.[1] Hopton himself merely says that he drew up the foot in the best order he could on the

[1] The Roundhead position was probably on the ridge 800 yards north of Braddock Down.

west side of Braddock Down. In front of the army he placed an advanced guard – a 'forlorn' he calls it – in little enclosures. The few horse and dragoons he placed on the wings in the customary manner. The artillery had been left at Bodmin, but Hopton had two little iron guns brought up secretly from Lord Mohun's house and planted 'upon a little Borough within randome-shott of the Enymies bodyes'. These he concealed from the Roundheads by placing little parties of horse in front of them. The Roundheads had more cavalry than the Cavaliers, but the Cornish foot outnumbered the opposing infantry.

For about two hours the two armies were content to skirmish: 'we saluted each other with bullets', says Grenvile. Both sides wished to 'keep their ground of advantage and to have the other to come over to his prejudice'. Hopton eventually decided to attack, only waiting to hold prayers at the head of each unit – 'mass' the Roundheads styled it.

This done, Hopton suddenly unmasked his two guns and ordered a salvo, then leaving the reserve of foot in position he advanced with the rest of his army. Both wings of horse charged. In the centre Grenvile, well seconded by the other infantry regiments, led the van, his men following him so gallantly down one hill and up the other that they struck terror into the Roundheads. The hedgehogs of pikemen, colours flying in their midst, striding forward with musketeers on either side must have been truly impressive. The Roundheads fired one ill-aimed volley before their opponents were well within range and then took to their heels in great disorder. All the way to Liskeard they ran, and there the townsmen rose against them. The Cavaliers pursued, and entered the town unopposed. At least 1,250 prisoners fell into their hands, with all the baggage and ammunition and many arms. Five guns were among the spoils. One was only an iron Saker, but the rest were brass and included one piece 14 feet long, probably a Culverin, with the Rose and Crown of the Tudors engraved upon it.

As a result of this battle Cornwall was now firmly in the hands of the Cavaliers once more. But the moral results of Braddock Down were even more important than the physical. Ruthin had only himself to thank for this abrupt conclusion to his series of triumphs, for he had acted contrary to the order of the Lord General, Stamford. Hopton, on the other hand, now emerged as a general of merit. Though a Somersetshire man himself, he had won the trust of the Cornishmen and had convinced them that he cared for their needs, both material and spiritual. He had been to great pains to arm them and to pay them properly; he had not thrown them into battle without time to offer up

a prayer. His personal courage and his industry were as well known as
his piety and integrity. But he had far more than the qualities required
of a good regimental officer: he had an eye for country, a flair for
tactics, and resolution in adversity.

On 20 January the Cavaliers rested and gave thanks for their
victory, but they were not content to rest on their laurels. The time
had come for a second invasion of Devon. Dividing their force they
directed one column against Stamford, who had got as far as Launceston before he heard of the disaster, but now beat a hasty retreat to
Tavistock. A second column under Hopton and Lord Mohun stormed
Saltash on 22 January, capturing 140 more prisoners, four guns and a
ship of nearly 400 tons mounting 16 cannon. Ruthin, who had been
working hard to fortify the place, escaped in a small boat to Plymouth.
Many of his followers, less fortunate than he, crowded into such craft
as they could find, swamped them and were drowned.

The threat to Plymouth was grave, but its garrison was still not
much weaker than the Cornish army, for once it crossed the Tamar
the trained bands refused to leave their own county. The Cavaliers
therefore endeavoured to blockade Plymouth, for a proper siege was
still beyond their resources.

Sir John Berkeley, after successfully beating up Major-General
James Chudleigh's quarters at Kingsbridge, tried the same game at
Okehampton on 8 February 1643. The Roundheads dispersed on
hearing of his approach but rallied at Chagford. There in a confused
dawn skirmish the Cavaliers lost one of the noblest of their number,
Sidney Godolphin the poet, who had been serving as a volunteer
throughout the campaign. He was in Sir Bevill Grenvile's words 'as
gallant a gent. as the world had'.

Despite this setback the Cavaliers continued to blockade Plymouth,
but it was at best a deadlock. A relief force was gathering at Kingsbridge; its task was none too difficult for the Cavaliers with detachments at Modbury, Plympton, and Ham were very scattered.

At 1 o'clock on 21 February the Roundhead force, under James
Chudleigh, fell upon Modbury. The fight raged all through the
afternoon and on into the night. After a stubborn resistance the
Cavaliers fell back to Plympton, leaving 100 dead, 150 prisoners,
1,100 muskets, and 5 guns. Next morning the Cornish army, having
sent their heavy carriages and guns across the river to Saltash, fell back to
Tavistock. Thus ignominiously ended their second invasion of Devon.

Stamford and Ruthin, happy to be rid of them, agreed on 28 February to a local cessation of hostilities. Hopton was merely playing for time; the Cornishmen were tired after the strain and hardship of their winter campaign and ammunition was short. Astonishingly enough the armistice spun out for forty days during which both sides prepared for the further struggle which they recognized as inevitable.

Stamford reorganized his army so that by 15 April he had 3,500 well-armed foot and eight troops of horse.

The truce expired at midnight on 22 April. Stamford, suffering from gout, was lying at Exeter and James Chudleigh, son of Sir George, a professional soldier who had fought in Ireland and already a Major-General at the age of 25, led the army. He marched out of Lifton with five troops of horse, 1,500 musketeers, and 200 pikemen, advancing over Polston Bridge to attack Launceston.

The Action at Launceston. 23 April 1643

Hopton occupied Beacon Hill (or the Windmill), with half of Grenvile's regiment and lined the hedges at its foot with musketeers. He had a magnificent observation post and a splendid position but not enough men to man it, though fortunately for him William Godolphin's regiment arrived about the time that battle was joined.

Chudleigh reached the outskirts of Launceston about 9 o'clock, but it was not until an hour later that he began to assault Beacon Hill, driving Grenvile's musketeers from the hedges.

About 11 o'clock Major Slingsby appeared with Lord Mohun's regiment, and Berkeley rode up with some troops of horse and dragoons. Thus reinforced, Hopton, who must have had nearly 2,000 men, held his ground throughout the day, inflicting considerable losses on the Roundheads.

About 7 o'clock in the evening Slanning and Trevanion joined him, but at the same time Chudleigh was reinforced by 700 of Sir John Merrick's London greycoats, and by 100 of Sir John Northcote's regiment. These reinforcements defended Polston Bridge from the Royalist cavalry.

Hopton, whose whole army had now arrived, decided that the time had come for a counter-attack. Re-grouping his foot into three separate columns under himself, Berkeley and Major-General Thomas Bassett, he charged Chudleigh's main body. Shaken by its previous losses and exhausted by the day-long struggle the Roundheads were quickly disordered, but a number of factors saved them from complete rout: the steadiness of the greycoats who covered their retreat, the gathering darkness, and the gallantry of their young commander. Chudleigh himself brought up the rear, and when some of his followers, eager to be gone, told him it was impossible to save one of the guns, he harnessed the oxen to it with his own hands. The explosion of a powder magazine which scalded a number of the Cornish discouraged them from further pursuit, adding to the lassitude which, even with the best of soldiers, is the inevitable reaction to the strain of a hard-fought day.

The Action on Sourton Down. 25 April 1643

On 25 April the Cavaliers, hearing from a friend that the Roundheads in Okehampton were in great disquiet, determined to fall upon them at dawn the next morning. The Cornish army now consisted of 3,000 foot, the five voluntary regiments, 300 horse and 300 dragoons. They had four guns, including the two 12-pounders taken at Braddock Down, and Hopton thought his army 'the handsomest body of men that had been gotten together in those parts all that war', but pride comes before a fall. Chudleigh with 100 good cavalry was on the alert, determined to waylay them in the dark.

Lord Mohun and Hopton with Berkeley and Bassett were 'carelessly entertaining themselves in the head of the dragoons' when suddenly they saw the Roundhead party within carbine shot. Chudleigh's party fired a volley and charged, led by Captain Drake who shouted, 'Fall on, fall on, they run!' The dragoons panicked and fell back upon the horse and the Roundheads riding amongst them routed half the army. Mohun and Grenvile made a stand by the guns, and Hopton sent word to Slanning to bring the rearguard up to them.

The Roundhead cavalry were eventually beaten off, but not before they had killed some 60 men. To follow up his success Chudleigh sent to Okehampton for the rest of his men, 1,000 foot.

The Cavaliers manned an ancient trench and planted 'Swedes' Feathers' — sharp stakes about 6 feet long — in front of their guns. Soon, through the dark, sultry night, they saw lighted matches approaching. As soon as these came within range they fired two cannon at them, and at this the hearts of the Roundhead infantry failed them. But their cavalry made yet another charge, this time as far as the 'Swedes' Feathers'. Surprised perhaps by this unexpected obstacle, Chudleigh retired to his quarters. A fierce tempest broke over the moor drenching the discomfitted combatants and adding to their terrors.

Sourton Down was a disaster to the Cavaliers both morally and materially. They fell back to Bridestowe in disorder, leaving behind many weapons and horses, five barrels of powder and Hopton's portmanteau with all his papers. In it were letters from the King, from which, though they were in cipher, Stamford learned that the Cavaliers had orders to march into Somerset and join hands with Hertford and Prince Maurice. This combination the Earl determined to prevent.

Stamford spared no pains to prepare for the next bout, ordering his own forces to rendezvous at Torrington, there to join with such contingents as could be spared from the garrisons of Barnstaple and Bideford. Ample stores of food and ammunition were collected. Sending Lieut.-General Sir George Chudleigh and 1,200 horse to surprise the Cornish Posse Comitatus at Bodmin, the Earl crossed into Cornwall on 15 May and advanced to Stratton where he took up a strong position on the hill that now bears his name. He had 5,400 foot, 200 horse, and 13 guns.

To meet this invasion Hopton could muster only 2,400 foot and 500 horse, for he was compelled to leave garrisons at Saltash, Millbrook, and elsewhere. Nevertheless, he was eager for battle once more, for his administrative difficulties compelled him to seek a swift decision.

The Battle of Stratton. 16 May 1643

On the evening of 15 May Hopton, who had advanced via North Petherwin and Week St. Mary, was in contact with the Roundheads at Efford Mill south-west of Stratton. That night the Cornish commanders held a Council of War 'where it was quickly resolved, notwithstanding the great visible disadvantage, that they must either force the enemies' camp, while the most part of their horse and dragoons were from them, or unavoidably perish'.

The Roundhead position was indeed a strong one. Stamford Hill runs north and south, and is about 200 feet above sea level. On the east it is steep and thickly wooded, an obstacle inaccessible to cavalry and difficult for infantry. Elsewhere the slope is about 1 in 6 or 10. On the summit an ancient circular earthwork[1] served as a magazine.

During the night most of the Cornish army crossed the stream at

---

[1] The oval-shaped earthwork on the summit of Stamford Hill does *not* date from the time of the battle, but was there long *before* 1643. Though, from its shape, it cannot have been used as a battery, it may well have served as a powder magazine.

Efford Mill and occupied enclosures on the east side. They stood to
their arms all night, but there was no fighting until daybreak, when a
fire fight began with the Roundhead infantry lining hedges not more
than 200 yards away.

Hopton brought up the rest of his army, and divided the whole into
four columns of foot each about 600 strong, giving each two cannon.
The first column under Lord Mohun and Sir Ralph himself was to
attack the south of Stamford's camp; on the west were two columns,
one under Berkeley and Grenvile, the other under Slanning and
Trevanion. Bassett and Godolphin were to assault from the north.
By attacking in an arc in this way Hopton forced the enemy to fight
with their backs to the difficult precipitous slope which made their
position impregnable from the east. In reserve he kept Colonel John
Digby with 500 mounted men upon a sandy common, which is now
Bude Golf Course.

The battle began at about 5 o'clock in the morning, the Cornish
foot pressing up the hill and the Roundheads fighting stubbornly to
keep them down. The fight continued doubtful until about 3 p.m. by
which time the Cornish had little ammunition left.

Major-General James Chudleigh chose this moment for a counter-
attack. Advancing with a stand of pikes he attacked Grenvile, who was
at the head of a similar party. Chudleigh charged so smartly that there
was some disorder in the Royalist ranks and Sir Bevill himself was
knocked over, but being relieved immediately by Berkeley, who led
the musketeers of this column, and by some of his own officers, he
threw in his local reserves and managed to capture Chudleigh.

The other three columns were doing equally well, and drawing
nearer to one another as they pressed on up the hill; the Roundheads
began to give way abandoning their dead and some of their guns.

Between 3 and 4 o'clock the Cavalier commanders 'happened to
meet all together in one ground near the top of the hill, where having
joyfully embraced one another they pursued their victory, and
recovered the top of the hill, which the enemy had quitted in a rout'.
This passage is important as showing that all four columns did not
converge on the summit of the hill, but somewhat short of it: in other
words the columns 'bunched' – a common tendency. One Roundhead
officer says the Cavaliers came in on his rear because the left wing
failed, and so it seems that the two right-hand columns of the Cavaliers
pushed along the top of the plateau, rolling up Stamford's line.

All was over; Stamford fled to Bideford and thence to Exeter, leaving 300 dead and 1,700 prisoners. The Cavaliers took 13 brass guns, a mortar, 70 barrels of powder and a very great magazine of provisions, a timely prize when they had not four barrels of powder left, and when officers and men had lived for the last three or four days on a dry biscuit apiece.

Sir George Chudleigh hearing of this disaster beat a hasty retreat from Bodmin, many of his troopers falling into the hands of the Cornish.

Hopton now occupied Launceston where he heard for certain that Hertford and Maurice were marching westwards. His victory at Stratton gave him the opportunity to join them and although Plymouth and Exeter were still in the hands of the Roundheads, he advanced without delay.

Stamford deserves to be blamed for sending away his cavalry while the Cornish army was still in being. This looks like over-confidence. But in the battle he and his men had fought stoutly enough, which makes the Royalist victory all the more remarkable.

From his conduct of the counter-attack at the battle of Launceston there can be little doubt that the bold tactical idea of an assault by converging columns was Hopton's own invention. No doubt it was his voice that suggested this daring plan to the Royalist Council of War. The battle was fought out by the infantry. There is little reference to the guns in the accounts of the battle; the Royalist cavalry were kept in reserve and the Roundhead horse, only 200 strong, were too few to intervene effectively: 5,400 foot massed on Stamford Hill, with skirmishers well out in front during the early stages, were gradually forced back by four bodies, each the strength of a battalion. In the end the Roundheads must have been massed in great clumps on the top of the hill, with the Royalists gradually advancing from south to north, outflanking each hostile body in turn. It was a remarkable achievement against odds of more than two to one and speaks volumes for the Cornish infantry, their regimental officers and the Cavaliers who led the four columns. The Civil War saw many bigger battles than Stratton, but few as hard fought.

CHAPTER 4

The War in the North, 1643 – I

DURING THE OPENING three months of the Civil War there had been little observable strategy in the plans of the high command on either side. Indeed, for all practical purposes it resolved itself into a struggle for the capital with a series of disconnected local struggles for the supremacy. But with the turn of the year and the coming of spring 1643 signs of a more comprehensive strategy became evident in the Royalist camp. In modern terms it can be described as a concentric movement on London from north, northwest and west – the strategy of exterior lines.

In the last chapter we saw the first steps in this grand plan where in the extreme south-west, Sir Ralph Hopton always had London as the ultimate goal. In the centre we have seen the King consolidating his advanced position around Oxford within four days march of London. In the North a third army was gathering under the Earl of Newcastle whose ultimate aim was also to push southwards towards London. This can be described in modern parlance as 'a pincer movement' by the Western and Northern armies, with a third army in the centre prepared when the time came to advance on the common objective in co-operation with the other two. No written document in such specific terms is known to exist, but the evidence for the plan is circumstantial and compelling, and its gradual development and unfolding through the greater part of the year 1643 forms a fascinating study.

No such grand strategy is discernible on the Parliamentary side. Whereas the Royalists had a single command, the King being the supreme and undisputed commander, the Roundheads had a host of independent-minded leaders, over whom the Earl of Essex, the Captain-General, had but little influence or control. The war, in practice, was conducted by an unwieldy committee, the control being in the hands of the Houses of Parliament in London.

In the previous chapter we have traced the inception of the Grand Plan as we have called it. We will now follow its development in the North. Yorkshire was a kind of debatable land and the issue had to be decided there before any advance on the capital could be contemplated by the Cavaliers. The King had at the outset of the war taken so many men from that county that the remaining forces were fairly evenly balanced, although the Earl of Newcastle, having secured the town whose name he bore, was raising men apace among his friends and tenants in the four northern counties.

Newcastle's responsibilities were heavy. He controlled the only major port through which the King could be supplied with the arms, ammunition, men, and money that the Queen was raising on the Continent; supplies without which the Cavaliers had little hope of carrying on the war.

At the age of 50 the Earl was completely lacking in military experience, his chief qualification for high command being that he had the financial resources to raise himself an army. But he had many officer-like qualities; he was active, fearless, the foremost horseman of his day, and a good fencer. As a general he knew well enough how to play the part and indeed enjoyed it, but, rightly or wrongly, he referred everything to the discretion of Lieut.-General James King, a Scots officer of great experience and ability. King was to Newcastle what Ruthven was to Charles, and what Hopton had been to Hertford; we may call him his chief of staff.

In the other camp the old Lord Fairfax,[1] who had taken upon himself the command, had the solid backing of the clothing towns of the West Riding, Leeds, Bradford, Halifax, and Wakefield, with their sturdy Puritan population. Still more important, he had as his right hand man his elder son, Thomas, a man of 30 and already a soldier of experience in the Dutch Wars, who was to prove the outstanding leader of the Roundhead armies in the First Civil War. The Hothams from behind the double walls of Hull, the strongest fortress in the kingdom, menaced the Cavaliers of the East Riding. They were allies rather than subordinates, reluctant to acknowledge Lord Fairfax as their chief, even after his commission had arrived from London.

In the North Riding Sir Hugh Cholmley, a man no less independent than the Hothams, held Scarborough Castle for the Parliament; other Roundheads were raising troops in Richmond and Cleveland.

[1] Ferdinando, second Baron (1584–1648).

Faced with this situation the Yorkshire Cavaliers while negotiating with Lord Fairfax, had already appealed to Newcastle for assistance as early as 26 September, a month before Edgehill. The Earl, though willing to forward the King's service in any way, made certain propositions. 'First that I have all your consents and promises that the army be paid whilst they are in that county.' In addition he asked 'that all manner of provisions fit for an army be prepared and brought to the army the first day it enters'. This care for the good administration of his men is hardly what one would expect of the dilletante Clarendon has described. Newcastle, unlike many of the Civil War generals, opposed the system of free quarters, so common at the time and so destructive of discipline, leading as it inevitably did to pillage and waste. His last proposition is of even greater interest: 'That since this army was levied a purpose to guard her Majesty's person, that it shall not be held a breach of any engagement betwixt us if I retire with such number as I shall think fit for that service.'

The danger to the Yorkshire Cavaliers was very real. As early as 4 October the younger Hotham had taken Cawood Castle, 10 miles south of York, breaking the treaty between Fairfax and the Cavalier leaders, and by 21 October Lord Fairfax had taken the field.

When at length at the end of November Newcastle moved, he did so with remarkable speed. Securing his communications by fortified garrisons at Newcastle, Tynmouth Castle, the little port of Hartlepool and a few other places, he marched south at the head of an army 8,000 strong, some 2,000 being horse and dragoons.

The younger Hotham with no more than three troops of horse and four companies of foot boldly advanced to meet him and on 1 December vainly contested the crossing of the Tees at Piercebridge. Newcastle reached York without further opposition. His advance had decidedly tipped the strategic balance, but in young Sir Thomas Fairfax the Cavaliers were now faced with a tactician of the first rank.

Though never at the head of forces comparable in numbers with Newcastle's Cavaliers, such were Fairfax's eye for country and his gift for leadership that the early months of 1643 were studded with astonishing exploits by the Yorkshire Roundheads. Few of these actions can be graced with the name of battle, and indeed the Fairfaxes were usually too short of cavalry to engage in the open field, nevertheless by holding hastily barricaded towns, and by beating up quarters 'Fiery Tom' Fairfax imposed endless delays on his numerically superior enemy. He had already been in action at Bradford where with about 300 men he had resisted Sir William Savile and over 700 Cavaliers.

A few days later the Roundheads had moved on against Leeds, which the Cavaliers had abandoned without resistance, encouraging Lord Fairfax to advance to Tadcaster, only 10 miles from York, a bold move for a man who had no more than 1,000 men. He was now posted along the river Wharfe covering the West Riding from which he drew his supplies. Sir Thomas Fairfax with 300 foot and 40 horse was sent to guard the crossing at Wetherby and a fight typical of this phase of the Northern War ensued.

Sir Thomas Glemham led 800 men from York and marching through the woods, unseen by the Roundhead outposts, surprised the town at 6 o'clock one December morning. Sir Thomas Fairfax himself was the only man ready mounted – no doubt on his famous white horse:[1] 'One came running to me, and told me the enemy was entering the town. I presently galloped to the Court of Guard, where I found not above four men at their arms . . . which stood with me when Sir Thomas Glemham with about six or seven commanders more charged us; where, after a short but sharp encounter (wherein Major Carr was slain) they retired.'

During the fight the Roundheads' magazine blew up, causing a panic among the Cavaliers, who instantly retreated thinking that Fairfax had got some cannon. The Roundheads pursued for some miles, taking many prisoners. Fairfax had lost no more than 10 men.

After these repulses the Cavaliers were more than pleased to see Newcastle's great host appear.

The Action at Tadcaster. 6 December 1642

On 6 December the Cavaliers appeared before Tadcaster where Lord Fairfax had concentrated his force, probably about 1,500 strong. His Council of War judged the place untenable, but before he could draw up his men on an advantageous piece of ground nearby Newcastle's army was upon them.

The Earl's plan was to attack from the east with his main body, while his Lieut.-General, the Earl of Newport, with a column consisting of most of the horse and dragoons, fell upon the enemy from the west. This simple plan came to grief through Newport's failure to carry out his part.

But if his lieutenant had failed to appear Newcastle had not yet shot

[1] He was affectionately known to his side as The Rider on the White Horse.

his bolt. Four thousand men, divided into brigades, came close up to the works and tried to storm them. The Roundheads held their fire until the Cavaliers were very near, and then poured in such a volley that they were forced to retreat for the time being and take cover behind some ridges. From 11 in the morning until 5 in the evening the battle swayed to and fro, the Cavaliers, fighting resolutely, at one time took part of the town and manned two or three houses: Fairfax's men bravely recaptured the houses and burnt them. And so as it grew dark the Cavaliers withdrew into the fields nearby, resolved to try again next day.

Lord Fairfax heard from the country people that the Cavaliers had lost about 100 men. But after this hot day's work he had scarcely any ammunition left and a withdrawal was imperative although his own losses had not been heavy. He chose, mistakenly, to retreat to Selby, thus uncovering the clothing towns. Newcastle promptly occupied Tadcaster next day, cutting off the Fairfaxes from their friends in the West Riding and capturing a number of his men, who had stayed behind.

Newcastle's next move was to secure Pontefract Castle, which lay directly between the Roundheads in the West Riding and the Hothams at Hull. This done, he sent Sir John Henderson, a Scots veteran, to secure Newark and the vital passage of the Trent, without which it would be impossible to send men or arms to the King. Newark was doubly important, for its Royalist garrison watched over much of Nottinghamshire and Lincolnshire.

Writing from Selby on 10 December Lord Fairfax pointed out to the Committee at Westminster that when Newcastle had crossed the Tees almost all the North Riding Roundheads had disbanded, and Sir Hugh Cholmley, with 700 men, had shut himself up in Scarborough. Colonel Sir Matthew Boynton had taken his 800 men to Hull and there he remained. No help was forthcoming either from Sir John Gell of Derbyshire or from Sir Anthony Irby of Lincolnshire. With part of the army at Selby and part at Cawood under the younger Hotham, now his Lieutenant-General, he awaited, not without misgivings, the further onslaught of the Cavaliers.

Despite the winter season there was some fighting in Yorkshire during January 1643, but Newcastle, with his army in winter quarters, was content to levy more men and wait for the spring.

At this time Sir Thomas Fairfax was at Bradford. He raised a body

E

of foot by calling in the countrymen and on 23 January marched to attack Leeds. Arrived within cannon shot of the fortifications he sent in a trumpeter and summoned the Cavaliers to surrender. When the summons was rejected Fairfax stormed the place. He described the affair as follows: 'The business was hotly disputed for almost two hours. But after the enemy was beaten from their works, the barricados were soon forced open to the streets, where horse and foot resolutely entering, the soldiers cast down their arms, and rendered themselves prisoners.'

This swift bold action, typical of 'Fiery Tom', in which about 50 men were killed, caused Newcastle some concern. The Cavaliers quitted Wakefield and Pontefract and fell back to York. Newcastle recalled his soldiers from Newark, leaving Henderson to hold it with the local levies. This reopened the Parliamentary communications between Lord Fairfax at Selby and the clothing towns. However, the Earl soon recovered from the shock Leeds had given him, and re-occupied his former quarters at Pontefract.

The Queen landed at Bridlington Quay on 23 February despite the attentions of Captain William Batten and four ships of the Round-head navy, who, failing to intercept her, bombarded the house where she spent her first night ashore. 'I assure you that it was well marked', she wrote to her husband, 'for they always shot upon it.' The Dutch Admiral Martin Van Tromp, who with Frederick Henry's connivance had escorted Henrietta Maria to the English coast, eventually forced Batten to desist, and she arrived safely at York on 7 March.

The Queen, like Goring and King before her, brought arms, money, and officers for the Cavalier armies, and the train of artillery with which she was to march to Oxford constituted a very considerable addition to the Royal artillery.

But if the Royalists were slowly gaining ground in Yorkshire their fortunes elsewhere were at a low ebb. Rupert after storming Ciren-cester on 2 February had been foiled at Bristol early in March. Waller, fresh from a series of minor triumphs, set up his headquarters there towards the end of the month, so that the Oxford Cavaliers, whose main army was still in winter quarters, now had Essex to their east and 'William the Conqueror' to their west, though the former had not yet taken the field. In Cornwall the forty-day truce was still in being, but in Cheshire, after a similar period of neutrality, Sir William Brereton had won several successes for the Parliament. Lancashire, like Cheshire, had contributed generously to Charles' army in the previous autumn: with so many of their best men away with the King, the local Cavaliers were gradually losing ground at home.

An Eastern Association comprising Essex, Suffolk, Norfolk, Cambridge and Hertford had been established on 20 December. Five days earlier a Midland Association, Leicester, Derby, Nottingham, Northampton, Buckingham, Bedford, Rutland and Huntingdon, had come into being. The one was headed by Lord Grey of Wark and the other by Lord Grey of Groby, son of the Earl of Stamford.

On 27 February Major-General Ballard with a makeshift army from Lincolnshire, Nottinghamshire and Derbyshire appeared before Newark. Henderson fought a delaying action on Beacon Hill, burnt the Spittal and then fell back into the town. Next day the Roundheads stormed the town from both the north and the south, fighting their way to within pistol shot of the works. Sir John Gell, whose Derbyshire contingent formed a brigade with the men of Nottingham, seems to have made the most progress, and the Lincolnshire levies were moved round to support him. Seeing this, Henderson, who had the advantage of interior lines, massed on the south side of the town. For three hours he held the Roundheads in play and then at 6 p.m., sensing that his assailants had shot their bolt, he led a sortie. The Roundheads fell back in disorder, leaving three guns behind them.

Ballard drew off next day, his men grumbling that his treachery or incompetence had caused their defeat. The Roundheads had lost their best opportunity of taking Newark, whose fall would have been a serious blow to the Royalist cause, for without it the King could not hope to receive reinforcements and munitions from Newcastle. The Eastern Association had made no attempt to assist in this operation.

A month went by without any notable action, and then as the weather began to improve the Cavaliers were encouraged by a number of successes. The first was diplomatic rather than military. Sir Hugh Cholmley was persuaded by the Queen to change sides and Scarborough with its port and its strong castle fell to the Cavaliers.

The next success was more creditable.

The Action on Seacroft Moor. 30 March 1643

As time went on Lord Fairfax found his position at Selby growing more and more precarious, and decided to retreat to Leeds. Newcastle, who was well aware of his intentions, posted his army on Clifford Moor, meaning to intercept him.

To cover his father's march Sir Thomas Fairfax advanced on Tadcaster. The garrison fell back to York without fighting and the Roundheads began to destroy the defence works. This move perplexed Newcastle, who suspected some design against York. He reacted quickly, sending General Lord Goring with 20 troops of horse and dragoons to retake the town.

George Lord Goring, now a man of 34, had long been Colonel of a foot regiment in the Dutch service. At the siege of Breda in 1637 a shot in the ankle-bone had lamed him for life. In the second Scots War he had commanded a brigade of foot.

Historians, following Clarendon, have never tired of condemning Goring both as a man and as a general. It must be granted that he was an ambitious intriguer and an extravagant gamester; he was unquestionably fond of the bottle, and lacked the steadiness to stick to any plan of campaign requiring deliberation and patience. But with all this he was a brave and skilful officer. Bulstrode who served on his staff says of him: 'He was without dispute as good an officer as any served the King, and the most dexterous in any sudden emergency that I have seen.' Such was the man who was about to cross swords with Fairfax for the first time. They were to meet three times more before the war had run its course; at Wakefield, at Marston Moor, and at Langport.

Fairfax had just left Tadcaster when Goring came up and although the bridge had been broken down he crossed the river. Sir Thomas had only three troops of horse and was therefore at a grave disadvantage, for he had now to cross Bramham Moor, a large plain. He ordered his foot to march off while he fought a rearguard action in the narrow lanes leading to the Moor. Goring with about 800 horse pressed on, not waiting for General King, who was marching to his support with foot and guns.

There was a good deal of firing but numbers told, and Fairfax, having gained, as he hoped, time for his infantry to get out of danger, was forced to give way. Imagine his wrath when emerging on to the open Moor he found his foot where he had left them! Undismayed he marched on across the plain with his foot in two divisions and his horse in the rear. The Royalists followed about a musket shot behind with their men in three good bodies. At first the Roundheads kept good order, and Goring merely marched along behind them, biding his time. And so Fairfax got across Bramham Moor on to Seacroft Moor, which is smaller. His men now began to think that they were safe and became careless. It was a hot day and the officers had great trouble getting them out of houses where they had gone in search of drink. Goring's moment had come. He gave the word, the trumpets blared out, the Cavaliers struck their spurs into their chargers' sides and came galloping across the moor into the flank and rear of Fairfax's little army.

Almost at once the countrymen flung down their arms and fled and the rest of the infantry soon followed. Fairfax had too few pikemen to form a hedgehog and stave off Goring's horse. Rallying a few officers he retreated with much difficulty, losing his cornet in the rout. Two hundred Roundheads fell and 800 were taken.

'This', Fairfax admits, 'was one of the greatest losses we ever received,' – but it was some consolation to find on reaching Leeds that his father and his forces had arrived unmolested.

Goring was not the only distinguished cavalry officer in Newcastle's army. The Earl had another in Charles Cavendish (1620–1643), second son of the Earl of Devonshire, a natural soldier, who had served in the 1641 campaign under the Prince of Orange and had fought as a volunteer in the Lifeguards at Edgehill. He soon made his name in a series of hack-and-thrust affairs. In the spring Newcastle sent him south with a small flying column to join hands with Colonel General Henry Hastings' forces in the Midlands and with the Lincolnshire Royalists. With the help of Henderson and the Newark garrison he stormed Grantham on 23 March. His next success was the action on Ancaster Heath on 11 April, when he defeated a combined force of 1,500 Roundheads under Lord Willoughby of Parham and the younger Hotham.

Newcastle's gradual advance southwards was beginning to cause grave concern in the Eastern Association, the real core of the Roundhead resistance. Oliver Cromwell, now a colonel, was already at Huntingdon by 10 April with six or seven troops of horse. Early in April he had summoned 12,000 men from Cambridge, Norfolk, and Suffolk. Of these 5,500 under Lord Grey of Wark marched on 10 April to join Essex at Reading. The others were intended to make head against Newcastle whose army now amounted to about 16,000 well-armed men, of whom nearly 3,000 were horse and dragoons. This number must have included garrisons as well as the forces of the Queen and General Cavendish, but it was nevertheless a formidable host. If Newcastle moved south with this great army the Eastern Association would be hard put to it to bar his path. That he was unable to do so was largely due to the continued activities of Lord Fairfax and his diminutive army.

Cromwell now posted his forces across the path of the northern Cavaliers. On 22 April he established his headquarters at Peterborough, where his troopers amused themselves by burning the books in the Cathedral and by acts of iconoclasm.

Cromwell had come to the front rapidly since his return from the Edgehill campaign. Already in February 1643 we find him referred to as Colonel – there is no evidence that he ever held the rank of major or lieutenant-colonel – and besides being a Member of Parliament he was also a member of both the Eastern and the Midland Counties Associations. His name now begins to figure in the contemporary newspapers: he is already as important in his sphere as Hampden and Hazelrig, more so than Strode and Stapleton. And already he was recruiting his troopers among 'the godly'; according to Whitelocke 'most of them freeholders and freeholders' sons, who upon a matter of conscience engaged in this quarrel'. In a well-known letter of 29 August 1643 Cromwell tells us much of how he selected his officers: 'I had rather have a plain russet-coated captain that knows what he fights for, and loves what he knows, than that which you call a gentleman and is nothing else. I honour a gentleman that is so indeed.

'I understand Mr Margery hath honest men will follow him: if so, be pleased to make use of him. It much concerns you good to have conscientious men.'

It was not only the Cavaliers that looked askance at such officers. The Earl of Manchester, Cromwell's immediate superior, speaking three years later, complained, doubtless with a measure of exaggeration born of the malice between them, 'Col. Cromwell raising of his regiment makes choice of his officers not such as were soldiers or men of estate, but such as were common men, poor and of mean parentage, only he would give them the title of godly, precious men. . . . I have heard him oftentimes say that it must not be soldiers nor Scots that must do this work, but it must be the godly to this purpose. . . . If you look upon his own regiment of horse, see what a swarm there is of those that call themselves godly; some of them profess they have seen visions and had revelations.' It is evident that the Ironsides were far from typical of the men who served the Parliament. Quantity rather than quality was sufficient for most commanders; countrymen armed with clubs, Royalist prisoners and deserters, pressed men of every description were to be found in the ranks of Essex, Fairfax and Waller. The Cavaliers too raised men where they could. To Cromwell belongs the credit of being the pioneer of 'personnel selection'.

On 25 April he joined forces with Sir Miles Hobart, a Norfolk colonel, and Sir Anthony Irby in beseiging a Royalist cousin, Captain Cromwell, who had made a garrison at Croyland. The place surrendered after a three day siege, which is only remarkable as being Cromwell's first. Indeed it seems that it was the first time he had been in action since Edgehill. Thus well had Fairfax kept the Royalist wolf from the Eastern Association's door.

At the end of April the Roundheads were holding their own in the West, while in the Thames Valley Essex was actually advancing. It was only in the North that things looked black for the Parliament. The Cavaliers were concentrating at Newark and an invasion of the eastern counties seemed imminent. On 2 May the Commons ordered Cromwell, Irby and seven others to secure Lincolnshire.

Accordingly Lord Grey of Groby and Oliver Cromwell received orders from Essex to rendezvous at Stamford with Sir John Gell, and with the Nottingham forces, and then to join the Lincolnshire Roundheads. But this ambitious combination broke down largely because Grey was afraid Hastings might attack Leicester.

Action near Grantham. 13 May 1643

This skirmish deserves some notice as a stage in Oliver Cromwell's military education, but the records of it are very incomplete and its importance has been greatly exaggerated: S. R. Gardiner goes so far as to say: 'The whole fortune of the Civil War was in that nameless skirmish.'

A Parliamentary force under Lord Willoughby of Parham, Sir John Hotham and Cromwell had eventually concentrated at Sleaford on 9 May. Their intention was to make another attack on Newark – so long a thorn in their side. They made little haste, for though they reached Grantham on 11 May they were still quartered there and in the neighbouring villages two days later.

This delay gave the Cavaliers time for a counterstroke. They concerted their plans with great secrecy, Cavendish bringing his men south from Gainsborough and meeting Henderson with the Newark horse near Grantham in the dead of night. Their combined force amounted to 21 troops of horse and three or four of dragoons, perhaps 1,200 men in all.

In the early hours of the morning of 13 May Cavendish surprised three of Lord Willoughby's troops quartered at Belton and practically destroyed them, killing 70 and taking 40 prisoners with trifling loss to his own side. Such Roundheads as survived owed their escape to the darkness.

Late in the evening of the 13th the Cavaliers advanced again and faced the Roundheads within two miles of Grantham. Cromwell, our only source for the details, himself tells us what then took place.

'So soon as we had the alarm, we drew out our forces, consisting of about twelve troops, whereof some of them so poor and broken, that you shall seldom see worse. With this handful it pleased God to cast the scale. For after we had stood a little above musket-shot the one body from the other and the dragooners having fired on both sides for the space of half an hour or more, *they not advancing towards us, we agreed to charge them*,[1] and advancing the body after many shots on both sides, came on with our troops *a pretty round trot, they standing firm to receive us;*[1] and our men charging fiercely upon them, by God's providence they were immediately routed, and ran all away, and we had the execution of them two or three miles.'

The Cavaliers lost 100 killed and wounded, and 45 prisoners. Cromwell says quaintly 'we lost but two men *at the most* on our side'.

It is doubtful whether the Roundheads were really outnumbered in this fight, for *Special Passages*, a Roundhead newspaper, in its number for this very week credits Cromwell alone with '2000 brave men, well disciplined', and there were also the contingents of Lord Willoughby and Hotham. It is likely that the two sides were fairly evenly matched.

The Roundheads won because, although they took half an hour to make up their minds to it, they attacked. The Cavaliers lost because they stood still to receive the charge. The Roundheads did not charge very fast, but they did at least resort to shock action, and cavalry battles are seldom won by any other means. That much Cromwell learned at Grantham, a flash of insight into something that was obvious from the outset to professionals such as Balfour and Goring.

Those were pious times and it was customary for commanders on either side to ascribe their tactical successes to the Almighty. In his letter Cromwell does so no less than three times. It is evident that he was relieved, even surprised, by the first success in which his regiment had shared. The result confirmed his belief in the men he was raising, but to regard Grantham as a tactical gem is going altogether too far. It was an elementary lesson in the Art of War.

[1] Our italics.

Despite their success the Roundheads seem to have abandoned their attempt on Newark, which leaves one with the suspicion that both sides had had enough for the time being.

The Storming of Wakefield. 21 May 1643

To return to Yorkshire, on 21 May Sir Thomas Fairfax made a night attack on Wakefield. The object of the operation was simply to take prisoners who could be exchanged for the Roundheads taken by Goring at Seacroft Moor. Believing that the Royalist garrison was only 800 or 900 strong, Sir Thomas set out with about 1,500 horse and foot collected from Leeds, Bradford, Halifax and Howley House.

The Roundheads met at Howley House at midnight and reached Wakefield about 4 o'clock in the morning, only to find the Cavaliers on the alert, their works manned and 500 musketeers lining the hedges around the town. Fairfax and his officers held a brief consultation and decided to attack none the less. The Parliamentary foot under Major-General John Gifford and Colonel Sir William Fairfax stormed the works in three places and after two hours fighting some of the foot carried one of the Royalist barricades and tore it down. Sir Thomas charged through the gap at the head of his own troop followed by two others. The street was full of Royalist foot, but Fairfax charged right through them, leaving them to be mopped up by his own infantry.

The two senior Royalist commanders were Goring and Sir Francis Mackworth, the Sergeant-Major-General of Newcastle's foot. Goring was sick of a fever, but with the presence of mind which seldom failed him in an emergency, rose from his couch, and swiftly mounting, led a counter-attack. 'And presently', wrote Fairfax, 'we were charged again with Horse led by General Goring, where, after a hot encounter, some were slain, and himself taken prisoner . . .'

Meanwhile the Royalists had been reinforced by Sir William Lambton's regiment which had come to the aid of the garrison while the fight was in progress. Pushing on single-handed Fairfax found himself in the market-place, face to face with this fresh unit and three troop of horse. Luckily for him he was well mounted and putting his horse at one of the Royalist barricades he got clear away.

Meanwhile Maj.-General Gifford had brought a captured gun into action from the churchyard and a second charge by the Roundhead horse drove the Cavaliers out of the town. Most of their horse got away, but about 1,500 prisoners and much ammunition fell into the hands of the victors. The Roundheads were astonished to discover that they had attacked a garrison of not less than 3,000 infantry and seven troops of horse. Four guns were taken. Mackworth was among those who managed to escape.

With the capture of the impetuous commander of his cavalry Newcastle was compelled to lean more than ever on the methodical General King. Once more 'Fiery Tom' had made his presence felt and this at a moment when things elsewhere were beginning to go badly for the Roundhead armies. In the West Hopton had just won his victory at Stratton; in the centre the first convoys of munitions had just reached Oxford.

By the end of May Lord Grey of Groby had concentrated an army of between 5,000 and 6,000 men at Nottingham. There were troops from Derbyshire and Lincolnshire besides Cromwell and the younger Hotham, but the commanders quarrelled and their army did little or nothing to prevent the Queen's army marching south.

Henrietta Maria, who had left York with some 4,500 men on 4 June, set out from Newark on 21 June. Cavendish stormed Burton-on-Trent on 2 July and the Queen was able to join forces with the King on 13 July.

Not only did she bring reinforcements sufficient to tip the balance in the South Midlands but her absence left Newcastle free to concentrate on his main objective – Lord Fairfax. Relieved of responsibility for the Queen's safety the Earl advanced rapidly and on 22 June he took Howley House, between Pontefract and Bradford.

The Battle of Adwalton Moor. 30 *June* 1643

The end of June found Lord Fairfax still holding Bradford, and Newcastle marched to attack it from the east. A moorland ridge (now partly built over) runs east from Bradford, reaching its highest point near the little village of Adwalton, five miles away. On the morning of 30 June Newcastle reached Adwalton and, hearing that Fairfax was approaching, halted and occupied a position astride the ridge, which here is about 1,500 yards wide. His position ran some 700 yards west of Adwalton, with its right embracing the road to Bradford and its left a short way down the southern slope. His army was about 10,000 strong, horse, foot, and artillery. The latter included two demi-cannon, nicknamed *Gog* and *Magog*.[1] The Roundhead army con-

---

[1] A cannon-ball from one of these guns, and several smaller ones, are now kept in the village school. They probably included some Drakes, for there is a Drake Lane just in rear of the village.

sisted of about 4,000 trained troops and an unspecified number of country folk armed with agricultural implements and devoid of discipline.

Despite this disparity in numbers Lord Fairfax had moved off at about 7 or 8 o'clock in the morning and advanced straight up the Adwalton road. One and a half miles short of that village he drove in the Cavalier Forlorn Hope posted on a small hillock called Westgate Hill. He pushed on, and coming in sight of his opponents' position he deployed his army on a line some 500 yards short of them. He himself commanded the centre or reserve, General Gifford the left and Sir Thomas Fairfax the right. The latter's division was posted on the southern slope of the hill, where it was entirely out of sight of the remainder of the army.

The battle that ensued consisted for the most part of a series of cavalry charges on the part of the Royalists and of counter-charges by their opponents. These counter-charges were delivered with great spirit, especially on the southern flank. Sir Thomas Fairfax was holding an enclosure, with his musketeers, about 1,000 strong, lining the hedges next the moor, 'which', he writes, 'was good advantage to us who had so few Horse'. His dragoons were dismounted and he kept his five troops of cavalry in support.

Ten or 12 troops of horse charged him, striving to get through a gate from the moor where only five or six could enter abreast. The few that broke in 'found sharp entertainment' from Fairfax's cavalry, while those that stayed in the road 'got as hot welcome from the musketeers that flanked them in the hedges'. In the end the Cavaliers, who had lost their commander, Colonel Thomas Howard, were forced to retreat and the Roundheads 'gained ground of them'.

The Cavaliers, 13 or 14 troops, led this time by Colonel George Heron, came down again and charged. Fairfax's men defended themselves as before, but this time with much more difficulty, for many of the Cavaliers got in among them. But in the end they were beaten off and their leader slain.

After the second charge 'Fiery Tom' led an impetuous charge after them along a convenient ledge of fairly level ground that led up to a hedged lane named Warren Lane, leading down the hill to the south 600 yards from the Roundhead position. The charge came to a halt at this lane and Fairfax prudently recalled his troops to their original position. As he withdrew the Royalists let off one of their guns and by a strange chance hit four men of Captain Copley's troop, who while their comrades were fighting about them had been stripping Colonel Heron's dead body. Fairfax, who was a strictly religious man, regarded this an Act of Divine Justice.

Meanwhile on the left wing, where Gifford with a similar force was engaged with the Royalist foot, things were also going well for the Roundheads whose resolute bearing had made Newcastle think of retreating. Indeed he had given his orders, and some of the Cavaliers had actually marched off the field.

This was the climax of the battle.

Now came one of those sudden and unexpected changes of fortune which so often decide the fate of a battle. Colonel 'Skirton',[1] 'a wild and desperate man', Fairfax calls him, desired his General to let him charge once more.

This initiative was rewarded. Advancing with a stand of pikes – most of Fairfax's foot were musketeers – he broke in upon Gifford's wing which, being unsupported by the reserve, lost ground. Perhaps the Royalists struck a portion of the line held by the country levies. Sir Thomas Fairfax blames Gifford, 'who did not his part as he ought to have done', and also some disaffected officers. He does not explain how it was that his father did not throw in his reserve.

The Cavaliers were not slow to see their advantage and to pursue it, bringing up fresh troops. The Roundheads lost heart and beginning to flee were soon broken. Newcastle's horse charged again, and the Royalists turned their guns upon the main body of Lord Fairfax's horse, killing many and routing them.

Once the rot was started the whole of the Roundhead left followed by the reserve gave way and fled down the road to Bradford.

Incredible though it may sound, Lord Fairfax had not warned his son that he was falling back – or perhaps his messenger failed to get through – and the latter, as we have seen, was out of sight of the rest of the army. He maintained his ground, and when at long last someone got through with orders to retreat he found himself practically surrounded, the Cavaliers having cut the Bradford road.

Accordingly he withdrew to the south down the main road to Halifax, eight miles away. Arrived there, and finding that Bradford was still holding out, he turned sharp to his right, and despite the fact

---

[1] Who was this hero of Adwalton Moor? There seems to have been no colonel of this name in the Royalist Army. Probably he was Colonel Posthumous Kirton, a veteran of the Dutch service who fell with the Whitecoats at Marston Moor.

that his foot had marched fifteen miles that day and fought a battle, he pushed on till he had reached the town. Only a general who had a tight hold on his troops and an iron will could have accomplished this. Next morning he took command of the town, his father having made off for Leeds. Sir Thomas' general conduct that day was the brightest spot in the Parliamentary army, but he may be censured for failing to keep in touch with the troops on his left during the battle. The Roundheads lost three guns, 500 killed, and 1,400 prisoners. The Royalist losses, though they included several senior officers, were relatively light.

Newcastle could move fast when he chose. That night he arrived before Bradford and made his approaches. Next day his two batteries came into action very near the town on hills within half musket shot. The Roundheads had two Drakes on top of the tower, which was lined with woolpacks, but the Cavaliers battered it so that nobody could stay on it. By Sunday night the attackers had gained both ends of the town, and the Roundheads were down to their last barrel of powder. Sir Thomas Fairfax and Maj.-General Gifford broke out that night with a party of 50 horse, but his foot were less successful and the garrison, 300 strong, surrendered next day.

Lord Fairfax tried to secure Leeds but 700 Royalist captives broke out of the prison and seized the magazine with 1,500 arms and 12 cannon, holding the town until Newcastle relieved them. Lord Fairfax, his army now reduced to three or four troops, beat a hasty retreat to Selby.

Hotham had chosen this moment to declare for the King, but when things seemed most desperate the citizens of Hull secured him, and after a hazardous journey the defeated Roundhead commanders made their way there through a host of enemies. It was 60 miles, but after a desperate journey they reached the only stronghold left to them in Yorkshire. To Sir Thomas things must have seemed black indeed. His wife had been captured in the flight from Bradford and he himself wounded. But things might have been worse. Fairfax's wound healed well, and the courtly Earl of Newcastle, who disdained to make war on women, sent Lady Fairfax to Hull in his own coach.

Behind the walls of Hull the Fairfaxes began to raise new forces and in a short time had 2,500 foot and 700 horse.

The Eastern Association still lay between Newcastle and London, but with his victory at Adwalton Moor the initiative lay more than ever with the Cavaliers.

While Newcastle was conquering Yorkshire the Roundheads were equally successful in Lancashire, but this was a sideshow, for events there had little influence on the main campaigns of the war. The Earl of Derby, like Hertford in the West, greatly overestimated his personal influence. A loyal and gallant man, he had little military talent and by June 1643 nothing remained to the Cavaliers but Lathom House, held by his brave countess, and Greenhalgh Castle.

CHAPTER 5

The War in the Centre — I

W HILE IN THE West the Cornish Cavaliers were carrying all before them, and in the North Newcastle and Fairfax were striving for the mastery, operations in the Centre were of a more episodic and disconnected nature, making it more than usually difficult to 'see the wood for the trees'. It will perhaps assist the reader to open this chapter with a summary of the course of events, before relating the more important actions in greater detail.

At first the initiative lay with the Roundheads, who outnumbered Charles' main army very considerably. In the Thames Valley Essex faced the King, while there was another Parliamentary army in the field under Sir William Waller, operating further south.

The Royalist army as we have seen had already proved too weak to capture London without help from the North or the West, and during the winter the King was content to improve his central position by enlarging the territory he held round Oxford. In this he was not entirely successful, for Waller cut off and destroyed two regiments of his Edgehill army at Winchester on 12 December. Rupert's capture of Cirencester on 2 February 1643 was the Cavaliers' chief success at this period.

Essex was content to hibernate and the only sign of life given by his army was an abortive attempt on the Royalist outpost at Brill on 27 January. John Hampden led the attackers, but he was repulsed with loss by Sir Gilbert Gerard and two Lancashire regiments of foot.

Waller on the other hand was most active and in addition to his success at Winchester took Farnham Castle, Arundel Castle and Chichester in the same month. These exploits which, except for Winchester, were victories over ill-armed local levies, won him great popularity with the citizens of London, and the title of 'William the Conqueror'. Much more important, they won him the command of the Western Association, which was formed on 11 February 1643 and included Gloucestershire, Wiltshire, Somersetshire, Worcestershire, Shropshire and the City of Bristol, where he set up his headquarters in March.

Sir William Waller was a man of about 45; as a young man he had been in the Venetian service, and had later fought against the Imperialists in Bohemia and the Palatinate. No commander on the Parliamentary side had so rapidly won a reputation for energy and tactical skill. The Royalist Colonel Walter Slingsby, himself an experienced professional soldier, generously describes Waller as 'the best shifter and chooser of ground when he was not master of the field that ever I saw'.

By February therefore, the Oxford Cavaliers were in a distinctly dangerous position, with Essex in front of them and Waller barring the road to South Wales, one of their best potential recruiting areas. Lord Herbert, son of the Roman Catholic Marquis of Worcester, a man who spent altogether nearly a million pounds in the Royal cause, had already raised a small army of Welshmen. This force, owing to the shortage of trained officers, was as yet but imperfectly drilled and disciplined when on 24 March Waller fell upon it at Highnam and utterly routed it, taking nearly 1,600 prisoners.

Meanwhile the Royalists were active in the North Midlands, occupying Lichfield, Stafford, Tamworth, and Ashby-de-la-Zouch and paving the way for the approach of munitions and reinforcements from the Queen and Newcastle.

To oppose this movement Parliament sent Lord Brooke to command its forces in Warwickshire and Staffordshire. Hard fighting ensued – two sieges of Lichfield, the battle of Hopton Heath (19 March) and the storming of Birmingham by Rupert (3 April).

While Rupert was busy before Lichfield, his brother Maurice was sent to reckon with Waller and he conducted a brief campaign in the Forest of Dean thereby relieving the pressure on Herbert's Welshmen.

These successes, however, did nothing to help the King at Oxford, whose position went from bad to worse. In April Essex at last moved forward, laying siege to Reading on 16 April. Charles promptly summoned his nephews and marched to its relief, only to be foiled at Caversham Bridge (25 April). Reading fell on the 27th, and the road was clear for Essex to advance on Oxford. This was a grave reverse for the King, for clearly he would have to recapture the town before he could make a second attempt on London – a target that he kept constantly before his eyes. While the Roundheads held the capital they seemed bound to win the war in the long run.

Luckily for the Royalists neither Essex nor Waller was enough of a strategist to take advantage of this fleeting opportunity and in mid-May two events greatly improved the Royalist position. On 15 May the Queen's first great convoy, 40 wagon-loads of arms and munitions including 300 barrels of powder, reached Oxford. From that time forward the King's army was not notably worse armed than Essex's, and with reinforcements from the North and the addition of the Reading garrison, who had been allowed to march out with their arms, it was numerically at least as strong. The second factor was Hopton's victory far away at Stratton on 16 May. The King, knowing that the Cornish Cavaliers were short of cavalry, had already determined to send some to them, and on 19 May Hertford and Maurice marched west to join Hopton. From now on Waller's attention was focused on the Western army; he was no longer in a position to co-operate with Essex even if he had so desired, but he still barred the road to South Wales.

In July the King grew stronger still, for on the 13th he and the Queen met once more — on the field of Edgehill — and she had brought with her an army of about 3,000 men with eight or nine pieces of ordnance and 100 wagons. The Oxford army now definitely outnumbered Essex. The same day saw Waller's army virtually destroyed at Roundway Down by Lieut.-General Wilmot and Prince Maurice. Essex in the meantime had got no further than Thame and had not attempted to besiege Oxford.

The Battle of Hopton Heath. 19 March 1643

The northern outpost of the King's circle of fortresses round Oxford was Banbury, where Spencer Compton, second Earl of Northampton, was quartered with his regiments of horse and foot. A veteran of Breda and Lemgo, he was 41 years of age. Ordered to recover Lichfield, he marched north with his own and Prince Charles' regiments of horse and a handful of foot, joining forces near Stafford with Col.-General Henry Hastings and several of his mounted regiments. Their combined force numbered about 1,200.

To oppose them Sir John Gell co-operated with Sir William Brereton, the Cheshire leader, who now advanced on Stafford. Their plan was to rendezvous on Hopton Heath, about three miles north-east of Stafford, and launch a combined attack on that town, which Northampton had reached on the previous day.

F

At about noon on Sunday 19 March Gell's little army of horse and foot, about 750 strong, ascended the hill out of Weston on the Stafford road, whilst Brereton in similar strength was approaching from Stoke along the Salt road.

On hearing of Gell's approach, Northampton hurriedly collected his men from their scattered quarters and marched out up the long gradual slope to meet his opponent.

The roads from Sandon and from Weston to Stafford cross the ridge on the south side of the Trent valley 2,000 yards apart. This ridge runs due east-west and from its summit the church towers of Stafford may be seen. Gell was the first to ascend it, and he at once realized that it would form an excellent locality for the junction of the two columns and a good defensive position in case of attack. He therefore deployed his troops along it without waiting for the arrival of Brereton. Running along the east side of the Stafford road was the stone wall bounding Ingestre Park, on which Gell rested his left flank. On the right of the road a carriage road 300 yards in length ran along the ridge top, leading up to a country seat called Heathyards. The house was in the centre of a small park or enclosure 500 yards in diameter, and bounded by a stone wall.[1] On the south side the wall was about 200 yards down the gentle slope and provided an excellent line for Gell's foot and dragoons. The three heavy field guns were placed on the top of the ridge near the house, while the eight Drakes were pushed forward into the front line. Further to the west there were some hedges for a few hundred yards, opening on to rough 'moorish' ground, pitted with rabbit holes. Here Gell placed his main body, with his small force of cavalry on his extreme right, where they were shortly joined by Brereton's horse, while the Cheshire foot plodded along some distance in rear. When eventually they arrived they prolonged the line to the west, making it about 1,500 yards in all – an unusually long front for so small an army.

As the Cavalier horse approached they could see the Roundhead guns in the enclosure on the ridge with the wall of Ingestre Park on their right hand, and consequently they deployed to their left. There was a halt for 30 minutes within a few hundred yards of the enemy, during which dragoons were sent out to silence the opposing dragoons which they succeeded in doing. A sharp fight ensued.

The Cavaliers now dragged up a heavy 29-pounder, or demi-

[1] The house has since been replaced by a farmhouse, but vestiges of the boundary wall still remain on the north side.

cannon, named *Roaring Meg*. The Dunrobin MS[1] gives a graphic account of the havoc she caused. 'We drew up our cannon, which was one very good piece and did great execution, for the first shot killed six of their men and hurt four, and the next made such a lane through them that they had little mind to close again.' Gell's stand of pikes drawn up on the rabbit warren must have offered a magnificent target.

The Cavaliers now decided to make a general onslaught against the hostile centre. The first furious charge, led by the gallant Northampton in person, was completely successful, both Gell's and Brereton's horse being put to flight in less than a quarter of an hour. All but a few were driven from the field.

Northampton now rallied his horse for a second charge — 'a most desperate attempt' Brereton called it — against the remnants of the Roundhead horse who were sheltered by their infantry. The Cavaliers were met with a volley which did some damage, but rode over some of the hostile foot, and almost routed Gell's main body. However, they were then so pelted by musketry that they were driven back, though not before they had taken eight pieces of ordnance, including two carts of Drakes, in the hedges. The going over the rabbit warrens made things doubly difficult for the cavalry, but even so they overran the main battery.

But a disaster had befallen the Cavaliers, for Northampton was himself unhorsed — quite possibly owing to a rabbit hole — and was temporarily separated from his men. Surrounded by enemies he killed a colonel and several others with his sword. His armour was so good that he held his own until someone struck off his helmet with the butt of a musket. Summoned to surrender, he answered, 'I scorn to take quarter from such base rogues, as you are', and was killed by a blow on the head with a halberd.

Undeterred by this, Sir Thomas Byron launched a third charge, recapturing the guns, killing more of Gell's foot and driving the last remnants of his horse from the field; but now he also fell wounded with a shot in the thigh. Hastings essayed a fourth charge but this time the horsemen were so scattered and disorganized and their horses so blown, that he found it quite impracticable.

Dusk was now falling. Gell's men were also feeling the strain, and had reached 'the sticking point'. Three of their guns had been taken,

---

[1] Fresh and important light has been thrown on the battle by a MS unearthed in the archives of Dunrobin Castle. This Cavalier account has been published by the William Salt Society, Stafford.

retaken, and taken again. Their horse had long since abandoned the field, and under cover of the darkness the Roundhead foot of both Gell and Brereton slipped silently away, leaving the Royalists in possession of the field. In addition to the guns they had had about 500 casualties, while their opponents' loss was under 50, though many were officers.

The upshot of the battle illustrates a well-known military maxim – one on which Napoleon insisted – the danger of attempting to unite one's forces on the field of battle. Brereton was late at the rendezvous; had his infantry been in position in time, things would have gone hard with the Royalists. But Northampton's quick and bold initiative had completely foiled the Roundhead's plan. They retreated in widely divergent directions – Brereton to the north-west back to Stone and ultimately into Cheshire; Gell to the north-east to Chartley (where his errant horse rejoined him) and Uttoxeter. Their project of capturing Stafford by a quick *coup de main* had ended in disaster.

We have seen that Lord Herbert's force of Welshmen had been routed by Waller at Highnam, a village about two miles west of Gloucester, on 24 March. At the beginning of April Waller followed up his success by advancing into Monmouthshire, where the Welsh fell back before him. He marched as far west as Usk and then returned to Chepstow only to find that Prince Maurice had reached Tewkesbury, and joined forces with Lord Grandison, who, with a detachment of the Oxford army, had taken possession of that town. In those days there was no bridge across the Severn at Tewkesbury (though there was one over the Avon), but constructing a bridge of boats, Maurice crossed into the Forest of Dean with 2,000 horse and foot. The Prince deployed his men in a ten mile cordon hoping to cut Waller off from the Parliamentary stronghold of Gloucester. Sending his infantry, guns, and baggage across the Severn at Aust opposite Chepstow, the latter marched with his horse and dragoons against Prince Maurice. There was a clash at the village of Little Dean, but Waller fought his way through and made for Gloucester. The Governor, Lieut.-Colonel Edward Massey, came out to meet them and it was agreed that Waller's tired troops should hold Gloucester, while the garrison made a surprise attack on Tewkesbury. This plan was completely successful.

The Battle of Ripple Field. 1 3 *April* 1643
There are only two contemporary accounts of this battle, the best

being by Massey's chaplain, John Corbet, who — from the amount of detail he gives — would appear to have been an eyewitness. *Mercurius Aulicus* adds some interesting details, taken no doubt from the letters of Royalist officers. If either Prince Maurice or Waller wrote a narrative of the engagement it has long since disappeared.

No sooner had Massey's men taken possession of Tewkesbury (12 April) and broken Prince Maurice's bridge of boats, than they caught sight of the Royalists who were still west of the Severn. During the evening Waller and his cavalry rode in from Gloucester. He deduced, correctly, that Maurice was making for Upton Bridge six miles N.W. of Tewkesbury, the only bridge over the Severn below Worcester. Waller decided either to hold or to break down this bridge, so as to cut the Prince's communications with Oxford. However, his men had already marched 11 miles that day and it was not until next morning that he set out. Maurice, on the other hand, seeing his bridge of boats gone, pushed on without delay to Upton and seized the bridge.

On the morning of 13 April Waller marched north out of Tewkesbury across King John's Bridge which spans the River Avon, up the steep slope of the Mythe Hill, and — keeping the Severn on his left — followed the old road (not the modern A38) towards Worcester. This highway is marked by crosses set up by King John, the first being at Ripple, three and a half miles north of Tewkesbury. Beyond the village the ground slopes up gradually for about 400 yards to the crest of 'Old Nan's Hill',[1] a ridge running east and west, between the point where Ripple School[2] now stands, and the village of Uckinghall on the river, where there is another of King John's crosses. The ridge is not long and curves gradually south at the western end. To the north it falls sharply to the flat plain – Ripple Field. The first enclosure north of 'Old Nan's Hill' is known as Deadland Field, and the next is Scarlet Close.

From the ridge Waller could see Prince Maurice's army drawn up in three bodies at the north end of Ripple Field with its right flank resting on the river Severn. Maurice had about 2,000 men, and although his musketeers were concealed in the hedges on his flanks, it was not

---

[1] An eighteenth century corruption of Ordnance Hill.

[2] Anyone wishing to inspect the battlefield should go to the School, which is just north of Ripple on an old highway from Tewkesbury to Worcester, via Ripple. This highway lies between King John's route via Ripple and Uckinghall and the modern A38, which lies to the east of them.

difficult for Waller to estimate his strength. The Parliamentary army was probably at least 2,000 strong, but it was not a balanced force, for it contained only one company of infantry – Massey's own – which cannot have exceeded 200 even if it was at full strength. So small a body of foot could not possibly hold the full extent of 'Old Nan's Hill'. Waller had artillery with him, but, as Corbet tells us, 'neither shot prepared nor cannoneers that understood the business'.

Maurice was extremely wary of Waller (who was already known as an able tactician), and suspected that the latter would try to draw his Cavaliers into an ambuscade. When some troops of Roundhead cavalry advanced Maurice repulsed them, but pursued only across the open ground towards the foot of 'Old Nan's Hill'. This preliminary skirmish would account for the bodies buried in Deadland Field.

Some of the Parliamentary officers were eager for battle, but Waller, disconcerted perhaps by his failure to forestall Maurice at Upton, was in two minds about it. His subordinates – evidently without orders – opened fire with their artillery, but they did little or no damage. There is a flat ledge near the top of the hill, where several guns could have been planted, though elsewhere the hillside is too steep. From the ledge or from the crest their fire would plunge, and the cannon balls instead of ricocheting would bury themselves in the ground.

Discouraged by the repulse of his cavalry, and finding his position too extensive for a single company of foot, Waller now decided to withdraw. His route lay down the lane, from the rear of his right flank to Ripple village. To cover this movement Waller sent out his dragoons to face the Royalists in Ripple Field, and placed Massey's musketeers in the bushes at the mouth of the lane, while he drew off his cavalry – these last somewhat shaken by their earlier repulse.

By this time we may assume that Maurice had advanced to within about half a mile of Waller's position. At any rate the Parliamentary gunners had opened fire, which they would hardly have done at any longer range, and it is evident that the Prince could see what was going on. He could also see that 'Old Nan's Hill' had a much gentler gradient to the west than to the north. He decided therefore to make his main attack from the west.

Maurice's attack was well timed. It struck Waller's army just as it was entering the lane, and caused great confusion. The Roundhead dragoons were broken – probably by a holding attack – and disordered their own musketeers. Hot on their heels came the Cavaliers. The Roundheads were struck almost simultaneously by the right hand

Royalist column, which had dashed into Uckinghall, swung left, and now came galloping along the ridge from the west.

Massey at once sent to Tewkesbury for reinforcements, and Sir Arthur Hazelrig persuaded his own troop to charge, leading them on gallantly. His Lobsters and some of Massey's bluecoats fought hard to give the rest time to rally,[1] but after standing for a while 'in a maze' they suddenly faced about and ran like a flock of sheep. The last stand was made near a big barn which can still be seen at the northern entrance to Ripple.

Some of the Parliamentary troops made for the ford over the Severn at Uckinghall, but the road to it was already cut: in trying to swim the river a number were drowned. Most of the fugitives made off to the south.

The Cavaliers pursued Waller's broken men for nearly three miles towards Tewkesbury, but when the runaways reached the narrow track that runs up on to Mythe Hill, near the old house known as King John's Castle, they met Massey's reinforcements who had hastened across the Avon. The fresh troops, undismayed by the scene of confusion that met their gaze, checked the Royalists with a galling fire, and Massey himself fought hand to hand with their leader, Major Thomas Sheldon of Prince Maurice's regiment of horse. Most of the Roundhead cavalry had fled by this time but Massey was rescued by a handful of his officers. The remnants of Waller's force were able to fall back into Tewkesbury, and Maurice pursued no further.

This sharp reverse cost the Roundheads 80 killed; few of their infantry can have escaped from Ripple. The Cavaliers admitted no more than two men killed; but must have had a number wounded.

Prince Maurice, though a stout fighter, is not usually credited with much military skill, but he was the first Cavalier general to get the better of 'William the Conqueror'. Of the Roundheads only Massey and Hazelrig emerged with credit from the rout of Ripple Field.

Waller could have drawn up his men on top of 'Old Nan's Hill' in such a way as to make Maurice wonder whether he had a greater force in rear, but instead he advanced down the forward slope of the hill 'and discovered their weakness to full view'.

Maurice now retired to Evesham, whence he was soon recalled to assist in the attempt to relieve Reading. Waller soon recovered from

[1] One of Massey's men succeeded in shutting a gate in the faces of the pursuers. It is curious that its exact location on the road just north of Ripple can be told from a map of 1775.

his shock, and on 25 April he captured Hereford after a feeble resistance. There he lingered for about a fortnight, before withdrawing to Gloucester. He had not enough men to leave a garrison behind him. One feels that he might have been more usefully employed at so critical a period of the war.

The Chalgrove Raid

We left Essex immobile at Thame which he reached on 10 June. A week later he sent a party to occupy Islip and the passage of the Cherwell, and although his detachment did not push home its attack, Rupert felt that it was time for a riposte. A few days earlier Colonel John Urry, a Scots mercenary, had deserted to the Cavaliers. This officer, who was to change sides twice more during his career, was able to supply accurate information as to Essex's quarters. Moreover, he reported the approach of a convoy bringing £21,000 to pay the Parliamentary army.

Accordingly on the afternoon of 17 June Rupert set out across Magdalen Bridge with three regiments of horse, 1,000 in number; 350 dragoons under Lord Wentworth, and 500 foot, without colours, commanded by Colonel Henry Lunsford. Major Will. Legge led the Forlorn Hope of 100 horse and 50 dragoons.

Passing the River Thame at Chislehampton Bridge the Prince brushed past a Roundhead quarter at Tetsworth, and reached Postcombe in the early hours of the morning. Colonel Morley's troop slumbering too securely in its quarters far from the front, was quickly overwhelmed and Rupert pushed rapidly on to Chinnor. Legge charged in, and the Cavaliers made short work of Sir Samuel Luke's newly-raised Bedfordshire dragoons, taking three of their guidons – ' buff bibles on a black background'. About 50 men were killed and 120 surrendered, though some of the officers defended their quarters bravely.

Leaving Chinnor in flames behind him the Prince then hurried on hoping to surprise the convoy. But the escort warned by a countryman had driven the carts into the woods that fringe the Chilterns. All search was futile.

It was now high time to think of a withdrawal, but it was not until the Prince neared the River Thame that the Roundheads began to press upon his rear. Sending Lunsford to secure Chislehampton Bridge, Rupert drew up his horse in Chalgrove Field, about a mile and a half to the east of it, to face his pursuers until his foot could get into position. He placed his dragoons in ambush on either side of a lane leading to the bridge in his rear.

Pursuing horsemen appeared riding down Gilton Hill; a party of dragoons cantered ahead, dismounted, lined a hedge that separated the two sides, and opened fire. The hostile cavalry began to trot forward in line, for although they were outnumbered, they wanted to delay the Cavaliers until more horse could concentrate.

Rupert sat his horse calmly at the head of his Lifeguard, but when the carbines of the hostile dragoons emptied a saddle or two, his patience was quickly exhausted. 'This insolency is not to be endured', said he, and clapping spurs to his charger, he dashed forward, cleared a hedge, and leapt into the midst of the astonished dragoons. Sir Richard Crane and the rest of the Lifeguard, every man as best he could, 'jumbled after him', and as soon as about 15 had joined him, the Prince drew them up in a single rank until the rest could come up. The dragoons fled, but the Roundhead horse by the admission of a Cavalier, 'stood our first charge of pistols and swords better than they have ever done since our first beating them at Worcester.[1] But the Prince, with his life-guard charging them home upon the flank, put them in rout at the first encounter.'

While this was going on Lieut.-Colonel Dan. O'Neale with Rupert's regiment, and General Percy with his own had charged each flank of the Roundhead horse, putting them into utter confusion.

Somewhere near Wapsgrove House John Hampden, who as an infantry brigadier had no reason but his gallant and ardent spirit to bring him into a cavalry skirmish, received two bullets in the shoulder. Mortally wounded he rode painfully across country to Thame, where on 24 June he died.

Rupert rallied his tired troopers and fell back across Chislehampton Bridge, taking with him 100 more prisoners, and leaving 45 Round-heads dead in the field.

The campaign had done little to enhance Essex's reputation. Supine by nature he had allowed himself to be held up by the belt of fortresses around Oxford. He had his troubles — sickness, lack of money, shortage of reinforcements, but he had not the imagination to appreciate that the Cavaliers were suffering from much the same difficulties. He did not possess that essential faculty of the great commander, the power to see 'the other side of the hill'. Moreover he had not the strategic ability to

[1] Powick Bridge.

see the struggle as a whole, and in any case the headquarters of his army in the Thames Valley was not the best place from which to control the widely scattered Parliamentary forces. For this London was the only suitable location. Gradually, perhaps almost insensibly, the Captain-General abdicated his wider powers, devoting his efforts and attention more and more to his own army. Sir Samuel Luke, his Scoutmaster-General, whose reports and letters have survived, sent his spies ranging far afield, but generally they concentrated on discovering the movements and locations of the Oxford army. Essex was simply not in a position to plan operations against the Royalists in the North or in the South-west. It was perhaps inevitable, therefore, that the higher direction of the Roundhead armies should come from the Capital, where the dominant figure was still John Pym.

When the war broke out Pym had even less knowledge of military affairs than the King, and the latter had experienced officers constantly about him. It is true that the Parliamentary Committee which directed the war included the senior generals, but since they were usually in the field, Pym had not the benefit of their advice. Charles had Ruthven to act as what we may call his chief of staff; Pym had nobody to serve him in that capacity. It is hardly strange therefore that the Roundhead strategy was at first a fumbling affair. When, in mid-May 1643 the tide turned against the Parliament Pym's strategy was little more than an effort to cope with each successive emergency as it occurred. The war became a struggle to retain control of the territory still in the hands of the Parliamentary commanders.

However, Pym seems to have possessed a real grasp of grand strategy, for he took a number of measures which were to bear fruit in the long run. On 19 July, for example, orders were given to the Earl of Rutland, Sir Henry Vane (the younger) and three other members of the Commons to go to Edinburgh and arrange for the intervention of a Scots army. Three days later (22 July) the excise ordinance was issued. This measure by increasing the customs placed the finances of the Parliamentarians on a sounder footing, and provided the necessary sinews of war.

CHAPTER 6

The War in the West — 2

SHORTLY AFTER THEIR victory at Stratton the Cornish Cavaliers heard that a force under Hertford and Prince Maurice was marching west from Oxford to join them. With Devonshire as yet unsubdued — Plymouth, Exeter, Bideford and Barnstaple all held Roundhead garrisons — it was no mean feat on the part of Hopton to persuade his Cornishmen to march into Somerset; that he succeeded is the measure of their confidence in him. Leaving a force to blockade Plymouth and Exeter he arrived at the rendezvous at Chard on 4 June.

The combined armies included 2,000 horse, 4,000 foot and 300 dragoons, a force which, counting officers, totalled about 7,000. Hertford's contingent amounted to 1,500 horse and 1,000 new-levied foot; the Cornish were all comparative veterans. At first there was a certain amount of suspicion and ill-feeling between the two parts of this army. Hopton complains of the plundering propensities of the horse, while Captain Richard Atkyns tells us that the Cornish, though splendid marchers and fighters were a mutinous lot and would let fly at their own cavalry if they saw them drawn up in a cornfield! Despite all this the two elements soon fused into a formidable army.

More serious was the question of command, for the Royalists had two sets of generals. Hertford, the senior officer present, was, as we have seen, no soldier, and seems to have been content to act as a mere figurehead. But there was a grave danger that friction might arise between Hopton and Prince Maurice; the one had his Cornish victories behind him, the other had already defeated Waller at Ripple Field, and it was with Waller that the Cavaliers had now to deal. It is impossible to be certain how this difficulty was overcome, but the indications are that Hopton, besides acting as a kind of Chief of Staff, actually commanded the whole force in the field; while Maurice was content to confine his activities to the mounted arm. As usual operations, except when actually in close contact with the enemy, were directed by a Council of War consisting of the senior officers of both contingents. Such was the army that was now to try conclusions with 'William the Conqueror'.

With Bristol and Gloucester firmly in his hands, Waller had concentrated his field army about Bath, where he had been reinforced by 1,200 horse and dragoons sent by Stamford. Besides these he had Hazelrig's 'Lobsters' and his own cavalry which had followed him from London. The exact strength of his army is unknown, but it can scarcely have been less than that of his opponents, while in cavalry it certainly outnumbered them. His infantry, however, were not to be compared with the Cornish, who were a far more experienced and homogeneous force.

The Cavaliers did not at once advance against Waller, but occupied Taunton, Bridgwater, Dunster Castle and Wells without much opposition. There was no serious engagement between the two armies until 10 June, when there was a sharp cavalry skirmish near Chewton Mendip eight miles north of Wells. It was not until the end of the month that the Royalists advanced and reached Bradford-on-Avon six miles south-east of Bath.

The City of Bath is bounded on its southern side by the River Avon, a deep and sluggish stream. It was decided to outflank it from the east. From Bradford therefore the Cavaliers advanced north to Monkton Farleigh. But Waller did not budge and after an ineffectual skirmish on 3 July the Cavaliers decided to continue their turning movement. Next day therefore they pushed on to a point six miles north-east of Bath. Waller now sensed that their intention was to attack Bath from the north, which would give them the commanding ground of Lansdown Hill and would avoid the necessity of crossing the Avon. In order to forestall this move Waller was obliged to march out of Bath and occupy Lansdown Hill himself. Thus on 4 July we have the two armies marching roughly parallel in a northerly direction. By evening, whilst a certain amount of bickering went on between the horse on each side, Hopton, who had been placed in command for this operation, halted for the night at Marshfield. Waller halted on the northern edge of Lansdown Hill, nearly five miles north of the city, the same distance separating the rival armies.

The Battle of Lansdown. 5 July 1643
Early next morning Waller sent a strong party towards Marshfield,

driving in the Royalist piquets and causing a general alarm throughout their quarters. Without delay the Cavaliers marched out two miles towards Lansdown where they could see the Roundhead army which was drawn up on the crest of the hill, with breastworks of earth and faggots, manned by their musketeers, with cannon at intervals. On either flank Waller's position was strengthened by the thick woods which clothed the steep slopes of the hill: here he had placed more musketeers, while his reserves of horse and foot were drawn up on the plateau in rear of his breastworks; in the works of Lieut.-Colonel Slingsby, 'Thus fortified stood the fox gazing at us when our whole army was ranged in order of battle upon the large cornfield near Tughill'.

Two hours passed in bickering between the cavalry outposts, and then the Royalists, seeing that the Roundheads would only fight with the advantage of their seemingly impregnable position, faced about and began to march back to their quarters.

Waller in fact had done too well! He had chosen such a strong position that the Cavaliers would not oblige by assaulting it. In order to harass his retreating enemy Sir William now sent nearly 1,000 horse and dragoons under Colonel Burrell to charge their flank and rear.

The dragoons advanced unseen under the cover of hedges and poured a heavy fire into the Royalist cavalry who withdrew in considerable disorder, falling foul of their own foot in the process. The Parliamentary horse charged the rear of the Cavaliers, routing two bodies of cavalry, but were held up by some little bodies of Cornish musketeers. Hopton, acting on Maurice's advice, had posted these men on the flanks of the cavalry to support them, a tactical device which Prince Rupert was wont to employ, and which his younger brother had obviously learned from him. The Cornish stubbornly held their ground until counter-attacks by Hertford's Lifeguard and Carnarvon's regiment swept the Roundheads back to a point half a mile north of Lansdown Hill. Meanwhile the Cornish musketeers beat back the Parliamentary dragoons.

This done, Prince Maurice advanced with his cavalry supported by some Cornish foot, drove back the enemy cavalry over Tog Hill and right back to their main position, the Cornish musketeers inflicting severe casualties in the valley between Tog Hill and Lansdown.

By about 2 p.m. the Royalists were back in the position they had reached and quit in the morning at the foot of Lansdown Hill. But this time their blood was up, and the Cornishmen, seeing the line of cannon drawn up on the opposite height, clamoured to be allowed to 'fetch those cannon' (Slingsby). Such was their ardour and confidence

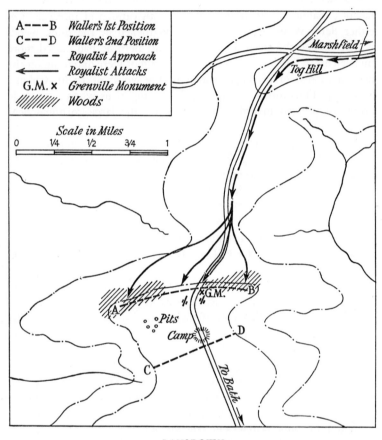

LANSDOWN

that Hopton acceded to their request and ordered a general attack on the hostile position.

This position must now be described.

The long flat-topped Lansdown Hill runs for nearly four miles north by west from Bath, ending suddenly in a steep escarpment with a drop of 150 to 200 feet. Just on the right of the road at the top of this escarpment is a tall obelisk erected to the memory of Sir Bevill Grenvile. This monument marks the centre of the position and the approximate centre of the breastwork that had been erected the previous evening, along which the seven Roundhead guns were posted. The road descends the hill diagonally to the right, after which it ascends Freezing Hill and so on to Tog Hill. The escarpment is covered with a belt of trees on both sides of the road, though at the time of the battle they were in the immediate vicinity of the road, thinly scattered but further to each flank were woods (as there are today). The surrounding country was for the most part unenclosed, but there was a long stone wall 'half a culverin shot' in rear of the breastwork. There is today such a stone wall about 400 yards in rear which is very likely the wall in question.

It was well on in the afternoon when the Cavaliers advanced to assault the formidable position directly to their front. As seen from Freezing Hill (which must have been the Royalist command post), a breastwork astride the road at the summit of the hill appeared to mark the centre of the position, but its flanks could not be exactly determined owing to the woods. No account states where precisely the flanks did rest, but as Waller sent musketeers forward into both woods to move down the hill under cover of the undergrowth we can take it that both woods were occupied for their full extent.

Hopton's intention was, in his own words, to send out 'strong parties of musketeers on each hand to second one another, to endeavour under the covert of the enclosed grounds to gain the flank of the enemy on top of the hill. . . .' He does not specify what precise role he allotted to the horse, or whether he intended to rest them in reserve, so we are left guessing.

What actually happened was that the infantry entered the woods as ordered and ascended the hill, and the cavalry followed them over the fairly open central space. Thus we get the usual dispositions reversed – the foot on the two wings and the horse in the centre.

The musketeers on the flanks secured entry into the woods without much difficulty, but in the centre pikes and horse received the plunging fire of the guns as they crossed the dip and began to ascend the steep hill.[1] The scene is graphically described by Richard Atkyns, a troop commander in the Royalist army. Signs that the enemy was flying made

[1] It has been asserted that the attackers while climbing the hill would be immune from hostile artillery fire as the guns could not be depressed sufficiently to hit them. This is not so. The problem is fully dealt with in *More Battlefields* by Col. A. H. Burne, pp. 169-171.

Lieut.-Colonel Sir Robert Welsh 'importunately desire the Prince to have a party to follow the chase, which he gave him the command of and me of the reserve. . . . As I went up the hill, which was very steep and hollow, I met several dead and wounded officers brought off; besides several running away, that I had much ado to get up by them. When I came to the top of the hill, I saw Sir Bevill Grinvill's stand of pikes; which certainly preserved our army from total rout, with the loss of his most precious life: they stood as upon the eaves of an house for steepness but as unmovable as a rock; on which side of their stand of pikes our horse were, I could not discover for the air was so darkened by the smoke of the powder that for a quarter of an hour together (I dare say) there was no light seen, but what the fire of the volleys of shot gave; . . .'

Meanwhile the Royalist musketeers were making steady progress through the woods, and eventually the crest of the hill was attained all along the line. But at heavy cost. The cavalry in particular melted away; Hopton says that at the end of the day 'of 2,000 horse there did not stand above 600'. This does not mean that the remainder were killed or wounded as some accounts would seem to imply. Then what did happen to them? Clarendon is quite candid about it. They ran away. Some did not draw rein till they reached Oxford where they, as he shrewdly puts it, 'according to the custom of those who run away, reported all to be lost, with many particular accidents which they fancied very like to happen when they left the field'.

The sheer fighting qualities of the Cornishmen had accomplished the seemingly impossible. The position was captured and the Roundheads fell back to the shelter of a lateral stone wall about 400 yards in rear. This they loopholed and manned with their guns, all of which they managed, somewhat surprisingly, to withdraw. There was every sign that the next stage of the battle would begin. But nothing happened. The Royalist cavalry had shot their bolt; the infantry were exhausted by their arduous climb; the guns were short of ammunition (though they did get to the top of the hill). Thus both sides sat and glared at each other as darkness fell.

Both armies were by now in an unenviable position, especially the Cavaliers. Except on the right, where they had crept forward into some pits that still exist, they were perched on the very edge of the hill, 'like a heavy stone upon the very brow of the hill, which with one lusty charge might well have been rolled to the bottom', Slingsby puts it; the momentum of the attack had died out, the casualties had been severe, ammunition was scarce, extreme fatigue pervaded the ranks after a long day of marching, counter-marching and fighting, and deep gloom had descended over the Cornishmen at the death of their leader Grenvile.

But the aspect of things is so different when viewed from 'the other side of the hill'. Waller too had his difficulties, which seemed great to him, but which in reality were much less than those of his opponents. So far from counter-attacking, he was contemplating a retreat to within the walls of Bath. Both sides, in short, were played out. That deadening condition of mind and body, that *lassitudo certaminis*, which always supervenes on the evening of a hard-fought battle, had done its work – on both sides. It is in situations such as this that the mark of a great general becomes apparent. Which man, Sir Ralph Hopton or his old-time friend, Sir William Waller, would show that supreme quality (so strikingly displayed, as we have seen, by the King himself after Edgehill) of 'sticking it out'? In the upshot it turned out to be the general who had the greater excuse to retreat who held his ground, and the other who abandoned it. The Cavaliers hung on, the Round-heads retreated.

During the night they slipped away unnoticed and took refuge within the walls of Bath.

Thus Hopton had wrested victory from what had threatened to be disaster. But the course of war is unpredictable. Early next morning Fortune struck the Cavaliers a double blow which completely reversed the strategical situation. Let Richard Atkyns tell the story in his own inimitable way·

'Major Cheldon[1] and myself went towards the Lord Hopton, who was then viewing the prisoners taken, some of which were carried upon a cart whereon was our ammunition, and (as I heard) had matches to light their tobacco. The major desired me to go back to the rear, while he received orders from his lordship. I had no sooner turned my horse and was gone three horse lengths from him but the ammunition was blown up and the three prisoners with it together with the Lord Hopton, Major Cheldon, and Cornet Washnage who were near the cart on horseback, and several others. It made a great noise and darkened the air for a time and the burnt men made lamentable screeches. As soon as the air had cleared I

---

[1] Major Thomas Sheldon of Prince Maurice's regiment.

G

went to see what the matter was. There I found his lordship, miserably burnt, his horse singed like a parched leather, and Thomas Cheldon (that was a horse length further from the blast) complaining that the fire was got within his breeches, which I tore off as soon as I could, and from as long a head of flaxen hair as ever I saw his head was like a Black-Moor. . . .'

Sir Ralph Hopton was put into a litter, blind and incapable of motion. Thus suddenly deprived of two of its trusted leaders and bereft of almost all its ammunition, the Western army with drooping spirits turned its back on Bath and its opponents and marched towards Oxford.

Thus did the fickle goddess of war sport with the victors of Lansdown field.

COMMENTS

In neither the preliminary movements nor in the battle tactics did either commander distinguish himself. It should be remembered that although both men had warlike experience on the Continent in the Thirty Years War, their actual command of troops in the field had been limited; nor does it appear that they had (as Prince Rupert for example had) systematically studied the art of war before they had leadership thrust upon them.

The most important moment in a battle is the last. That moment is the supreme test of generalship, and judged by that test Sir Ralph Hopton is entitled to be considered a great general.

The Cavaliers had shown vacillation in their preliminary motions and questionable judgment in their use of cavalry, and Waller, who had a reputation for an eye for country, had been deceived by the seeming strength of the position which he selected to hold. He did not fully realize the weakness of this position with much dead ground immediately in its front and the weakness of its flanks, which could be approached under cover of the woods.

The Roundheads, encouraged by the news of the explosion of the Royalists' ammunition, lost no time in recruiting their army, drawing reinforcements from the garrison of Bristol, and when on 7 July the Cavaliers marched from Marshfield to Chippenham they moved after them. Despite their victory the Cavaliers were in low spirits. Slingsby tells us: 'Our horse were bad before but now worse, our foot drooped for their Lord [Hopton] whom they loved, and . . . as I remember we had then but nine barrels [of powder] left: . . .' To make matters worse the country people seeing that Waller was now pursuing the Cavaliers 'begins to desert us; so that we could get neither meal nor intelligence, two necessary things for an army: . . .'

The Royalists halted at Chippenham for two days but early on Sunday, 9 July on the approach of the enemy, they resumed their march and reached Devizes that night. Waller fell on their rear, and hustled them into the town whereupon Prince Maurice ordered Slingsby with Mohun's regiment to hold a ford north-west of the town until he could draw up the army 'upon the hill by the town'— Roundway Hill. This position was probably Rowde Ford, about two miles north-west of Devizes Castle on the way to Chippenham. His men held the line of a brook for half an hour, losing nearly 60 casualties, for there was little or no cover.

Next day (10th) Waller with his whole army faced the Royalists on Roundway Down and they, not caring to give battle, withdrew into Devizes placing their artillery in the Castle. The Roundheads came down the hill and encamped in the valley north of the town.

That evening the Cavaliers held a Council of War in the house where Hopton lodged, Sir Ralph, in his own words, 'being then not able to move himself from thence but as he was carried in a chair'. The Council unanimously resolved that Hertford and Maurice with the horse should break out that night, and march with all speed to Oxford, while Hopton with the foot and guns would defend Devizes until relief could come from Oxford. This plan was put into execution and that night the cavalry got out without loss. They were only just in time, for next day, the 11th, Waller beleaguered the town, posting his men within carbine-shot of it in many places and raising a battery upon a slight hill east of the town. Day and night he poured great and small shot into the place.

The Cavaliers had no better defences than hedges and banks, but they barricaded every avenue to keep out the besiegers' horse.

The shortage of ammunition in the town was serious, for not only powder, but match was lacking, and Captain Pope, the comptroller of the ordnance, reported to Hopton that, having issued ammunition for the first action, he had only 150 pounds weight left. But the indomitable Hopton was not at a loss to amend this deficiency; he sent a guard from house to house to gather together all the bedcords in the town, and to have them beaten and boiled in resin. This expedient produced 15 cwt. of match.

Meanwhile Maurice, skirting round to the south-east, had eluded Waller and, covering 44 miles during the night – a remarkable achievement – had reached Oxford on the morning of 11 July. The King was already aware of the needs of his Western army. As early as the 9th the Earl of Crawford with 600 horse had been sent west from Oxford with a convoy of ammunition, while on the 10th Lord Wilmot, Lieut.-General of the horse, with his brigade was ordered to march thither, for it was appreciated that Waller's cavalry outnumbered that of the western Cavaliers. Sir John Byron's brigade was now added to Maurice's own horse and on the 12th they set out to join Wilmot and go to the relief of the Cornish foot. Hertford, exhausted by his recent exertions, stayed at Oxford to recuperate.

To return to Devizes, Waller spent the 10th and 11th July in continual but fruitless attempts to storm the town. On the 12th he sent in a trumpeter to arrange for the free passage of Sir Bevill Grenvile's body, and took the opportunity to let it be known that his cavalry had intercepted Crawford's convoy and beaten it off. He therefore offered Hopton terms of surrender. Sir Ralph, glad to give his men some rest and to spare his ammunition, spun out the negotiations for seven or eight hours. But help was now at hand.

The Battle of Roundway Down. 13 July 1643

Wilmot, the commander of the relief force, made his rendezvous at Marlborough. He had with him his own brigade and Byron's beside Crawford's contingent, altogether 1,500 horse of the Oxford army. To these must be added some 300 of Maurice's horse, who despite their tiring marches, were still fit to fight. Wilmot had no infantry at all and only two light guns – probably two of the 'galloping guns' the gun detachments riding on horses, the earliest form of horse artillery. Thus on the morning of 13 July Wilmot, with only 1,800 men marching along the old Bath road was nearing the besieged town. He had arranged that when he drew near he would fire off both cannon, as a signal to notify the garrison of his approach.

Waller had decided to assault the town on the evening of that day. As a preliminary he subjected it to a heavy bombardment from the hill 600 yards to the east. Part of this bombardment was deliberately aimed at St. John's Church, and pretty good practice was made, the marks of which are still visible.

But Hopton still hoped to be able to hold out long enough to allow of reinforcements arriving. This he calculated would not be for a few days, so he was pleasantly surprised on the afternoon of the 13th to receive the welcome news that Wilmot and Maurice were on their way.

An interesting situation was developing. Let us examine it. In the town were perhaps 3,000 Royalist foot. Approaching from the north-east were 1,800 Royalist horse. In between the two was the Roundhead army, consisting of 2,500 foot and 2,000 horse, with 8 field guns.

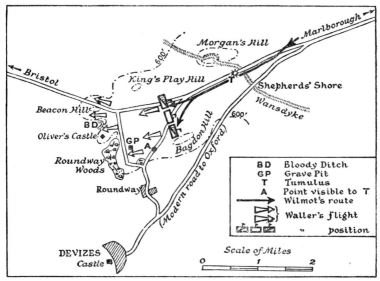

ROUNDWAY DOWN

Thus the Roundheads heavily outnumbered each of their opponents, and the only chance for the latter would seem to rest in a combined attack. Wilmot evidently realized this, and hoped for assistance. Unfortunately the messenger with this plan seems to have been captured, and though the signal guns were heard (a surprising fact at four miles range, unless the wind was north-east) it was suspected in the town that the withdrawal of the besieging army was a ruse to entice them out. This, at least, is the explanation given by Hopton, though it does not seem very convincing. Waller had indeed drawn off his army to confront the new opponent, and if Hopton was aware of Wilmot's approach his right course was to join in the battle, ruse or no ruse.

Hopton, with his soldierly instinct, saw this, and tried to convince his Council of War whom he had summoned to his bedside. But the majority were averse to this course. Now it is difficult to lead an army from a sick-bed and in his physical state the wounded commander may not have exerted the same forcefulness in the Council as he would have done had he still been in vigorous health. At any rate, he did not feel equal to ordering his subordinates against their will to march out to battle while he stayed behind; he reluctantly acceded to the opinion of the majority, and the army remained inactive.

Thus Wilmot was left with his 1,800 horse to face an army roughly thrice his own strength, for Waller had left only a few guards for the heavy guns and wagons, and with the remainder of his army he had ascended the hill on to the top of Roundway Down.

There are, as usual, conflicting views as to the precise site of the battlefield, and they are dealt with in the Appendix. The course of events was as follows:

The road from Oxford and Swindon to Devizes did not take its present course via Shepherds Shore, four miles from Devizes, but left it two miles farther on (see sketch-map). It crossed Wansdyke 500 yards to the north-west of Shepherds Shore at a spot that is still a point of great archaeological interest. It is marked by a tumulus, and was evidently the junction of two sections of Wansdyke. From this point the track runs west-south-west for 2,000 yards and then bends to its left, and makes straight for Devizes. When Waller, having ridden up to the top of the hill, reached A on the Sketch-map, he saw the Royalist horse approaching direct from the tumulus, which is visible from this spot, and is marked by a small clump of trees. In front of him was a wide plain in the shape of a shallow valley, with gentle slopes to north and south – a beautiful arena for a battle (as Richard Atkyns observed). Its breadth is about 1,500 yards. The hill to the south is marked Roundway Hill on the O.S. map, but at that time it was called Bagdon Hill. The hill to the north is called King's Play Hill. In this shallow valley, then, Sir William Waller decided to offer battle to the on-coming foe.

From the tumulus, just two miles from Point A, Wilmot would catch sight of the leading men of Waller's army appearing over the brow of the hill and on the summit of Bagdon Hill; and it was probably at this point that he brought his two guns into action and fired the signal. He then proceeded to form up and deploy his tiny army. Observing that Waller was doing the same, he had no need of speed. Delay, rather than speed, was his policy for the moment; for time was required for Hopton to marshal his army and march out of the town and up the hill. At least an hour was consumed in this fashion, and the afternoon must have been far spent when all was ready.

Waller had formed his line in the conventional fashion, his foot in the centre, astride the track, his horse on the two wings, his guns in the intervals between horse and foot. Sir Arthur Hazelrig's cuirassiers, the Lobsters, were on the right, probably on the summit of Bagdon Hill. Having marshalled his army in line, as described above, Waller for some curious reason moved his whole army forward some hundreds of yards.[1] Meanwhile Wilmot had deployed his column with two brigades abreast, his own on the left, Byron's on the right, with a third, Crawford's, in support. Wilmot seems to have moved off slightly before Byron. He directed his advance against Hazelrig's regiment which was simultaneously advancing to meet him. Thus the clash took place slightly in front of Waller's main line. Very shortly afterwards Byron's column engaged the Parliamentary horse on the other (north) flank, and the cavalry battle became general. Hazelrig's Lobsters proved a tough proposition. In an apt phrase Clarendon described them as 'that impenetrable regiment'. It took Wilmot a long time before he got the better of them and drove them off the field. Meanwhile Byron on the other wing was also hotly engaged. Crawford, of whose men Wilmot had a poor opinion, now made a timely intervention on Byron's outer flank. The defeat of the Lobsters shook the morale of the rest of the Roundhead Cavalry.

Thus the curious situation had arisen in which Waller's foot – the bulk of his army – stood unemployed in the centre while hot fights raged on both sides of them. They dared not open fire with musket or cannon for fear of hitting their own people; they could only stand and gape. In the course of the fray four of the Roundhead guns were captured, and turned against their own side. This was all the fire the infantry had to encounter.

At the end of about 30 minutes the issue was decided, the Round-head cavalry turned and fled from the field, hotly pursued by the triumphant and exultant Cavaliers. Instead of retreating on the line on which they had approached the field, the bulk of the fleeing troopers took a westerly direction. The natural inference is that some

[1] Sir John Byron asserts this and his account is the best of all. The British Museum copy is badly catalogued so we give the press-mark: 1103.d.77/5.

of Wilmot's troops had swept over Bagdon Hill and prevented flight in that direction. The ground on the actual line of their flight sloped upwards very gently and with perfect uniformity. It is beautiful cavalry country, and being unhedged, offered ideal ground for shock action.

After retreating in this direction for 2,500 yards, with their pursuers thundering behind them, they saw, to their horror, suddenly yawning in their front a huge semi-precipitous slope with a drop of about 300 feet. There was no pulling up, the enemy being hard on their heels. They were indeed 'twixt devil and deep sea'. Down the hill they stumbled and plunged and rolled willy-nilly – a hill 'where never horse went down or up before'. In their impetuosity some of the pursuers could not pull up their horses in time and shared the fate that overtook their adversaries. The bottom of the hill became a shambles. A ditch marks its foot, and it is now known as 'Bloody Ditch'.

Waller's cavalry was utterly routed, and he himself escaped with difficulty, almost certainly down the Bristol road. Never can quite such a dramatic and harrowing scene have been witnessed on an English battlefield. The Roundheads no doubt fanned out in the course of their flight: some would strike the 'precipice' by Beacon Hill, some by Oliver's Castle, and some in Roundway Woods (see Sketch-map).

Meanwhile the Parliamentary foot, after witnessing the downfall and destruction of their own horse, had been left on the position intact and unmolested but without a leader, without an enemy and even without a mission. And so there they stood motionless, alone on what a few minutes ago had been a bloody battlefield.

We must now return to the other portion of the Royalist forces – Hopton's army. Hearing the sounds of battle and receiving definite messages from Wilmot, Hopton had no further difficulty in securing agreement for an advance. The troops who had probably already received a 'warning order' were assembled rapidly and marched out up the hill, meeting with no opposition on the way. On reaching the top, they could see the Roundhead infantry drawn up in a body about 1,000 yards away, while isolated bodies of Wilmot's horse were beginning to come back from the pursuit and to engage the hostile foot. Wilmot had managed to collect the majority of his troops on the brow of the hill with a view to launching an attack on what remained of Waller's army. But he showed admirable coolness. He reckoned that Hopton's Cornish infantry must be on their way, if indeed he did not see them.

There was therefore no immediate call for haste. Quietly he collected and marshalled his disordered ranks and not till he saw the Cornishmen on the hill-top and about to engage did he launch a concerted attack. Then the unfortunate Roundhead infantry faced the fate that had overtaken their own horse. Threatened if not actually attacked by the fresh Cornishmen from the south, charged by Wilmot's elated horse-men from the north, their guns captured, their commander missing, they were quickly overwhelmed. Over 600 were killed; the remainder were captured; scarce a man got away. Waller's army had been wiped out by an inferior force as completely as any army in the whole course of our civil wars. It was the most sweeping victory the Royalists had won.

COMMENTS

The battle of Roundway Down was the most dramatic of the whole Civil War. One might add that it was one of the most interesting strategically; for it involved a situation on 'exterior lines'. It is an illustration of the inherent difficulty of ensuring and co-ordinating the two attacks by the side holding the exterior position. Unless this co-ordination be effected the advantage lies with the army who is on interior lines. The Royalists were in the exterior position, and they did not succeed in launching a simultaneous attack at the outset. Moreover they were numerically inferior, even when combined. How, then, can one account for the victory of the Royalists? This question brings out another cardinal feature of war – the power of morale. Hopton's army had won a series of victories and their morale though temporarily damped by casualties to their leaders, was in the ascendant. Their cavalry were still imbued by that almost contemp-tuous feeling of superiority over their opponents that they had exhibited at Edgehill. The war was still only in its first year, and the Roundhead cavalry – as yet – had little to be proud of. Then we must remember that it was only the Parliamentary horse that was defeated by the Royalist horse; the downfall of the foot was achieved by joint action on tactically exterior lines – Wilmot's horse from the north combining with the Cornish foot from the south. If, as it appears, Wilmot deliberately delayed his attack on the foot till the Cornishmen arrived, he was ensuring that co-ordination and simultaneity of attack which, as we have seen, is essential to success. Wilmot also showed sound instinct (if indeed it was his deliberate action) in avoiding contact with the infantry in his first attack. In so doing he brought about a situation which has scarcely a parallel in battle, that of the two wings engaging, and the main body of the defenders being left with no opponents in their front.

This brings our attention to Sir William Waller. What was the Parliamentary commander doing while his horse were being dispersed and his foot were standing disengaged? History does not relate. Sir William afterwards wrote about the battle, but apart from blaming the Earl of Essex for not coming to his assistance, he does not indicate the reason for the disaster nor his own movements in any detail. He presumably fled with his cavalry; he certainly must have made off in that direction, nor did he stop till he reached Bristol, nearly 30 miles distant, where he was the first to bring the tidings of his own defeat. Bad news travels fast; Waller travelled even faster. He afterwards proved himself quite a good general; Roundway Down was his black day. For his opposite number, Lord Wilmot, we can have nothing but praise on this occasion. His conduct at Edgehill had not been convincing, and it is possible that in this battle he was urged on by Prince Maurice, while Clarendon gives much credit to Carnarvon by whose advice Wilmot began by disposing of the Lobsters.

It is interesting to speculate as to what course the battle would have taken had Sir Ralph Hopton been in the saddle. It is natural to suppose that he would have had his own way at the council, and that his infantry would have joined in the battle simultaneously with, or very shortly after Wilmot's attack. The result could hardly have been more decisive than it actually was, but the battle might have been of shorter duration. That is all that can be said. One can picture and feel for the pent-up excitement of the general, lying within earshot of the battle, and powerless to influence it.

The Storming of Bristol. 26 July 1643

Roundway Down was a knock-out blow to Waller's field army, and the King's Council of War at Oxford was quick to seize the opportunity to complete the conquest of the West. On 18 July Rupert marched from Oxford to join the Western army.

He had three brigades of infantry under Lord Grandison, Colonel Henry Wentworth and Colonel John Belasyse, and two wings of cavalry under Sir Arthur Aston, now Major-General of the Horse, and Colonel Charles Gerard. There were in addition nine troops of dragoons. The train of artillery was commanded by Monsieur de la Roche, a Frenchman, and Captain Samuel Fawcett.

The Prince carried out his reconnaissance on the afternoon of 23 July, riding over Durdham Down.

The Roundhead defences are shown in the sketch map, but a brief description of their nature is necessary. The five forts were the chief

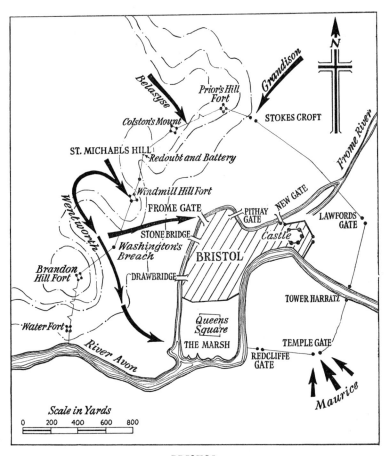

BRISTOL

defence. They were all self-contained, with dry ditches and palisades round them, but without artificial glacis thrown up in front of the walls to give additional protection against bombardment. They were connected by an earthwork about five feet high and three feet thick at the top. Outside was a ditch six feet broad and five feet deep. In places owing to the rocky ground the ditch was very shallow, but round the forts, except for Brandon Hill, it was eight or nine feet deep.

To man these works Colonel Nathaniel Fiennes had 300 horse and 1,500 foot, besides townsmen, and nearly 100 guns. The garrison had been weakened by the loss of 1,200 foot who had followed Waller to Roundway Down.

On 24 July Rupert summoned the City and began to throw up his batteries. Next day he crossed the water and held a Council of War with the commanders of the Western army. At this Council it was decided to storm the defences, rather than to proceed by sapping and the orders for the assault were agreed upon.

'Zero hour' was to be daybreak on the 26th; the password 'Oxford' and for easier identification every man was to wear green colours, either branches or such like, while nobody was to wear a band or handkerchief about his neck. Once inside the line the brigade commanders were to detail men to throw down the breastworks and fill up the ditch, to help the horse to get in.

During that evening Rupert held a conference. He gave the brigade commanders a free hand as to how they should attack the fortifications. They were to keep the Roundheads awake with alarms all night, and to make a general assault as soon as the two demi-cannon from Lord Grandison's battery should fire the signal shot. But the Cornishmen 'jumped the gun', beginning their attack about 3 a.m., and seeing this Rupert sent to have the signal fired.

On the left Grandison's brigade made a gallant attack – first on Stokes Croft, and later on Prior's Hill Fort. In the first attack Captain Fawcett fastened a petard on the gate of the work which only broke two or three of the bars. The Cavaliers got into the very ditch of Prior's Hill Fort, but were eventually beaten off, leaving the ditch full of their dead. Grandison himself was mortally wounded.

Belasyse was no more successful in his attack on Windmill Hill Fort. For lack of scaling ladders and faggots to fill the ditch they were held up, some taking cover under a stone wall. Rupert himself met some of the men retreating, and led them on again, having his charger shot under him in so doing.

Wentworth's brigade attacked between Brandon Hill and Windmill Hill Forts, but the ground was so bushy and uneven that the soldiers soon fell into disorder. As they pushed up the re-entrant between the two forts they came under very heavy fire, which made them run close up to the works as fast as they could so as to get into the dead ground.

Wentworth, Washington, and several other colonels led the way, and once they had reached the defences, they found themselves practically invisible from the forts. Hurling grenades over, they stormed the line, the defenders streaming back towards the town.

The Cavaliers now began to tear a breach with their halberds and their partisans, and even with their bare hands. Lieut.-Colonel Littleton galloped along the inside of the line with a blazing fire-pike in his hand, and the garrison fled crying out 'Wildfire!'

Major Hercules Langrishe had been posted to support the defending infantry at this point, but he failed to charge. Colonel Fiennes' horse eventually put in a counter-attack but 300 Cavaliers were already over the wall, and some musketeers lining a hedge beat off this troop. Fiennes' men came on again but some Cavalier officers ran at them with fire-pikes which was more than horse or man would endure.

The Western army had attacked in three brigades with Colonel Brutus Buck on the right; Sir Nicholas Slanning in the centre and Major-General Bassett on the left. Carts and wagons were provided to be driven into the ditch to serve as a bridge, but it proved too deep. Prince Maurice had foreseen this and had provided faggots and scaling ladders. The Cornish fell on resolutely, but after half an hour were driven back by showers of stones and bullets. Their losses were very heavy. Slanning, Buck, and Trevanion were all killed or mortally wounded. Bassett and Sir Bernard Astley were wounded, and Slingsby helping to push a cart into the ditch, fell in himself in his armour and was carried off unconscious.

It was now about 4 o'clock. More by luck than judgment Wentworth's men now captured Essex's work. The defenders saw some Cavaliers running towards them and fled, though their fancied assailants were in fact trying to avoid some Roundhead cavalry! Wentworth consolidated this position, until joined by Belasyse's brigade and some horse under Aston. He then pushed on to College Green, and towards the Quay; Belasyse, supported by Aston advancing on Frome Gate, where for two hours the fight raged, the Roundheads sallying out with covering fire from windows behind them, while some 200 of the women of Bristol laboured to make a bulwark of earth and woolsacks inside the Gate. Here fell the gallant Colonel Henry Lunsford, shot through the heart on the stairs, known now as Christmas Steps. Belasyse himself was badly wounded in the head, and his men were getting tired when part of Grandison's brigade came up, and beat the Roundheads into the town.

Once his men were in the suburbs the Prince posted himself at Washington's Breach, where he could best receive intelligence and send back directions. His command post was within easy range of two important forts, but the Roundheads were losing heart. The Prince, determined to reinforce success, sent to Maurice for 1,000 of the Cornish foot, but the fight was done. Before they could arrive Fiennes sent to ask for a parley.

Fiennes was violently attacked as a coward and a traitor. Court-martialled and sentenced to death, he owed his life to the good sense of the Earl of Essex. With a city behind him whose wealthier inhabitants were certainly hostile to him he had fought hard. His force even with modern weapons was inadequate to hold a line over three miles long. This does not detract from Rupert's achievement; for when five out of the six Royalist brigades were held up he prosecuted his one success with relentless vigour. The forcing of Frome Gate when the troops were already fatigued was a splendid feat of arms.

CHAPTER 7

The War in the Centre, 1643 — 2

The Relief of Gloucester

WITH BRISTOL IN his hands Charles and his Council of War deliberated at length as to their next move. While the Roundheads were still dispirited by Rupert's great victory, the Earl of Carnarvon overran Dorset, capturing Dorchester (4 August), Weymouth and Portland. Sir Walter Erle abandoned the siege of Corfe Castle and shut himself up in Poole, and in the rest of the county only Lyme held out.

Meanwhile Maurice with the old Western army went to complete the conquest of Devonshire, where Exeter and Plymouth were still in the hands of the Parliamentarians.

With his central army the King now determined to besiege Gloucester and thus to complete the conquest of the Severn Valley. With Gloucester in his hands the road from South Wales to his forward area round Oxford would be open.

King Charles summoned Gloucester on 10 August, and met with a firm refusal from the Governor, Colonel Massey, the man who had fought so stoutly at Ripple Field. Massey had his troubles. He considered that the citizens in general were discontented, and he had only one regiment whose men could be described as regulars. The place was certainly not stronger than Bristol, and had Rupert been left to his own devices he would probably have stormed it, but at Bristol there had been heavy casualties, particularly among the senior officers, and this influenced the King's decision to carry on a formal siege.

Meanwhile in London Pym was making every effort to provide for the needs of Essex's army. Money, clothing, 2,000 recruits — to be pressed if necessary — were all forthcoming. Six regiments of the London Trained Bands, well-drilled if inexperienced soldiers, formed an additional brigade for his army. Meanwhile Waller, whose early popularity was not eclipsed by his disaster at Roundway Down, was given command of a new army to be raised in and around the capital.

The Roundheads at this critical moment were diligent indeed, and by 26 August Essex who had received orders to march to the relief of Gloucester was ready to move from Uxbridge. He had a well found army about 15,000 strong. Passing through the zone of Royalist defences north of Oxford, he crossed the Cherwell at Clifton near Aynho on 1 September, having covered only about 50 miles in five days. Wilmot was detached to observe his movements.

Suffering from lack of provisions Essex's men pushed on through the Cotswolds. Rupert's cavalry alone were insufficient to halt them or to engage them in a pitched battle and the King decided to break up the siege. On 5 September, when Massey had only three barrels of powder left and Essex was at Prestbury nearly ten miles away, the Cavaliers burnt their huts and retreated in a southerly direction. Essex, after a stormy night on Prestbury Hill — so rough that the sound of his cannon had not carried to the ears of the beleaguered Roundheads — marched slowly down through Cheltenham and relieved Gloucester on the 8th.

Charles' object was now to cut off Essex's retreat to London. If he could now bring him to battle on ground of his own choosing he might virtually end the war at a blow. Even before Essex had entered Gloucester, the King had posted himself at Sudeley Castle about 12 miles north-east of the town (7–12 September). On the 10th Essex quitted Gloucester, and marched up the Severn Valley to Tewkesbury. Here he ordered the construction of a bridge of boats over the Severn so as to make the Cavaliers believe he intended to attack Worcester. It has been mentioned that there was no bridge over the Severn at Tewkesbury in those days, though there was one over the Avon. To counter this threat Charles moved to Pershore, a move which also blocked the route back to London via Evesham and Warwick. But this time Essex meant to move round the south of the circle of garrisons round Oxford.

Turning south and east with the intention of regaining his base, London, Essex reached Cirencester on the night of the 15th, and next day Charles conformed, marching on a roughly parallel route. Essex spent the night of the 17th at Swindon, and Charles at Alvescot, 16 miles to the north-east. The Roundheads were now 20 miles from Newbury, which was their next objective, while the Royalists were a good eight miles farther away. It looked as if Essex would win the race for Newbury, but Prince Rupert delayed their march in a skirmish on the Berkshire Downs at Aldbourne Chase next day, so that they only reached Hungerford, nine miles short of Newbury. However, the Royal army also did a slow march, being still in some uncertainty as to the objective of their opponents. Thus they spent the night at Wantage, 16 miles from the vital town. It looked as if the race was already as good as won by the Parliamentarians. But military operations are not decided by a pair of dividers on a map; the human equation is often the deciding factor. In this case there has been curiously little speculation or comment on the slowness of the Roundhead march next day; but one suspects that the main cause was a kind of 'delay action', resulting from Prince Rupert's aggressive attitude on the previous day. Or it may be that Essex had knowledge of the King's position at Wantage, and that he reckoned without the agility and drive of the King's nephew. Whatever the reason, when the Roundhead quartermasters, pushing on ahead, were leisurely chalking up billets in the town of Newbury late in the afternoon, they were rudely disturbed by Prince Rupert, who thundered into the town, dispersed the escort and took prisoner many of the said quartermasters. A few hours later the main body of the Royal army arrived, and the Cavaliers were now between Essex and the capital.

Though the Royalists had won the race, there was no time for celebration, for at any moment their enemies would be upon them. The King, who surmised that Essex would approach south of the River Kennet along the road from Kintbury, led his army out of Newbury and bivouacked on its southern outskirts. Charles had guessed right. Essex halted for the night near Enborne, two miles to the west of the Royal army which now lay planted directly in his path to London. Charles had won that round decisively; and his men retired to rest, tired after a four day's march, but exultant.

There was every prospect of a battle next day on the ground between Newbury and Enborne. It is time therefore to describe the terrain over which the battle was destined to be fought.

The First Battle of Newbury, 20 September 1643
The general slope of the ground can be adequately portrayed by a single contour, that of the height, 400 feet, which has been adopted in the sketch map on p. 100. It will be noted that the essential feature is the plateau extending over the southern half of the field. To the north the ground shelves gently down to the River Kennet. All this northern part of the field is flat and was well enclosed – much as it is today. But,

H

curiously enough, whereas over most parts of England enclosures have increased since the seventeenth century, the ground on the northern slopes of the plateau – that is, over the centre of the battlefield – was more enclosed than it is today. A huge field of at least 30 acres now

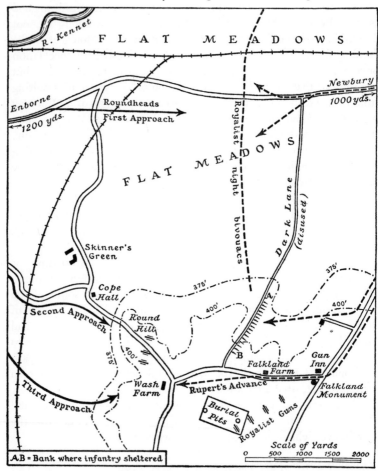

FIRST BATTLE OF NEWBURY

takes the place of the many 'closes' of which the chroniclers speak, but the southern half of this field has now been built over (1957). Among the hedges that have disappeared is that at which Lord Falkland met his death. The 400 feet contour shows two fingers or ridges jutting out to the north. The eastern one is marked on the one-inch ordnance map by the crossed swords denoting the site of the battle; the western one, when viewed from the low ground to the north, has the appearance of a round hill, rather than the end of a ridge. This fact is of great importance, for it explains much that is otherwise obscure – that is, the position of the 'round hill' to which contemporary writers such as Byron so frequently refer. Byron, from his position to the north-east would naturally describe it as a round hill, and for convenience we have named it Round Hill. At the present day it is crowned with some trees and a house, which should not be confused with Wash Farm, which is 400 yards farther to the south on the top of the plateau. This plateau, then known as Enborne Heath, is almost dead flat and featureless except for the so-called burial pits (more probably tumuli) to the south-east of Wash Farm. Even today there are some signs of heath.

No one knows for certain the respective sizes of the two armies. That of the King may be estimated at about 12,000 or a little more. The Parliamentary army had shrunk considerably since its arrival at Gloucester. It will probably be near the mark if we consider both armies of equal numbers. But the Royalists were still greatly superior in cavalry, both as regards numbers and quality. Seldom can an English army have ridden forth to battle that contained a greater proportion of men of noble blood. Cold contempt had they for their opponents, a contempt that the upshot was to prove unmerited.

In infantry the two sides were fairly evenly matched, but we are rather in the dark as regards artillery. Firth, in his *Cromwell's Army*, points out regretfully, 'I do not know of one single account of any English battle of the period that was written by an artillery officer'. It seems, however, that the Royalists had at least one really heavy gun, probably a culverin, for there is a well authenticated story of a cannon-ball reaching the village of Enborne during the course of the battle, at a range that must have been at least 2,500 yards. This would mean that the piece was elevated to the utmost that the carriage would allow, and fired at 'random range'.

The King went to bed in the town of Newbury on the night of 19 September in a cheerful and confident frame of mind. He had won the race. He had obtained ample supplies of food (collected in the town for his opponents), though his powder was dangerously short. The rebels had been outmanoeuvred and cut off from London. To continue in their design of reaching the capital they must cut their way through. The King was happy to let them attempt this; indeed, it had been his

aim throughout the campaign to make Essex fight a battle at a disadvantage. It was principally for that reason that he had abandoned the
siege of Gloucester – mistakenly as some thought. Many of his troops
were comfortably disposed in billets for the night, whereas the Roundheads were forced to bivouac out in the open on a damp chilly autumn
night.

Now let us move across to the Parliamentary camp. The army was,
in truth, in a bad way. The men undoubtedly in low spirits, wearied,
footsore, homesick (in the brigade of London Trained Bands desertion
had been rife); moreover they were short of provender. But one point,
and an important one, was overlooked by the Royalists, that despera-
tion breeds courage; a cornered animal fights the more fiercely. The
Roundheads resolved to fight fiercely that day, if necessary. The Earl
of Essex enheartened his men, not by promising them easy victory and
a happy return home, but by stressing the hardness of the road. 'The
enemy have all the advantages,' he exclaimed to his troops: 'the hill,
the town, hedges, and river.' Thus steeled for the fight, the Roundheads drew up in battle array at the approach of dawn on 20 September
1643.

Essex had, as we have seen, approached Newbury via Kintbury and
Enborne. He parked his baggage and artillery train at Hampstead
Park, just west of the village of Enborne, which was no doubt his
headquarters. His army lay in bivouac 1,000 yards farther forward,
stretching from the River Kennet on his left to Skinner's Green on his
right. Thus the two armies faced each other head-on during the night.

We must now hark back to an event, seemingly unimportant, of the
previous evening. It obviously would not do for the King to leave the
plateau on his left entirely unoccupied, and a body of cavalry was
accordingly despatched to make it good. We can picture them trotting
up the Andover road as far as the cross-roads now marked by the
Falkland memorial column. Here they turn to their right along the
lane as far as Wash Farm, where, from the edge of the plateau they
get a good view to their front and to their left. It appeared to be a good
vantage-point for the protection of the left flank, and so the horsemen
settled down for the night, sending out patrols to the front during the
hours of darkness. But they had been guilty of one omission. They had
not made good 'Round Hill', the northern end of the spur pointing
towards Skinner's Green. Fatal omission! A study of the map will
show that the Roundhead line of approach to this hill from Skinner's
Green would be invisible from Wash Farm; the enemy could thus

gain the hill unobserved. Failure to secure the hill may be attributable
to the lateness of the hour at which the Royalist cavalry were posted,
or to a casual assumption on the part of the commander that some other
unit was to hold it, or merely to sheer laxity and weariness. Whatever
the reason, the Roundheads took advantage of this lapse, and during
the night or at dawn they crept up the hill and, as daylight advanced,
brought up on to it two light guns. These guns immediately opened
fire on the Cavaliers in the plain below them, thus proclaiming in
unmistakable terms that 'Round Hill' was occupied by the enemy.

The Cavaliers' first task in the battle was clearly to eject the enemy
from 'Round Hill', and to strengthen their hold on the rest of the
plateau. The latter task was given to Prince Rupert with the bulk of the
cavalry, and he carried it out satisfactorily. The position on the Wash
Common was secured and guns were brought up to the plateau.
A battery was formed near the Falkland memorial corner in a north-
westerly direction and as more guns were gradually brought up on each
side, a protracted artillery duel developed at a range of about 1,000
yards, the Royalist guns being just behind what is now the Recreation
Ground, and the Roundheads on 'Round Hill'.

Meanwhile the infantry had deployed along the Andover road, with
their right on the Newbury road and their left a few hundred yards
south of Gun Inn. From this line they advanced to the attack, but
were soon held up. Few seem to have got beyond Dark Lane, and Sir
Nicholas Byron's brigade took cover from the hostile artillery fire
behind the bank marked A–B on the sketch map. In one regiment no
less than 11 out of 12 ensigns had fallen and the cry went up 'Horse!
Horse!' Presently Sir John Byron came up with two regiments of
horse, which he halted while he went forward to view the ground.

In view of Falkland's death – an event with which the battle is most
generally associated – it is desirable to determine the spot from which
Sir John viewed the ground. Actions in battle usually take a simple,
natural course. The Roundhead guns on Round Hill were engaged
with the Royalist guns on top of the plateau and the Royalist cavalry
would naturally prefer to attack them from a flank, i.e. from north or
north-east, and would instinctively swerve away from the cannon-
balls sweeping the plateau. The cavalry could hardly have climbed the
steep bank, marked A–B, which rules out an advance over the northern
spur. There is no mention of hilly ground, but rather of 'closes', which
were mainly on the flat ground to the north of the hill. Everything
therefore combines to place Byron's reconnaissance at the foot of the

plateau, and within musket shot of the defenders of Round Hill. The likely spot is indicated on the map.

Byron probably formed up his two regiments a few hundred yards to the east on what is now completely open ground. We can now from our vantage point picture the whole scene as Byron, somewhat breathlessly, describes it.

'I went to view the ground, and to see what way there was to that place where the enemy's foot was drawn up, which I found to be enclosed with a high quick hedge and no passage into it, but by a narrow gap through which but one horse at a time could go and that not without difficulty. My Lord of Falkland did me the honour to ride in my troop this day, and I would needs go along with him, the enemy had beat our foot out of the close, and was drawn up near the hedge; I went to view, and as I was giving orders for making the gap wide enough, my horse was shot in the throat with a musket bullet and his bit broken in his mouth so that I was forced to call for another horse; in the meanwhile my Lord Falkland (more gallantly than advisedly) spurred his horse through the gap, where both he and his horse were immediately killed.'

Byron continues:

'The passage being then made somewhat wide, and I not having another horse, drew in my own troop first, giving orders for the rest to follow and charged the enemy, who entertained us with a great salvo of musket shot, and discharged their two drakes upon us laden with case shot, which killed some and hurt many of my men, so that we were forced to wheel off and could not meet them at that charge.'

While Byron was rallying his men the Roundheads drew off their two field guns. He then sent in Aston's regiment which 'beat them to the end of the close, where they faced us again, having the advantage of a hedge at their backs and poured in another volley of shot upon us, when Sir Thomas Aston's horse was killed under him, and withal kept us off with their pikes. . . .' The Cavaliers wheeled off, and the Roundheads hastily retreated into 'another little close' and thence into Skinner's Green Lane. Byron's horse now charged yet a third time, but the hedges were too high to allow of pursuit. He had lost 100 men from his regiment alone. His uncle, Sir Nicholas, advanced and consolidated the ground he had won.

The course of the battle was confused and formless. The fortunes of the day swayed to and fro, but the general trend seems to have been an attempt by each army to turn their opponents' flank, i.e. the southern flank upon the plateau. Fighting in the enclosed terrain down in the meadows reached a deadlock, and reinforcements were pushed by each side farther south. The struggle thus centred about Round Hill and the ridge connecting it to Wash Farm. The tactical value of this ridge for the Roundheads was considerable. Until they could obtain a firm foothold on the plateau their guns were practically useless. If they came into action at the foot of the plateau their view would be limited to the crest of the hill above them, whereas, once established on the top they could command a great deal of the plain to the north, and also the plateau itself. This illustrates and explains the intensity of the struggle for Round Hill and the Wash ridge. At one period of the day the Royalist cavalry captured the gun position on the hill, but only managed to drag away one gun, probably a Drake. But for the most part the Royalists managed to retain the Wash Farm, and the Roundheads Round Hill.

Meanwhile the artillery duel continued, heavy guns (Culverins) being brought into action on each side. (This we know from the discovery of 15- and 20-lb. cannon-balls on the field.)

Little more of value can be said about the fight. Some of the Royalist infantry lacked spirit, as we have seen; whereas the young troops of the London Trained Bands performed splendidly, on the testimony of one of them that is generally accepted, though young soldiers, animated by a wholesome *esprit de corps* are apt to over-colour the picture.

Darkness fell, and with it came the alarming news to the King that the ammunition was running short. Indeed, a Roundhead testifies of his opponents: 'Powder and shot was so far spent that they were not able to answer one shot for three.'

Fresh supplies of powder were expected from Oxford, but unfortunately they had not arrived. The King, who is variously reported as being (1) on the plain, (2) on the side of the hill, (3) leading a cavalry regiment forward, now decided that his army, lacking ammunition, would not be able to withstand a resumption of the attack next morning, and regretfully gave the order to fall back on Oxford during the night. Had he decided to bluff it out next day, it is by no means certain that Essex would have persevered with the fight. Certain it is that he completely lost touch with the Royalist army in the night, and next morning fired a single round into what he supposed were the hostile lines, oblivious of the fact that the King was by that time many miles

to the north, on his way to Oxford. But the silence on the part of the
enemy soon disillusioned Essex and he resumed his march to London.

Losses on each side are problematical, but probably the Royalists
lost the most: in Rupert's brigade alone there were 300 casualties, and
not only Falkland but Carnarvon also was killed.

In view of the fact that the Royalist withdrawal was mainly due to
shortage of gunpowder, it can be asserted that this was the only battle
in the whole of the war in which the result was due to the influence
(whether positive or negative) of the artillery.

Essex had achieved his strategical aim, and the result of the battle
was as much a victory for the Roundheads as Edgehill had been for the
Royalists. A few days later his ragged army marched proudly into the
capital amid the plaudits of the citizens.

Although Falkland was not in fact a soldier his loss was to have a
baneful influence on the Royalist cause. George Lord Digby, brilliant,
charming but thoroughly unreliable, after being wounded at Powick
Bridge, Lichfield and Aldbourne Chase was now ready to exchange
command of a regiment of horse for Falkland's office of Secretary of
State. For the next two years he had the King's ear, and an influence
second only to that of the Queen. The Cavalier who shot Hampden did
not strike a more deadly blow than the Roundhead that slew Falkland.

Historians have never tired of condemning Charles for his resolution to besiege Gloucester, proclaiming that this siege was the ruin of
his cause. His critics say the King should have pushed forward up the
Thames Valley, with Maurice advancing parallel with him through
Hampshire and Sussex, and with Newcastle's army pouring southwards through the Eastern Association. But Newcastle, as we have
seen, was still held up by Hull and had only managed to get as far
south as Lincolnshire. The Western army though it had co-operated
with the main army at Roundway Down and at Bristol had still much
work to do in its own area. The King's own army was, as we have
seen, too weak to advance unaided against the capital. By besieging
Gloucester, Charles lured Essex far away from his base and won the
opportunity to fight another pitched battle with his old opponent of
Edgehill.

The short campaign which ended with the first battle of Newbury
is full of strategical interest. Everywhere the Royalists were triumphant, another success now and their cause might well be crowned with
final victory. Stamford, the Fairfaxes and Waller each in turn had gone

down before the conquering advance of the Cavaliers, but Essex still
barred the direct route to London. A victory over Essex in the summer of 1643 might well have changed the whole course of history.

APPENDIX

Since this chapter was written a document has come to light among
some Royalist Ordnance Papers in the Bodleian Library (Add. MS.
D.114, ff. 131[1]). It is a list of ordnance, ammunition and artillery
equipment of every kind, returned into the stores at New College,
Oxford, on 25 September 1643. It shows that the King had 20 guns
at Newbury, 16 of them brass.

At Edgehill also the Royalists had 20 guns but 14 of them were of
very low calibre. The improvement was probably due to the capture of
seven Parliamentarian guns at Edgehill, and the arrival of others
purchased by the Queen in Holland.

	Edgehill	*Newbury*
Demi-cannons	2	2
Culverins	2	2
12-pounders	–	2
Demi-culverins	2	–
6-pounders	–	5
Sakers	–	1
Mynions	–	2 (Iron)
3-pounders	–	4
Fawcons	6	–
Fawconetts	6	–
Rabonetts	2	–
Bases	–	2 (Iron)
	20 [2]	20

At Naseby, according to de Gomme's plan, the King had 12 pieces
of ordnance. Sprigge mentions the capture of the two demi-cannons,
and also records that two mortars were taken.

Unhappily similar details are not forthcoming for the Parliamentarian armies, but there is still a mass of undigested Ordnance
Papers in the Public Record Office.

[1] We are indebted to Mr. Ian Roy, of Magdalen College, Oxford, for a
copy of this list.
[2] *Journal of the Society for Army Historical Research*, Vol. XXXV, No.
144, pp. 146-7.

CHAPTER 8

The War in the North, 1643 – 2

A FTER ADWALTON MOOR it was to be expected that Newcastle would advance southwards, but he showed no great alacrity. Indeed the next blow was struck by the Roundheads. On 20 July Lord Willoughby of Parham surprised and captured Gainsborough, thus cutting Newcastle's communications with Newark. This was a very considerable success, but General Cavendish was still in the field and on 25 July Parliament sent orders to Meldrum and Cromwell to go to Lord Willoughby's assistance.

Meldrum, Cromwell, and the Lincolnshire troops met at North Scarle on 27 July, their forces, 20 troops of horse and four companies of dragoons, amounting perhaps to 1,200 men. They had wasted no time in coming to the rendezvous and now they marched on Gainsborough without delay. North of the river Lea they came upon the Forlorn Hope of Cavendish's army. The Parliamentary dragoons, without dismounting, tried to beat back the Cavaliers, who charged them, hurling some of them to the ground. The Lincolnshire troops, who led the van of the Roundheads, now drove the Royalists back to their main body which was drawn up on top of a steep hill with three regiments in front and Cavendish's own strong regiment in reserve. He had altogether 30 troops of horse and dragoons.

The Roundheads continued the advance, still led by the Lincoln men. The 'battle' or main body consisted of five troops from Northampton and Nottingham under Meldrum, and Cromwell brought up the rear with six or seven troops of his own regiment. The going was difficult, for the ground was broken by rabbit warrens. The Lincoln men fought their way uphill, and difficult though the tracks proved, they struggled to the summit. By so doing they allowed their main body to deploy just within musket-shot of their opponents.

Before the Roundheads were properly drawn up the main body of the Cavaliers advanced, hoping to take them at a disadvantage, but the

Puritan horse were undismayed. Cromwell gives the best account of what followed: 'in such order as we were, we charged their great body, I having the right wing. We came up horse to horse, where we disputed it with our swords and pistols a pretty time, all keeping close order, so that one could not break the other. At last they a little shrinking, our men perceiving it, pressed in upon them, and immediately routed this whole body, some flying on one side, others on the other of the enemy's reserve; and our men pursuing them, had chase and execution about five or six miles.'

He goes on to describe how he kept back three of his troops from the chase to oppose General Cavendish, who with his regiment, the reserve, was also facing four of the Lincoln troops.

'At last', says Cromwell, 'the General charged the Lincolners, and routed them. I immediately fell on his rear . . . which did so astonish him, that he gave over the chase, and would fain have delivered himself from me, but I pressing on forced them down a hill, having good execution of them, and below the hill, drove the General with some of his soldiers into a quagmire. . . .' where he was killed.

The victory could hardly have been more complete. Some credit is due to the Lincoln troops, but there is no question that Cromwell's good tactics and his hold over that part of his regiment which he kept back from the chase, were the deciding factors. There is a tone of decision in Cromwell's account of this fight that was lacking in his account of Grantham. This time there is no question of 'we agreed to charge' – the commander gives the order: the troops obey. This shows a marked advance in Cromwell's military career. He was gaining confidence in himself and his troops were reposing confidence in him.

Nothing now prevented the relief of Gainsborough, and the Roundheads lost no time in putting powder and provisions into the town. This done they advanced against another small force of Cavaliers which was reported to be a mile away. Reinforced by 400 of Lord Willoughby's foot they were eager to try conclusions with this new enemy.

Cromwell quickly routed two troops near a mill, but then coming to the top of a nearby hill, found himself, to his astonishment, in the presence of Newcastle's whole army. A great body of horse and foot – 50 infantry colours were counted – was advancing to lay siege to Gainsborough.

The Roundheads hastily made a plan. Cromwell was sent to order the foot to retire, and to withdraw the horse. Willoughby's infantry though they had little more than a quarter of a mile to go fell back in disorder; the Royalist horse came galloping down on them and did some execution.

At first the cavalry too fled in confusion, but after about half a mile they came to a narrow lane at the end of an open field. Here Cromwell, Whalley, and Captain Ayscoghe, the Lincolnshire commander managed to rally them.

'With these', says the official report of the Parliamentary commanders, 'we faced the enemy, stayed their pursuit, and opposed them with about four troops of Colonel Cromwell's and four Lincoln troops, the enemy's body in the meantime increasing very much from the army. But such was the goodness of God, giving courage and valour to our men and officers, that whilst Major Whalley and Captain Ayscoghe, sometimes the one with four troops faced the enemy sometimes the other, to the exceeding glory of God be it spoken, and the great honour of those two gentlemen, they with this handful faced the enemy so and dared them to their teeth in at least eight or nine several removes, the enemy following at their heels; and they though their horses were exceedingly tired, retreated in this order, near carbine-shot of the enemy, who thus followed them firing upon them; Colonel Cromwell gathering up the main body and facing them behind those two lesser bodies, that, in despite of the enemy we brought off our horse in this order without the loss of two men.'

In this manner the Roundheads got back to Lincoln.

After this there could be no question that Cromwell had become a very able regimental commander. In attack or in withdrawal he could handle a regiment of horse. Newcastle had now lost both his best cavalry commanders; Goring was a prisoner, Cavendish was dead.

It must be pointed out that only three or four out of the six or seven troops of Cromwell's regiment appear to have been among those who distinguished themselves during that long day.

The immediate results of this victory were disappointing. On 30 July Willoughby surrendered Gainsborough, his army melted away and it was not long before he was forced to abandon Lincoln as well.

Lord Fairfax, who by a Parliamentary ordinance of 22 July had been made Governor of Hull, and Sir Thomas, undismayed by their defeat at Adwalton Moor, soon collected a fresh army of 700 horse and 2,000–2,500 foot.

Newcastle, acting perhaps on the advice of General King, but doubtless influenced by the Yorkshire Royalists, now decided to lay siege to Hull. Accordingly he set out at the head of an army of 15,000 men. Driving the Roundheads from Beverley, he laid siege to the town on 2 September. Strong though the fortifications were, Lord Fairfax decided to flood the country beyond the walls, cutting the breakwater which held back the Humber. This distressed besieged and besiegers alike, for while it swamped Newcastle's works, it made it practically impossible for Fairfax's cavalry to find any fodder for their horses.

But the Cavaliers could hardly claim to have done everything in their power to distress the garrison for on 26 September Lord Willoughby and Cromwell were able to cross the river and enter the besieged city for a conference. The upshot of it was that the very same day Sir Thomas Fairfax was sent with 25 troops of horse across the Humber into Lincolnshire. Henderson, the Governor of Newark, attempted to interfere with this movement, but he was not in sufficient force to prevent it. With 15,000 men Newcastle, however, might well have spared 5,000 to occupy Barton and cut off the garrison from their friends in Lincolnshire. Nor did the unenterprising Marquis, as he now was, pay much heed to a message sent direct from the King urging him to advance towards London.

The Earl of Manchester, who in August had been appointed commander of the forces of the Eastern Association, seems to have felt no great alarm for the safety of Hull, for he himself had been engaged since his arrival in a siege. Lynn had been fortified by the local Royalists under a pretence of neutrality. The place capitulated on 16 September, and Manchester then found it possible to send Meldrum with 500 well-armed foot to reinforce Lord Fairfax in Hull. They arrived on 5 October.

The Action at Winceby. 11 October 1643

On the fall of Lynn Manchester advanced to Boston where he was met by Cromwell with his contingent of horse and dragoons, and Fairfax with his detachment. The foot were reported to be 6,000 strong and the combined horse at least 1,500 strong.

While this army was assembling the Cavaliers were in motion. Sir William Widdrington, who since the death of General Cavendish was the senior Royalist commander in Lincolnshire, and Sir John Henderson, had received orders from Newcastle to take a mounted force to the succour of Bolingbroke Castle, which was now threatened by Manchester. This castle lay three miles south-west of Spilsby, seven miles south-east of Horncastle and 15 miles north of Boston. The Cavaliers, by milking the garrisons of Newark, Lincoln, and Gainsborough, managed to scrape together a scratch force of between 1,500 and 2,000 horse and 800 dragoons. Having collected his army

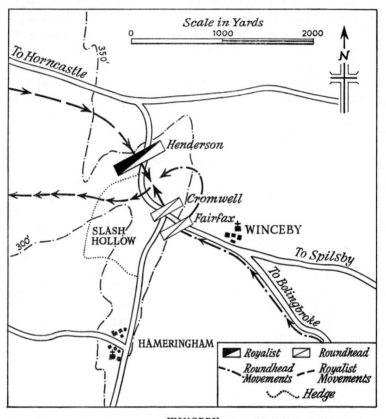

WINCEBY

at Lincoln, Widdrington set out for Horncastle, some 20 miles to the east.[1]

On 10 October the advanced guard of Manchester's foot marched from Boston and laid siege to Bolingbroke Castle. Meanwhile Manchester had sent Fairfax forward to throw out a cavalry screen far to the west, for information of the Royalist approach had been received.

[1] Contemporary accounts place Henderson in command but this on the whole would appear to be a mistake.

Fairfax carried out his task well, steadily falling back before the enemy.

By noon on the 11th the whole army was concentrated on Boling-broke Hill, where Manchester held a Council of War to decide whether to take the offensive and seek a battle. Cromwell advised against it, saying that his horses were exhausted (so also were those of the Royalists). But Manchester overruled him and ordered an im-mediate advance to meet the enemy.

Thus the two armies met head-on half way between Horncastle and Bolingbroke, on the southern edge of the Wolds near the tiny village of Winceby (distance four miles from Horncastle and three from Bolingbroke). On reaching the crest 500 yards beyond the village Manchester's advanced troops saw the rival army deploying for battle on the next ridge towards Horncastle about 600 yards away. There was a shallow dip between the two ridges, not more than 100 feet in depth. On the right hand the two ridges curved round and joined up; thus the terrain was like a horseshoe lying on its side, the toe being to the Roundheads' right. The ground was quite open, except that a few hundred yards away on the left a hedge marked the boundary between the parishes of Winceby and Scradfield.

The Earl of Manchester decided to take up a position on the ridge top, and he formed up his army as follows. In front was the Forlorn Hope under his Quartermaster General, Colonel Vermuyden. Behind that came the van, consisting of the regiments of Cromwell and Manchester, under the former. In the second line, or reserve, was Fairfax with his own contingent. Behind that came the foot (under Colonel Sir Miles Hobart), still some distance in rear, for the cavalry had advanced at speed. After deploying his mounted troops in the above order Manchester apparently went back to hasten forward the lagging infantry.

The Cavaliers were drawn up with their dragoons in the van. The main body of horse was drawn up in three 'divisions' and in rear were some more horse. Sir William Savile commanded on the right and Sir John Henderson on the left.

When both armies were ranged in battle order there was a pause, neither side making any sign of attacking.

The battle seems to have begun at last by the Royalist dragoons advancing across the dip between the two armies. On seeing this Vermuyden conformed with his dragoons and a short sharp contest followed. Contemporary writers stated that he 'charged'. There have been instances of mounted infantry charging, but what is probably meant here is that they advanced to close range, dismounted and opened fire. We know that the Royalist dragoons dismounted. While it was proceeding the Cavalier first line also crossed the dip. In response to this Cromwell led his two regiments down the hill at a trot. The distance cannot have exceeded two hundred yards, and during this short advance the Royalist dragoons had time to fire two volleys at them, the second being at point-blank range. A bullet from this volley killed Cromwell's horse and its rider was brought to the ground. While the fight was going on between the two bodies of horse Cromwell managed to extricate himself and rose to his feet, but a moment later Sir Ingram Hopton knocked him down, without wounding him, presumably recognising the already well-known Roundhead colonel. It is thought that the Cavalier was anxious to take him prisoner, but Hopton himself was killed in the mêlée. Presently a trooper brought up 'a poore horse' which Cromwell mounted – and after that silence descends on his activities in the battle. This silence of the sources has not prevented historians from exercising their imaginative gifts in the matter. A modern biography of Cromwell asserts that he 'rallied his troops and drove home the victory'. Not one of the five writers present in the battle mentions such a thing.

In the confusion of a mounted action where each man is intent on killing and avoiding being killed, it is only natural that detailed and reliable accounts of individuals should not be forthcoming, but it is possible that the expression 'a poore horse' may have some special significance; that the troop horse that was brought up proved rather restive and unmanageable, and that by the time Cromwell was well established in the saddle of his new mount the battle had rolled forward past him. This might account for the sudden silence of the contemporary accounts.

The Cavalier first line had recoiled on to the second, creating some disorder as it did so on the right of the line. The mêlée now became general in the bottom of the dip, and lasted for about 15 minutes. Meanwhile the Roundhead second line was inactive. We can picture Fairfax sitting his horse at the head of his men, looking down on the battle, chewing his moustache and wondering how he could best intervene in the fight. To join directly in the mêlée in that confined space seemed fruitless; a charge into the hostile flank was more in keeping with his nature. But which flank? To attack the enemy's right offered no attractions: it would entail charging up hill, the movement would be visible to the enemy right from its inception and the hedge on his left might constrict his movements. But the ground on the other side seemed specially designed for such a manoeuvre. By skirting round the top of the ridge, just out of sight, he could wheel round to his left and crossing the ridge-top charge down into the unsuspecting flank of the enemy on a slope admirably suited for a mounted charge.

'Fiery Tom's' decision was made: 'Come, let us fall on,' he cried, and he suited the action to the word, leading his troops round to the right and then wheeling to the left over the crest. Just as the Roundhead horse came into sight a body of Royalist horse was also starting to charge, while Henderson had disordered the Roundheads opposite his wing. On came Fairfax's men at a rapid pace, making straight for the enemy, but before they could get into them Savile's divisions turned and fled. Their example was followed by the other divisions and soon the whole body disintegrated and took to flight – except the dismounted dragoons, whose horses were not at hand and who consequently were killed or made prisoners.

Fairfax pressed his advantage to the full, pursuing relentlessly. Now, owing to the direction of his attack many, possibly most, of the Cavalier horse were pushed off their direct line of retreat which was the road towards Horncastle and forced away into a south-westerly direction. This took them along the hedge that we have mentioned, and at a sharp salient angle in it there was a gate. The hedge being presumably unjumpable, the fleeing horsemen found themselves converging on to this gate in a dense mass. Unfortunately the gate was made to open inwards, and owing to the press and excitement both of man and beast the gate could not be forced open and the fugitives fell easy victims to the Roundhead swords. To this day the spot is known as Slash Hollow.

The battle was over; the victory complete. The bulk of the Royalist troops were either killed, captured or scattered over a wide area of country without a semblance of cohesion or order. The defeated leaders were quite open about the extent of their defeat. Next day Sir William Widdrington wrote a pathetic letter to Newcastle announcing the disintegration of the army and containing this pregnant sentence: 'Their Horse are very good, and extraordinarily [well] armed; . . .'

Fairfax continued the pursuit into and beyond Horncastle before drawing rein, and Manchester billeted his infantry in the town for the night. They had not fired a shot.

The Royalists now abandoned Gainsborough and lost Lincoln. Before long Newark itself was blockaded.

I

COMMENTS

The importance of the battle of Winceby was out of all proportion to the small numbers engaged in it and to the brevity of the conflict.

(1) Fairfax relates in his brief account how, as the battle was ending he heard heavy gunfire from the north,[1] which proved to be a successful sortie from Hull (made by his father) which resulted in the abandonment of the siege by Newcastle; and he goes on to surmise that it was those two successes, occurring simultaneously, that induced Newcastle to abandon his march on London, thus bringing to naught the King's grand strategic plan for 1643. Fairfax was no doubt right in this estimation.

(2) The fame of Cromwell's horsemen rapidly grew as a result of the victory. It was the first big success of the Roundhead over the Cavalier horse and the morale of the whole Roundhead army was correspondingly raised.

(3) The victory raised the reputation of Cromwell. He had now been engaged in three consecutive victories, and they had come at a time when the Parliamentary fortunes were on the wane. Cromwell's military future was thereby assured; his foot was firmly planted on the ladder of fame.

This last point brings us to a consideration of Oliver Cromwell's part in the victory. Modern writers are practically unanimous in regarding Winceby as *his* battle and *his* victory.[2] Four of them contrive to describe the battle without even mentioning the names of Manchester or Fairfax; it was Cromwell first and all the time. But it was not always so. The flyleaves of the original tracts describe the battle as Manchester's. Indeed it was clear from the accounts of eyewitnesses that owing to his accident so early in the day Cromwell could not have had much practical influence over the course of the battle. Nor could he be given the credit for issuing the orders that led to victory. So far from that, he had been averse to fighting a battle, as we have seen. But Cromwell was a Member of Parliament and already in the public eye, and his early successes had attracted more attention in the capital than those of the distant Yorkshire squire. Yet it cannot be disputed that the battle was ordered and organised by Manchester; his was the responsibility and therefore, in general terms, his was the victory. Of the

[1] Hull is nearly 40 miles from Winceby, a long way for the sound of ordnance to travel. The wind must have been in the north.

[2] Mr Maurice Ashley in *The Greatness of Oliver Cromwell* is an exception and states that Fairfax 'routed the enemy'.

actual executants, there can be no doubt that Sir Thomas Fairfax played the predominant part, and his name should ever be closely associated with the Roundhead victory. Revealing light on this point is afforded by careful reading of Manchester's despatch to the House of Lords announcing his victory. Of Cromwell he wrote somewhat coolly if not perfunctorily that he 'behaved himself with honour'. Far different is the tone of his reference to Fairfax: 'Sir Thomas Fairfax (who is a person who exceeds any expression as a commendation of his resolution and valour) . . . performed what he was commanded with readiness and success.'

'Resolution', 'valour', 'readiness', 'success'. Note in particular the last two words:

(1) *Readiness.* Fairfax had shown himself ready (indeed eager) for the fray. Cromwell had not.

(2) *Success.* Fairfax's successful part in the battle and pursuit had been obvious to all. That of Cromwell had not been so evident.

Colonel Cromwell can hardly have relished the terms of this despatch, and thus may have been sown that seed of mutual antipathy that was to come to a head twelve months later.

But if, by the fortune of war, Cromwell was not in a position to influence the course of the battle, he deserved full credit for having forged such a splendid fighting weapon as his Ironsides had now become. Training and morale won the battle of Winceby and for this a considerable part of the credit must go to Oliver. But how much of it should be ascribed to Sir Thomas? His horse also had been consistently successful and were plentifully imbued with morale, even though they may not have been as vociferous psalm-singers as Cromwell's troopers. If Cromwell's influence was most evident in the training camp that of Fairfax shone most brightly in the battle. The opinion of Whitelocke deserves quotation in this connection. Sir Thomas was 'a person of as meek and humble a carriage as ever I saw in great employment. . . . But in action in the field I have seen him so highly transported that scarce anyone durst speak a word to him, and he would seem more like a man distracted than of his ordinary mildness.'

Of the Earl of Manchester it is more difficult to speak. Certainly he seems to have impressed eyewitnesses with his vigour in the field. One of them wrote of him that 'he took wonderful pains' to get his army concentrated. He is also described as showing 'vigilance and industry'. Perhaps we may call him a 'plodding' general – he is however open to criticism in that, having succeeded in concentrating his army in a suitable position on Bolingbroke Hill he allowed it to approach the battlefield in driblets.

The relative positions of Fairfax and Cromwell is obscure. According to Ludlow Parliament 'appointed Cromwell to command under him [Manchester] in the army at Boston.' If this be true the position may have been awkward when his superior officer Fairfax joined the army. But Parliament on appointing Cromwell could not have foreseen that Fairfax would also be present. In any case there is no first hand evidence or sign that the general served under the colonel. *The Parliament Scout*, a second-hand source compiled in London, asserted that Cromwell commanded the cavalry, but this broadsheet contained some glaring errors on the same page and it cannot be relied upon.

11 October 1643 was a memorable day for the Fairfax family, for, as we have seen, while Sir Thomas was winning fresh laurels at Winceby, his stout-hearted old father was leading a sortie from Hull. Two days earlier a fierce Cavalier assault on the West Jetty Fort had been repulsed and the Roundheads, encouraged by this success, determined to take the initiative.

At 7 o'clock in the morning the garrison got under arms without beat of drum. The guards on the north side lit many hundred matches and flashed powder in the pans of their muskets to induce the Royalists to expect a sortie there.

At 9 o'clock, 1,500 foot, townsmen, soldiers, and seamen, with four troops of horse, sallied out on the west. They were gallantly received, yet in a quarter of an hour the Cavaliers were driven out of their first work. Pushing on, the Roundheads got the next position, but a fresh body of Cavaliers quickly came marching up from their camp a quarter of a mile in rear of their line. These beat back the Hull men, putting them into disorder, and charging their rear, recaptured all the siege works. The Roundhead cavalry meanwhile faced a great body of Cavalier horse, which dared not advance within range of the guns of the town.

Lord Fairfax and Sir John Meldrum rallied their men and persuaded them to charge once more, and after desperate fighting they retook the Royalist forts, turning the guns on the besiegers. Among the ordnance taken was a 36-pounder, probably of Dutch origin, one of the pair called the *Queen's Pocket Pistols* or *Gog* and *Magog*; which weighed 5,790 pounds.

That night the Marquis broke up the siege.

CHAPTER 9

Hopton and Waller

S AN IMMEDIATE result of the first battle of Newbury the
Oxford army – the central prong of the Royalist trident –
re-occupied Reading. It was in fact back where it had been
in the early spring of the same year. But the Northern army was held
up before Hull and the old Western army, now under Prince Maurice,
was fully occupied in Devonshire, where it took Exeter (4 September)
and Dartmouth (6 October) only to be held up before Plymouth. The
two outer prongs of the trident were decidedly stuck.

But if regionalism was keeping the Yorkshire and Cornish Cavaliers
from the decisive scene of action – the approaches to London – the
King's Council of War at Oxford still had their eyes on the main prize.
Indeed they showed a grasp of the essentials of strategy quite unusual
for the mid-seventeenth century.

In the North they decided to form a new army in Cheshire. This
was to be commanded by Sir John Byron, who had recently been made
a baron, and who by a dubious intrigue had succeeded in supplanting
the gallant Lord Capel, previously the Royalist commander in those
parts. Byron was expected to destroy Brereton's forces and to reconquer Lancashire. That done he could join Newcastle in his struggle
with the Fairfaxes and the Eastern Association. The doings of this
army will be related in Chapter 10.

More important still a new Western army was to be formed. For this
the obvious commander was Lord Hopton, who was now reasonably
well recovered from his wounds. While the Oxford army was operating
north of the Thames against Essex himself, Hopton with this new
force was to clear Dorset, Wiltshire, and Hampshire and in his own
words 'so point forward as far as he could go towards London'.

On 29 September 1643 there was a Council of War in Oriel College,
Oxford, when Hopton was informed of the King's decision, and the
composition of this projected army was discussed. Even on paper it was

not a very formidable host. The foot numbered 2,000; and the 12 regiments of horse could muster only 1,580 men between them. Even so there were good regiments among them.

Soon after two old regiments from Munster landed at Bristol. They were about 500 strong and well officered, but the soldiers were (as Hopton puts it) "shrewdly infected with the rebellious humour of England'. When, shortly after, they mutinied, Hopton promptly executed two or three of the ringleaders and the two regiments gave no further trouble.

Money, as usual with the Royalist armies, was the chief difficulty. Hopton was promised £6,000, of which only £1,500 was received from Oxford, but he raised £3,000 in Bristol and was able to take the field at the beginning of November. To improvise an army in just over a month was quick work and speaks volumes for his administrative ability.

Once more his adversary was to be Sir William Waller, who had taken the field in mid-October and who on 4 November was formally appointed to command the forces of a new South-eastern Association – Kent, Surrey, Sussex, and Hampshire. While Essex remained strictly on the defensive round St Albans and Newport Pagnell, Waller advanced on 7 November from Farnham, not against Hopton who was still very weak in numbers but against Basing House, which since the summer had proved a thorn in the side of the Roundheads. There can be little doubt that Waller made a grave error in not seeking out his opponent's main field army before it could get into its stride, but the Parliamentary commander, still shaken by Lansdown and Roundway Down, credited Hopton with an army he no longer had.

Waller's own army, like Essex's, included a brigade of the London Trained Bands, who were to prove even more mutinous than Hopton's 'Irish'. On 12 November a Westminster regiment refused to obey orders and two days later the Londoners, when ordered in to the attack, deserted with loud cries of 'Home! Home!' Waller, long the hero of the City, hanged none of them. He fell back to his base at Farnham, having lost fully 300 men in his abortive siege.

Hopton had wished to begin his campaign by reducing the remaining Parliamentary fortresses in Wiltshire and Dorset so as to clear his back area, but Sir William Ogle surprised Winchester about this time and Hopton was drawn in that direction.

During November Hopton was reinforced by troops from the West country and by others lent him from the Oxford army, and his field force, not counting those detailed to blockade the Roundhead garrisons of Portsmouth, Southampton, Poole, and Wardour Castle, must have numbered at least 5,000 men. With this 'very handsome little army' as he calls it, he twice tried to bring Waller to battle near Farnham Castle, but Sir William was taking no chances and drew up his men close under the guns of the fortress. Hopton therefore turned his attention to Arundel Castle, which was in his hands by 9 December. The Royalists were elated by this success, but it was to prove short-lived. Their small army facing Waller was strung out on a front 27 miles as the crow flies, its regiments dangerously exposed to defeat in detail.

The Roundheads now struck Hopton three telling blows in quick succession. First, Colonel Richard Norton, the Governor of Southampton, beat up the two regiments quartered at Romsey, causing both of them serious losses. Then Waller, marching through the woods from Farnham under cover of night, fell upon the Earl of Crawford at Alton on 13 December.

At 7 o'clock on the evening of 12 December Waller, who had paraded 5,000 horse and foot in Farnham Park, moved off in the direction of Basing, marching that way so as to mislead any Royalist scouts who might chance to spy his column.

At one o'clock in the morning Waller gave the order to turn south, avoiding the main roads, which he thought would be patrolled. A hard frost had made the going good for his marching columns, and at about 9 o'clock in the morning his army appeared undetected on the west side of the town. Crawford's men, it seems, were only patrolling the main Farnham-Alton road, which was, to say the least, unimaginative of them. When the fight began the Earl with his cavalry broke out of Alton leaving Colonel Bolle and his foot to defend themselves as best they could.

The first attack was made by Waller's own regiment of foot, supported by five companies of Sir Arthur Hazelrig's and five of Kentishmen who went in from the north and the north-west, taking what cover they could behind hedges and bushes. The Cavaliers firing fast from a great brick house near the church did some damage, but were dislodged by gunfire, for Waller had some leather guns with him.

The London regiments of redcoats and greencoats and four companies from Farnham Castle now came up and attacked a half moon and a breastwork. There was hot work for a time, but then the Green Auxiliaries, colours flying, got into the town and set fire to a thatched house. The smoke blowing into the faces of the defenders made an effective screen and soon the Londoners were in the Market Place.

Bolle manned the churchyard and a great work on the north side of it and hung on for two hours more. The Cavaliers had erected scaffolding in the church and kept up a heavy fire from the windows.

The men of the Red and the Yellow regiments of the London Trained Bands got the better of the fire fight in the south-east corner of the churchyard. The Roundheads could still see muskets sticking over the wall and suspected an ambush, but as no enemy put his head over the wall to fire they eventually concluded that the defenders had fled, and – not without misgivings – advanced into the churchyard. Simultaneously some of the Red regiment broke in driving the Cavaliers back into the church, and following so close on their heels that they prevented the barricading of the door.

A desperate struggle took place in the churchyard, the Roundheads laying about them stoutly with halberds, swords, and musket-stocks, while some threw hand grenades into the church windows. Colonel Birch is said to have been the first man to enter. The sight of the enemy waiting to receive him with their pikes and muskets, behind a breastwork of dead horses in the aisles, might well have appalled a fainter heart. Many bullet marks within the building still testify to the severity of that half forgotten fight.

Richard Bolle, the Royalist commander, had no thought of surrender. Swearing to run his sword through the heart of the first man that called for quarter, he slew seven Roundheads before he was struck dead by a blow from the butt of a musket, and fell surrounded by a circle of enemies. His death took the heart out of the defence, though a few – 'desperate villains' a Parliamentary officer calls them – still refused quarter and were slain in the church.

Wildly differing accounts are given of the losses sustained by the Cavaliers, but their losses were certainly severe: 700 is probably a fair estimate of the number of prisoners alone. Hopton was greatly depressed by the disaster.

The psychological shock to his self-esteem as a commander was very great – indeed out of all proportion to the realities of the defeat he had sustained. Perhaps he felt a sense of shame at having left his men exposed to such an attack; perhaps he experienced some feeling of guilt, however unjustified, because, try though he did, he had failed to come to their rescue in time.

It will be recalled that he had been wounded and then blown up at

Lansdown in July, a shattering experience whose effects in those days may well have been underrated by his friends and colleagues. The mental shock of Alton, coming comparatively soon after the physical shocks of Lansdown made a changed man of Ralph Lord Hopton, and the changes were not for the better. Henceforth he lacked the old fire and decision which had marked his early battles; he became slower to make up his mind and too apt to change it – more of a second-in-command than a supreme commander, Clarendon thought. However depressed he may have been by them, the series of reverses which Hopton had sustained can be explained simply enough. He was being invited by the Royalist Council of War at Oxford to carry out an ambitious strategic plan with very inadequate forces.

On 6 January, after a fortnight's siege, Waller recaptured Arundel Castle. But just when 'William the Conqueror' was getting back into something like his old form of the pre-Lansdown period the snow set in and little more could be done that winter.

It was the same north of the Thames where, with the veterans at their disposal, the Oxford Cavaliers had done little enough. An attempt to threaten the Great North Road by making a garrison at Newport Pagnell had come to grief. A similar attempt to cut the Roundheads' communications between London and the North Midlands by occupying Towcester had also to be abandoned. Little serious fighting had taken place and then as the situation in Cheshire and Shropshire worsened the King had found it necessary to send Rupert to put things right. Neither the Queen nor Digby, one supposes, was sorry to see him go.

But though the Oxford army itself had little to boast of, this did not prevent its commanders losing confidence in Hopton. Perhaps they thought he had lost his cunning, perhaps they thought he was making too much of his difficulties. The upshot was that when at long last they sent him a respectable reinforcement, they sent at its head an officer much senior to him, Patrick Ruthven, Earl of Forth.

Forth was loyal, ancient, brave, and bibulous; vastly experienced and seriously gouty. Early in March 1644 he joined Hopton with a very handsome body of 1,200 foot, 800 horse, and four guns. Hopton's own men raised the army to a total of not less than 6,000, of whom nearly 3,000 were cavalry. A good administrator, he had seen to it that his men were well clothed; but it is the spirit that counts, and his new levies and his 'Irish' veterans – even if they were no longer mutinous – were not to be compared with the Cornishmen of Stratton and Lansdown.

Forth was a tactful old gentleman and, as Hopton tells us, it was with the utmost difficulty that he 'prevailed with him to honour him with his orders'. There can, however, be no doubt that from this time onwards the responsibility for the command of the army fell upon Lord Forth, but as he was suffering from the gout and could not move far from his coach all the practical work continued to fall upon Hopton, without the actual responsibility being his. This was a vicious system as we saw at Lansdown. An army should have a single commander and every man in that army should know who his commander is.

Sir William Waller, on the other hand, was in undisputed command of the Parliamentary army, and had been for five months. It was a firmly welded force, especially the cavalry, for the prestige of Sir Arthur Hazelrig's 'Lobsters' was still strong despite Roundway Down, a defeat which Waller himself, no doubt, was burning to avenge – even as Hopton was burning to wipe out his triple setback of the previous winter.

Waller's army outnumbered the Cavaliers by several thousand men, for in addition to his own cavalry he had at least 2,000 mounted men under Sir William Balfour, the best cavalry leader in Essex's army. Waller's infantry may have contained unreliable elements, but for the first time a Parliamentary commander was making ready for a really big battle with a strong cavalry force at his disposal.

The Earl of Essex, showing for once considerable strategic insight, had shifted the centre of gravity of the Parliamentary armies from the north to the south bank of the Thames. Cavalry, as we have so often seen, was the predominant arm in this war. Waller and Hopton had at first been fairly evenly matched. Then the King had lent Hopton 800 men; whereupon Essex sent 2,000 horse to join Waller, completely tipping the balance in his favour. The Cavaliers held the passages of the Thames above Reading and with the river barrier of Thame, Cherwell, and Thames to guard Oxford, were far better placed to play this game of shifting forces than Essex was. Generally speaking Cavalier strategy in the early years of the war was far superior to that of the Parliamentarians, but before Cheriton Essex loaded the dice in favour of his colleague.

Both sides were confident and eager for battle. Forth and Hopton actually issued a challenge in the mediaeval manner, offering to meet Waller at a prescribed place and time. If Sir William declined the challenge it was only because like the good tactician he was, he had resolved to fight whenever he could gain a favourable opportunity. Like all good generals, he preferred his dice loaded.

The Battle of Cheriton. 29 March 1644

On 25 March the Parliamentary army was approaching East and West Meon from the east, whilst the Cavaliers were assembling at Winchester. From this city they suddenly advanced two days later reaching Alresford the same day. Here they were just in time to anticipate Balfour's body of horse which Waller had sent forward with the same objective, forcing him to fall back to Hinton Ampner, four miles south of Alresford, where Waller's main body joined him.

There was bickering between the horse of both sides during the next 24 hours, while the two main bodies closed up to one another. By evening of the 28th the Cavaliers were drawn up along the ridge two miles to the south of Alresford, while the Roundheads were bivouacking in a large field at Hinton Ampner.

There is no dispute as to the site of this battle. Ample records, place-names and grave-pits pinpoint it. Between Alresford and Hinton Ampner lies a horseshoe ridge; its 'toe' points eastward and its 'heels' westward, thus forming two ridges which join each other to the east. In the centre, representing the hollow sole of a horse's foot, is a vast but shallow amphitheatre or arena, nearly a mile wide. The northern ridge is rather higher than the southern one, rising 100 feet above the mean level of the 'arena' as we will call it. It was in this arena – fit site for a battle – that the fighting took place. It was for the most part open common land, whilst the slopes to north and south of it were thickly enclosed with fields and lanes, which may be compared to the tiers of seats surrounding an actual arena. The toe of the horseshoe was, and still is, covered by an extensive wood known as Cheriton Wood.

When day broke on 29 March 1644, both armies were equally resolved to fight it out. The Cavaliers had managed overnight to gain possession of the southern arm or ridge of the horseshoe, and an out-post line of horse under Colonel George Lisle had been stationed there, while the remainder of the army took up position on the northern ridge. Here during the night Lisle lay unmolested, for a Parliamentary council of war on the previous afternoon had resolved on retreat. But with the dawn came a change of mind, though the exact reason for it is in some doubt.

It was a misty morning and Waller opened operations by sending a force from his London Brigade to seize Cheriton Wood. His well-known 'eye for country' here served him well, for this wood at the toe of the horseshoe was the potential key to the position. Whichever side obtained control of it enjoyed the double advantage of being able to gain the enemy's ridge by a covered line of approach and without

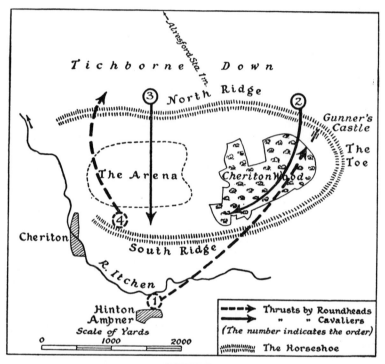

CHERITON

having to descend into the valley and attack uphill, besides being advantageously placed to threaten the flank of any hostile force that attempted to advance straight across the arena.

The Roundheads were successful in obtaining a lodgment in the wood, and this had the natural effect of inducing Lisle with his outpost to fall back on the main body, for fear of being outflanked and cut off.

But Waller was not the only soldier on that field gifted with an 'eye for country'. Lord Hopton also possessed it, and as soon as he realized what Waller was aiming at he countered it with a still stronger force. Cheriton Wood was vital for both sides and a battle royal took place for it. Whereas Waller had sent only infantry to seize the wood, Hopton sent infantry and guns to recover it. The guns came into action on top of the ridge, above and only a short distance from the edge of the wood. (This spot came to be known as Gunners' Castle.) As the enemy emerged in an inevitably ragged manner from the undergrowth the guns opened on them with deadly effect and they were driven back. Colonel Matthew Appleyard's foot carried on the good work begun by the guns. When he first advanced, with his 1,000 musketeers deployed in four 'divisions' he was held up for a time. Seeing this the Royalist general had ordered Lieut.-Colonel Edward Hopton with one of the four divisions, to run with all possible speed into the wood and outflank the Roundheads. Manning a convenient hedge they poured in a volley that sent their enemy to the rightabout, such was the confusion that the Royalist infantry actually captured the colours of a troop of horse and the Roundheads were completely ejected from the wood. Hopton himself, showing a very modern flair for minor tactics, had played a decisive part in the struggle. The first round had been won by the King's army.

The Parliamentary army was appreciably shaken by this early set-back and it would seem as if all that was now required of the Cavaliers was to follow up their initial advantage and sweep down the southern ridge from the wood, taking the Roundheads in their right flank. (The sketch-map should make this clear.) But it was not to be. The old and cautious Forth had, unfortunately, in spite of his gout managed to reach the battlefield and he restrained the younger and the more ardent Hopton, preferring to stand and allow the enemy to attack the strong position that he now occupied.

If this plan had been persisted in all might yet have been well, for Waller, an easily discouraged man, might have reverted to the previous day's decision to retreat. But the course of battles is never foreseeable. When all the known and ascertainable factors have been duly weighed there still remain the unascertainable factors, what we may call the imponderabilia of the battlefield – the unpredictable interplay of human nature, which often makes or mars a well-laid plan. In this case it marred it. A Royalist colonel, Sir Henry Bard by name, contrary to all orders suddenly took it upon himself to charge down into the arena at the head of his regiment, and up the other side against the enemy wait-

ing in a prepared position. Gardiner in his account is kind to this un-
disciplined cavalryman, enlarging upon his patriotic zeal, 'burning to
strike a gallant blow at the rebels he despised'. But this will not do. An
army in which the officers are so regardless of their orders is like a
cracked tool that may fall to pieces in your hand at any moment. Bard's
cavalry regiment was isolated, and Sir Arthur Hazelrig, in a timely and
brilliant manoeuvre, swung round their rear, cutting off their retreat.
The move was decisive; after a short combat every man in Bard's
regiment was killed or captured.

Now this happened under the eyes of the rest of the army. It was
hard to look on, leaving Bard's men tamely to their fate. Forth
made his second change of plan, sending another regiment down to
their succour. Much the same fate met this one. Regiment then
followed regiment down into the fatal arena in hasty ill-coordinated
and spasmodic charges. A long, tangled, planless, and formless struggle
swirled round and round in the arena bottom. The advantage was all
on the side of the defender, sitting securely behind his hedge or sallying
out when an isolated troop of the enemy provided a suitable opportunity, the Parliamentary guns belching forth from the higher ground
in rear.

Gradually the infantry were drawn in too, making the contest more
involved and more shapeless than ever. For several hours what can
only be described as a gigantic 'dog fight' went on in the arena, the
Cavaliers suffering very heavy losses particularly among the officers.
Two cavalry generals, Lord John Stuart and Sir John Smith fell that
day. Edward Walsingham, a gentleman in the latter's troop describes
his end. When he received Forth's order to commit his men to action
in the arena he was well aware that it would lead to disaster, but like a
good soldier, he proceeded to carry it out.

Smith's men were to charge a solid body of the enemy horse, protected by lanes and hedges lined with musketeers. He was almost
within pistol shot of one of the Roundhead cannon when it went off.
His horse reared and turned so that he had much ado to keep his saddle.
The Parliamentarians 'let fly at him as thick as hail. And in this
interim comes one amongst them clad in arms, like a lobster, who with
his carbine gives him this third and mortal wound in his belly, on the
left side beneath his armour. With this wound he falls and with him the
fortunes of the day.' Seeing their general fall the Cavaliers retreated in
great disorder, but Smith's own troop gallantly brought off their commander, and one of their number 'in a brave revenge' rode up to 'the

Lobster' who had mortally wounded him, and killed him with a pistol shot.

It must have been well on in the afternoon when the movement which decided the battle took place. It is related only by Lieut.-Colonel Slingsby, in a short passage that has apparently escaped the notice of the various historians of the battle. In the course of the 'dog fight' in the centre Royalist troops seem to have been gradually drawn away from their right wing. As it was on the open crest every movement could be seen from the other ridge, and on the Parliamentary left wing a regimental commander took advantage of it. Swinging his line to the right he outflanked the Royalist shortened right wing, and marching up the west end of the north ridge forced a withdrawal. The Cavaliers fell back over Tichborne Down for one mile and took up a fresh position on the ground where they had bivouacked the previous night, on a slight ridge half a mile south of Alresford railway station.[1] The Roundheads dragged up some guns and after three discharges the Cavaliers again fell back.

But ere this happened the far-seeing Hopton had ordered the artillery to fall back, and all except two of his 11 guns got safely away. The Earl of Forth now appears to have given the order for a general retreat, and the whole Royalist army streamed to the rear through the streets of Alresford. Forth and Hopton and the bulk of the army took the road to Basing House, which they reached that night; the remainder made for Winchester.

Waller advanced next day to Winchester where the city, but not the castle, surrendered to him. Soon all Hampshire was his, while Forth fell back on Oxford.

COMMENTS

Gardiner is unaccountably kind to the Earl of Forth. On paper, at least, it would seem that, with the capture of Cheriton Wood Hopton had 'the ball at his feet', as he himself represented to Forth. But either the nerve of the older man failed him or he played for safety, which comes to much the same thing. 'Fortune is a woman', but unfortunately for the Royalist commander, Napoleon's well-known maxim had not then been framed. Dame Fortune did not offer her favours a second time.

It is curious that Waller was content to accept defeat in Cheriton

[1] Secretary Roe claims for his master, that remarkable officer Colonel Birch, the credit for initiating this move.

Wood and that he made no definite attempt to retake it. For the remainder of the day there seems to have been practically no fighting in the wood. Not only must Waller be blamed for attempting nothing in this vital sector, but Forth must also be blamed for not taking advantage of it later in the day to intervene in the arena fight from that direction. The fact probably is that his command post on the centre of the northern ridge offered *too* good a view of the battle. It was laid out beneath him; almost every movement could be seen, and he would naturally become absorbed in what his own eye told him to the exclusion of other interests and considerations. He became too absorbed in the 'dog-fight', forgetful of everything else. Thus he missed the opportunity to profit by the favourable position on his left, and to rectify the unfavourable situation that supervened on his right flank.

One cannot share Gardiner's admiration for the action of Waller in posting his cavalry at the foot of the slope on the edge of the arena. Since only in the arena was there open ground favourable for cavalry it was the obvious place in which to post them. He would have been an imbecile to place them anywhere else, unless he placed them in reserve; for everywhere the slopes were studded with small fields, smaller apparently than they are today.

To sum up, it is difficult to detect generalship of a high order in either of the commanders on Cheriton Field. Secretary Roe admitted that 'it was indeed a victory, but the worst possible of any I ever saw'. To what then should we attribute the Parliamentary victory? The immediate cause was doubtless the happy manoeuvre of their left wing at the end of the day. But there were in addition factors of a more general nature. The first was Waller's great superiority in numbers, Essex having sent him 2,000 of his best cavalry shortly before the battle. Furthermore the Parliamentary army had attained a higher standard of training and it enjoyed greater homogeneity than its rivals. It was Waller's own army; he had trained the bulk of it himself; whereas the Royalist army was more heterogeneous, and it owned two masters.

Discipline was the better in Waller's army, and that old-fashioned military virtue – or rather the absence of it – proved the downfall of the Royalist army.

This was the last of the western prong of the Royalist trident. The King's central army was no longer as powerful as at Newbury: an important detachment had gone north with Rupert; desertions and casualties during the winter had further weakened it. Accordingly King Charles decided to add the remnants of Hopton's army to his own in order to make up his field army for the summer campaign. Clarendon's words were justified; the battle of Cheriton had 'altered the whole scheme of the King's counsels'.

CHAPTER 10

The Scots and the 'Irish'

———

THE WAR NOW enters its second phase. With the signing of the
Solemn League and Covenant on 25 September the intervention of the Scots was assured, though John Pym, its chief
author and thus far the undisputed leader of the Parliamentarians, did
not live to see its first fruits.

The 19th January 1644 may well be called the turning point of the
Civil War, for on that day the Scots army began to cross the Tweed.
The struggle between the English protagonists had become so nicely
balanced that the intervention of a well organized army of some
20,000 regular troops was bound to turn the scales.

The Marquis of Newcastle hastened north to join the Cavaliers of
Northumberland in an attempt to stem the torrent of invasion.

Since 11 October 1643 (the day of Winceby and the sortie from
Hull), which may be called the Black Day of the Northern Cavaliers,
there had perhaps been little likelihood that Newcastle's army would
ever play the part designed for it in the Grand Plan of the Royalist
strategists. To take its place the Oxford Council of War was, as we
saw in the last chapter, building up a second Northern army under
Lord Byron. This was possible because in September hostilities had
ceased in Ireland, permitting the Lord Lieutenant, the Marquis of
Ormonde, to send some of his English regiments to reinforce the
Royalist armies. First and last about 12 regiments of foot and one of
horse cross St. George's Channel; some landed in the south-west, but
the majority were shipped across to Chester. These reinforcements,
useful though they were, cannot be compared in importance with the
Scottish army.

Five of these foot regiments joined Byron in October 1643, and
with their aid he made considerable progress against Brereton. On
26 December he summoned a Roundhead detachment in Barthomley
Church. The first summons was rejected whereupon Byron stormed

the place and put the garrison to the sword. This action, revolting though it may seem, was strictly in accordance with the usages of war. But if not a crime Byron's act was an atrocious blunder.

Sir William Brereton single-handed was no match for Byron, but on 20 December Sir Thomas Fairfax had recaptured Gainsborough, and, obedient to the commands of the Committee in London, he set out on 29 December to march to the relief of his colleague. With Newcastle fully occupied watching the Scots Fairfax had nothing but his administrative difficulties – which were very considerable – to hinder his co-operation with Brereton.

The Battle of Nantwich, 25 January 1644

On 13 December 1643 Lord Byron laid siege to the little market town of Nantwich – the only remaining Parliamentary stronghold in Cheshire. On 18 January he delivered a general assault, which failed with heavy loss.

Collecting and reclothing his own mounted troops, to the number of about 2,300, Fairfax marched on 19 December via Derbyshire and Staffordshire to Manchester. Here he picked up about 3,000 foot, including some of his old comrades of Adwalton Moor. Sir William Brereton joined him with several Lancashire and Cheshire regiments. The army thus hastily assembled was a conglomerate affair and Fairfax was not happy about its constitution. A month later he confessed to Essex in a private letter, 'I have much trouble to command these forces I now have there being such divisions among the commanders, which doth much impair my health'.

Be that as it may, he set out for the relief of Nantwich on 21 January 1644.

In order to understand the events that ensued it is necessary to study the sketch-map on page 137. Nantwich is situated in almost flat country in the valley of the river Weaver, which here is some 20 feet wide. The river flows from south to north, passing along the western edge of the town. Dead opposite the town there is a bridge leading to Acton Church, one mile on. Half a mile downstream there was another, Beam Bridge by name. Just to the north of this bridge the beseigers had constructed a ferry the reason for which is not clear. The next bridge down stream was presumably at Minshull nearly six miles distant – north of the town.

On 24 January when the relieving army was passing through the forest of Delamere, where it had a successful skirmish with the

Cavaliers, a thaw and heavy rain set in. The river Weaver became so swollen that Byron hastily transferred his ordnance and most of his infantry to the far bank where the ground was slightly higher, keeping the horse under his own command on the eastern bank. He was just

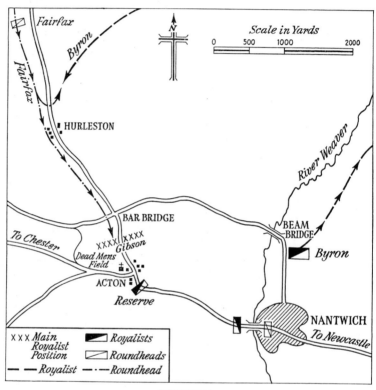

NANTWICH

in time, for next morning the flood swept away the ferry and rendered Beam Bridge impassable. As the townsmen now possessed the eastern end of the Acton bridge the Royalist army was split in two, separated by an unfordable river. To make matters worse news reached Lord Byron next morning, the 25th, that Fairfax was approaching with the relieving army. Byron,[1] full of contempt for his opponent, refused to

[1] Pleasantly described by Vicars in *God's Ark* as 'The Bloody Bragadochio Sir John Byron'.

relinquish the siege, and allowed his army to remain divided by the river. He with the horse was thus separated by about ten miles from the main body of his army. In this false position he heard on the morning of the 25th that the enemy was nearing Acton Church, evidently intending to deal with the forces on the other side of the river first. The Royalist commander took the only action possible under the circumstances – he marched down the eastern bank of the river as rapidly as possible, and crossed to the western side probably at Minshull. Here we must leave him for the moment.

The two armies that were about to confront one another were about equal in numbers, each having nearly 3,000 foot and 2,000 horse. The force on the western bank consisted entirely of foot. Moreover they were bereft of their commander, who had appointed his Major-General, Gibson (a temporary appointment), to command the foot in his absence.

Acton Church stands on slightly rising ground. About 400 yards to the north it slopes down gently and here Colonel Gibson drew up his force, astride the road to the North.[1] He held it with four out of his five regiments, two on each side of the road, while the fifth was kept in reserve, and entrusted with the special mission of watching and guarding the crossing over the bridge into the town. The ground was much enclosed with small fields and cut up by some deep miry lanes which made cavalry work difficult in the extreme. He had six small guns, which came into action near the church.

At 2 p.m. the Parliamentary army was within a mile of this position, and heading straight for it, when the alarming news reached Fairfax that a large force of hostile cavalry was rapidly approaching his left rear. (This was of course Lord Byron's own force.) The Roundheads had, it would seem, been adroitly caught between two fires by the 'bloody Byron'. It was enough to upset the equilibrium of any commander. We do not know what Fairfax's feelings were (he was always reticent about himself) but we can conclude from his actions that he was not unduly perturbed or unbalanced. In his report he merely states in matter of fact terms 'they told me the enemy was close upon our rear, so, facing about two regiments I marched . . .' straight for Acton Church. Fairfax had made a quick calculation and decided to take the bold course of attempting to crush the isolated force at Acton before Byron could close in on him.

The two regiments detailed to hold Byron had no difficulty in

---

[1] For the site of the battlefield see the Appendix to this chapter.

carrying out their mission; indeed Byron made no decided effort to break through to the assistance of his foot. The nature of the ground – small fields and hedges – undoubtedly was unsuitable for cavalry, but not impossible.

Meanwhile Fairfax did not interrupt the advance of his foot, and by 3.30 in the afternoon they were engaged all along the line. The battle that ensued took an unusual course. The Royalist regiments on the two wings (Richard Gibson's on the right and Robert Byron's on the left) rendered a good account of themselves, and inflicted heavy casualties on the attackers without suffering much loss themselves so that on the flanks the attack came to a standstill. Not so in the centre. One of the two regiments there – Warren's – fell back before the first charge, at push of pike. It was rallied by Colonel George Monck, afterwards to become famous, who was serving with it as a volunteer. But the Roundheads came on a second time, and now the regiment broke completely and streamed away to the rear.

But worse was to follow. We have seen how one regiment had been detailed, while acting as a reserve, to hold the western end of the Acton bridge. Byron had stipulated that 300 men should be detailed for this service, but Gibson sent only 100. Meanwhile the town defenders, seeing a battle for their relief developing, took the very proper step of organizing a sortie against the enemy's rear. A force of between 600 and 1,000 musketeers was assembled. Advancing across the bridge with a rush they had little difficulty in sweeping away the defenders, and following up their success they reached the church. Here they captured the carriages and possibly some of the guns of the Cavaliers, and so alarmed the men of the other regiment of the centre that they joined their comrades in flight. Thus a great gash was made in the centre of the Royalist line. It is to the credit of the two flank regiments that despite this discouraging setback they stood their ground.

Still a favourable situation had suddenly developed for the Round-heads and they were quick to take advantage of it. The Roundhead centre, horse, and foot, swept forward into the gap, and swinging out-wards assailed the inner flanks of the two regiments on the wings, while the attack on their front was resumed. Whether or not 'Fiery Tom' ordered this movement it was just the type of operation that he would approve.

The inevitable result quickly followed. The two gallant flank regiments were overwhelmed; the men retreated to the rear, and the bulk of the officers, with those of the two centre regiments, took refuge in Acton Church. Terms were granted and all the officers in the church, including three of the colonels, surrendered their arms. All the guns and colours, together with the train, half the officers, and about 1,500 other ranks were captured. The victory was complete. The *débris* of the Royalist army fled to the security of Chester. Byron led his cavalry there almost unmolested and intact, while stragglers from the foot regiments came in driblets in the course of the next few days. Ultimately about 1,200 of them rejoined but Byron's 'Irish' army had ceased to exist as an army and Nantwich was triumphantly relieved.

COMMENTS

At first sight it might appear that, the numbers being equal, the Roundheads must have been better soldiers, man for man. But there are other considerations to bear in mind. In the first place, the Royalist horse were scarcely engaged, whereas the Roundheads made good use of their cavalry in the final stages of the battle. Then, the incursion of the townsmen must have been most disconcerting, coming as it did at the critical stage of the fight. Moreover the bulk of Fairfax's foot were unknown to him and of doubtful quality, whereas Byron's had formed part of the garrison of Ireland and may be regarded as regulars. Thus, on paper we may rate the Royalist foot more highly than the opposing infantry.

To what then are we to attribute Fairfax's resounding victory? The answer seems indisputable – to better generalship and superior morale. Fairfax caught his opponents disunited, and he would not allow the threat to his rear to deter him from maintaining his true objective. It is not however clear why he elected to attack the forces to the west of the river rather than marching straight to the relief of the town which he could thus have achieved at very small cost. As for morale, the Roundheads had been worked up into fierce feelings against their opponents whom they conceived to be mainly native Irish Papists and against their commander Lord Byron for his severities. Byron's ferocity in ordering the massacre in Barthomley Church now rebounded on his own head. By contrast, the morale of the 'Irish' troops was lukewarm and in some cases suspect; some of the troops in the centre regiments, according to one story, actually went over to the enemy during the fighting. Bearing in mind all these factors it is not surprising that Fairfax won the battle.

Nantwich was one of the most clearcut and the biggest success that the Parliamentary armies had so far won. Sir Thomas Fairfax had established his reputation as a skilful and co-operative commander. When others made difficulties, Fairfax, obedient to his masters far away in London, was able to persuade his men to leave their own homes, march across England, and win a resounding victory.

The battle of Nantwich is peculiarly difficult to reconstruct. Many conflicting statements have to be reconciled and pieced together. The main cause of this is Lord Byron's despatch to the Marquis of Ormonde, in which he carefully disguises the part he himself played – or rather did not play – in the battle. This has made the disposition of his troops obscure and the course of events difficult to follow. Nor does Fairfax in his despatch do much to remove these difficulties. The cause of these unfortunate reticences must have been that Byron was ashamed of the futile part he himself had played in the battle and therefore tried to cover it up. To be more precise, Byron, while stating that his troops on the east bank marched to join those on the far bank, did not specify them, merely calling them 'a part of the army'. Nor did he say who was in command of this part. It is however quite certain, from various statements made by others, that he himself was in command of them and remained with them throughout the battle. He does not explain why he placed all his foot on the west bank, thus dividing his army when he should have concentrated it since he had warning of Fairfax's approach.

The utter inactivity of his 2,000 horse cannot be excused by the fact that the terrain was unsuitable for mounted action, for it did not prevent Fairfax's horse from charging. Even if Byron felt that it was impossible to make headway against Brereton's infantry he could have made use of his superior mobility to 'fetch a compass' round them and join up with Gibson's hard-pressed troops. Instead he sat idly looking on, and after the battle was over he retreated 18 miles to Chester.

Byron had shown himself a good commander of a cavalry brigade, but that was about the limit of his capacity.

After Nantwich it was clear to the King and the Council of War that Byron was not the man to reconquer Cheshire and Lancashire, let alone to succour Newcastle or fall upon the Eastern Association. So serious had the situation in the North become that Prince Rupert himself was selected to take over the command. He reached Shrewsbury, which he made his headquarters, on 19 February. He brought few troops with him, but he found that the remnants of Byron's army had just been reinforced by two more infantry regiments from Ireland under Colonel Henry Tillier, an old soldier.

The Relief of Newark. 21 March 1644

On 29 February Sir John Meldrum with a force 6,000 or 7,000 strong drawn from Derbyshire, Leicestershire, Lincolnshire and Nottinghamshire advanced on Newark.

The Governor, now Sir Richard Byron, could look for no help from Newcastle, yet the safety of Newark was vital to the Marquis, for its fall would set Meldrum free to operate against his rear, besides cutting the line of communications between York and Oxford. The garrison was less than 2,000 strong, but included 300 horse.

On 6 March the town was finally invested after a sharp fight at Muskham Bridge, but a heavy attack on the 8th was repulsed with loss to the besiegers, and in a sally a few days later the Cavaliers took 200 prisoners. On the other hand an attempt at relief by Colonel Gervase Lucas, the Governor of Belvoir Castle, was beaten off.

As early as 18 February the King had written to Prince Rupert recommending 'the succouring of Newark', and on 12 March when visiting Chester the Prince received positive orders to march to its relief. This was easier said than done for as yet Rupert had no army. Next day he hastened back to Shrewsbury sending Major Will. Legge ahead to select as many musketeers as could be spared from among the 'Irish' regiments in that garrison. Colonel Tillier with 1,120 men was sent down the Severn by boat to Bridgnorth where on the 15th he met Rupert and about 800 horse. Next day (16th) they marched to Wolverhampton where they were met by 300 of the garrison of Dudley Castle. On the 17th they reached Lichfield.

Meldrum had got wind of Rupert's approach and sent out his horse, 2,000 strong, under Sir Edward Hartop to prevent the junction of the various Royalist contingents. Hartop utterly failed in his mission and on the 18th at Ashby-de-la-Zouch the Prince was reinforced by Henry Hastings, Lord Loughborough, and Major-General George Porter. His strength had now risen to about 3,500 horse and rather more than 3,000 foot, all musketeers. There were three field guns with the force. If it was a makeshift army, most of the troops which formed it were experienced soldiers of high quality. There was magic in Rupert's reputation, even though most of his men had never set eyes on him before.

The Prince arrived at Bingham on the 20th and bivouacked undisturbed ten miles south-west of Meldrum's army, sending out spies to observe the enemy.

At noon on the same day (20th) Meldrum and his Council of War had resolved to send out their cavalry again, but before they could do so

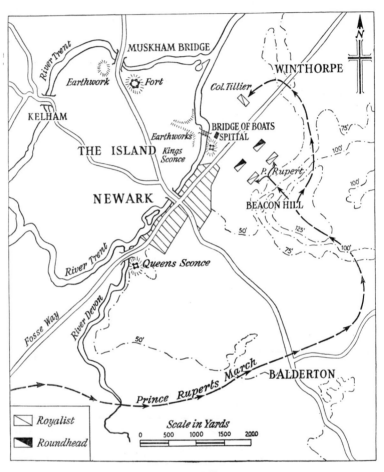

NEWARK

it was reported that Rupert and 8,000 men intended to quarter that night within eight miles of them. Sir Miles Hobart advised a retreat to Lincoln, but Meldrum resolved to concentrate his foot in the Spittal, and to send his horse across Muskham Bridge to bring in provisions.

During the night Rupert's spies brought him the news that the Roundheads were massing in one body, and fearing that this portended a withdrawal, he paraded his men at 2 a.m. and in the moonlight led the van of his horse 'upon the spurre' to overtake them. Approaching, through Balderton, he could see some of Meldrum's cavalry on the crest of Beacon Hill.

Meldrum had ordered his cavalry not to fight until the Cavaliers were within range of his guns, so they fell back and let Rupert occupy Beacon Hill unopposed.

Riding to the edge of the hill the Prince could see the main body of the Parliamentary army drawn up near the Spittal, with four great bodies of horse awaiting him on the lower slopes of the hill. Still fearing that Meldrum intended to retreat, the Prince decided to make a holding attack, although half of his cavalry and his foot were not yet in sight. He drew up his force in two lines with his own regiment, about 500 strong, on the right and the Lifeguard under his own command on the left. Major-General Porter's regiment and Lord Loughborough's troop were in support and Major-General Charles Gerard's troop was in reserve.

The Parliamentary horse did not much outnumber the Cavaliers, for Meldrum had sent the Derby horse into the island to cover a detachment that was building a fort. Colonel Francis Thornhagh commanded the right wing of their horse and Colonel Edward Rossiter the left.

The battle began about 9 a.m. The fighting was particularly bitter on the Roundhead left where Rossiter, doubling his files so that his men were six deep, charged the flank of the right-hand Royalist squadron. Captain Clement Martin of Rupert's regiment, whose troop was part of the next 'division', led his troop to the rescue, and by his intervention Rossiter was beaten off, but not before he had driven the Cavaliers back up the hill to their reserves. Charles Gerard's horse fell as he led a counter-charge and he was wounded and taken prisoner.

On the other wing the Lincolnshire horse fled at the outset, leaving the Nottinghamshire men to fight it out.

Prince Rupert had pierced deep into the ranks of the Roundheads, his troopers shouting their fieldword 'King and Queen', while the Parliamentarians raised the cry of 'Religion'. Set upon by a host of assailants he laid about him with his sword. When a Roundhead trooper laid hold of the Prince's collar Sir William Neale sliced the man's hand off.

Sir Richard Crane broke clean through the Roundhead right wing, pursuing the routed troopers to the works about the Spittal.

It had been a sharp fight, both sides had managed to rally and charge a second time, and Rossiter, at least, fell back in good order.

This fierce cavalry action was followed by a lull during which Rupert's infantry came up. While Meldrum's horse fell back across the bridge of boats into the island, part of the 'Irish' foot under Tillier made a detour and supported by detachments of cavalry fell upon the north-east side of Meldrum's position, trying to capture the bridge of boats. Tillier soon found the Roundhead position too strong for him and fell back out of range of Meldrum's guns.

Hearing from a prisoner that the Roundheads had only victuals for another two days, the Prince decided to starve rather than storm them.

Meldrum was hemmed in with Tillier to the north-east, Rupert to the south-east, and Newark itself to the south-west, and the Prince now completed his discomfiture by sending Sir Richard Byron and part of his garrison into the island to cut the lines of communication between the Spittal and Muskham Fort, whose defenders, after breaking down the bridge, departed without orders. These were not the only Parliamentary troops to misbehave: the Norfolk Redcoats mutinied, and Meldrum sent a trumpet for a parley. The Roundheads were permitted to march away with their drums, colours, horses and swords, baggage and personal belongings, but all guns, ammunition, and firearms remained as a prize for the victor. Over 3,000 muskets, and 11 brass guns and two good mortars were among the pieces taken. One of the guns was 'a Basiliske of Hull, four yards long, shooting 32. (pound) Ball'.

The Roundheads had lost about 200 killed and the Cavaliers less than half that number.

COMMENT

Rupert had surprised Meldrum by the speed and certainty of his movements. Although he had more mounted men than Meldrum, the decisive engagement was won before half of them had come up. The Prince's hastily gathered army obeyed him without question, because of his military reputation and his royal blood. The factious Roundhead commanders on the other hand had by their jealous wranglings nearly broken the heart of 'the poor old gentleman', as a Parliamentary writer called Meldrum.

Newark is not one of the better-known battles of the Civil Wars, but it was a quick and complete victory and deserves to be rescued from oblivion. Rupert's victory enabled the garrison to hold out for another two years.

Newcastle meanwhile having fallen back to Durham contented himself for some time with trying to cut off the invaders' provisions, in which he met with considerable success. On 20 March the Scots took a fort at South Shields and surprised a detachment of cavalry at Chester-le-Street. Thus provoked the Marquis decided to offer battle and advanced on 23 March to Hilton near Sunderland.

The Scots came out of their trenches round Sunderland and took up a position on Bedwick Hill.

Try as he would Newcastle could not bring on a general engagement, but at about 3 p.m. his foot attacked the Scots on the hillside. The fight continued until nightfall, and there was shooting throughout the night. Next day the Scots fell back to Sunderland, and Newcastle drew off towards his own quarters.

The Scots now attacked the Royalist rearguard with all their horse. Sir Charles Lucas with his brigade went to their support and charged so well that he forced the entire body, some 3,000 strong, to hasten back to their cannon, which were planted on a hill, doing much slaughter among the Scottish lancers.

Next day the Marquis again offered battle, but the Scots were not to be drawn, so the Cavaliers fell back to Durham. In the fighting they had had about 250 casualties while the Scots were reckoned to have lost about 1,000 men.

Newcastle had held his own fairly well thus far, but on 11 April the Fairfaxes stormed Selby, capturing John Belasyse and more than 3,000 prisoners. With his rear thus exposed Newcastle was forced to fall back from Durham. On the 18th he reached York with 5,000 horse and 6,000 foot, and on the 20th the Scots and Fairfax joined forces at Tadcaster and determined to lay siege to York.

APPENDIX

The Site of the Battle of Nantwich

The exact site of the battlefield appears to be lost. It is not shown on the 2½-inch Ordnance Survey map, and local opinion on the matter is vague as to the location. It may therefore be worthwhile to explain the reasons for locating it as we do.

Since Fairfax was approaching from the north the Royalists would naturally choose a defensive position astride the main road coming from that direction, which runs from Acton to the hamlet of Hurleston, 2½ miles distant. The ground between the two places is low lying and flat, all except the southern 400 yards, which form a plateau 25 feet above the valley level. The obvious position to hold would be the northern edge of this plateau which has a gentle slope to the front. Gibson would certainly not descend into the low ground farther forward, which must have been more or less water-logged. Moreover, we know that the position selected was visible from Hurleston, which would not be the case were it either farther forward or farther back. His force was sufficient to hold a frontage of about 1,000 yards astride the road at the point where it reached the plateau.

Both Byron and Fairfax place the battle near Acton Church which lies at the crossroads in the centre of the village only 400 yards in rear of the position. In addition the fourth field along the Wrexham road from Acton is still called Dead Man's Field. No doubt it marks the left flank of the Royalist position where some of the hardest fighting took place, and extends 400 yards to the north. Its northern hedge may well have been the actual battle line for Colonel Robert Byron says 'our army was drawn [up] in several enclosures'. It is certain that in this field many of the protagonists found nameless graves.

CHAPTER II

The Oxford Campaign

A T the beginning of April 1644 the Parliamentary Committee of Both Kingdoms had five great armies in the field, besides the local forces of Brereton, Massey, and others. In the North Lord Leven's Scots and Lord Fairfax's English were closing in on York, while Manchester was soon to lay siege to Lincoln. In the South Waller had just won his greatest victory at Cheriton (29 March) while Essex was preparing to take the field. The intervention of the Scots had tipped the scales against the King.

In the North the Marquis of Newcastle was hard pressed by Leven and Fairfax, though Prince Rupert, at Shrewsbury, intended to march to his relief. There was no Royalist army available to make head against Manchester. In the South Midlands Charles still held an extensive position – Oxford, Reading, Banbury, Abingdon, Wallingford, and a ring of well fortified garrisons – but in order to form a respectable field army he was compelled after Cheriton to absorb Hopton's army into his own.

In the West a small army, 6,000 strong, under Prince Maurice had been besieging Lyme since the middle of March. There was much despondency at the Royalist headquarters, and not without reason. Indeed it is obvious that had the five Parliamentary armies been directed by a single commander of even ordinary capacity they might well have ended the war in the summer of 1644. But the Committee of Both Kingdoms, although it numbered Essex, Waller, Manchester, and Cromwell among its members, was a far less effective instrument than the King's Council of War, which directed Royalist strategy. Its ablest soldiers were almost always absent in the field, and Sir Henry Vane and Oliver St. John were thus left the dominant figures.

The Cavaliers who discussed strategy at Charles' Council of War also executed its decisions. The Parliamentary generals regarded the often ambiguous instructions of the Committee of Both Kingdoms as

145

a basis for discussion rather than as orders. Quick to complain when pay or recruits were not forthcoming, they were yet more quickly wounded when ordered to carry out operations they had not themselves devised.

Nevertheless, things looked black for the Cavaliers.

On 6 April the Committee, not unreasonably, ordered Essex and Manchester to rendezvous at Aylesbury on the 19th and to advance against the King. Waller would thus be able to advance into the West and deal with Maurice. This promising combination quickly came to grief. Essex, who had no gift for seeing the war as a whole, took a gloomy view of the situation, and on 8 April wrote, not to the Committee, but to the remnants of the House of Lords saying: 'Newark is not taken, Lincolnshire is lost, Gloucester is unsupplied, and the last week there was but a step between us and death, and – what is worse – slavery.' After protesting his fidelity to the cause he continued in plaintive strain: 'You have been pleased to reduce my army to 7,000 foot and 3,000 horse, when my Lord of Manchester is allowed an army of 14,000 and receives £34,000 a month for the pay of it – since it is done by you I submit. . . .' But he was far from intending either to submit or to co-operate.

Manchester, indeed, was ready to take the field, but with Rupert's recent success at Newark in mind and with Lincoln still in the hands of the Cavaliers, he felt quite rightly that it was his duty to guard the Eastern Association. Though Rupert at Shrewsbury had as it happened not the least intention of attacking Manchester, the Earl was not to know that.

The 19th April came and saw no rendezvous at Aylesbury. Nor had Waller been able to follow up his victory at Cheriton, for the City regiments had clamoured to return home and by 12 April Sir William was back at Farnham once more. Taking advantage of his withdrawal the Dorset Cavaliers pounced on Wareham.

But if in fact all was not well with the Roundheads the King was, as yet, far from suspecting it. At Lyme Maurice was still held up by the future Admiral Blake, and with only the army around Oxford at his disposal Charles felt that he himself would be unable to hold his own. The danger seemed so great that he decided to send the Queen, who was expecting a baby, into the West Country and on 17 April she set out for Exeter. The departure of the She-Generalissima as she had once called herself, however sad for the King who loved and relied upon her, was an excellent thing from the military point of view, for she was a very poor strategist and had certainly used her influence against Rupert. No sooner was she gone than Charles wrote to his nephew summoning him to his side.

The Prince was quick to answer the summons, but he was intent none the less on marching to the relief of York where Newcastle was now besieged. Rupert was at Oxford from 25 April to 5 May and during that time expounded his strategic views, which were adopted. Reinforced garrisons were to be retained in Oxford, Wallingford, Abingdon, Reading, and Banbury. A good body of horse was to remain about Oxford free to manoeuvre in support of the garrisons. The Parliamentary armies would not be sufficient to overrun this extensive complex of fortresses, nor, it was considered, could they safely push farther west leaving it in their rear. This would permit Maurice, reinforced by some of the King's cavalry, to complete the conquest of the West, while Rupert himself went to the aid of Newcastle. Such was Rupert's plan.

The Prince returned to Shrewsbury and soon after his departure the King decided to abandon Reading, a decision which can probably be attributed to Lord Forth, who, despite Cheriton, was evidently still in high favour. Thus 2,500 men were added to the field army, though the position round Oxford was considerably weakened and on 19 May Essex and Waller entered the abandoned town.

There was some reason for the withdrawal from Reading, but the abandonment of Abingdon which followed on 25 May was a serious mistake, born, no doubt, of the despondency prevailing in the Royalist camp, for it gave the enemy one of the inner ring of fortresses round Oxford, while its garrison was not sufficiently strong to make an appreciable difference to the field army. Manchester had stormed Lincoln on 6 May and Maurice was still held up before Lyme. On the 24th Massey took Malmesbury and Essex entered Abingdon on the 26th. The same day the King, alarmed for the safety of Bristol, sent Hopton to secure that city.

Next day a Council of War at Oxford decided not to give battle against the combined armies of Essex and Waller, but to post the King's army in such a way as to keep the communications of Oxford open on one side. Then if the two Parliamentary commanders should separate, the Cavaliers would be strong enough to attack each in turn with a good chance of defeating them in detail. This excellent plan was evidently devised by Lord Forth. It can hardly have been coincidence that he was created Earl of Brentford on the very day this Council was held.

L

The King now withdrew his army to the north side of Oxford, realizing that it was high time to quit his capital if he himself was not to be besieged.

By 2 June Essex was at Islip and Waller at Newbridge; there were Roundheads at Bletchingdon and Woodstock, and also near Eynsham; the net was closing.

One of Charles' advisers even counselled surrender. The King, always at his best in the face of evident and immediate danger, said that 'possibly he might be found in the hands of the Earl of Essex, but he would be dead first'.

A 'grimace', as Lord Digby called it, towards Abingdon sufficed to induce Waller to fall back across Newbridge, and at nine o'clock on the evening of 3 June the Royalist army marched out of the North Port of the earthworks of Oxford, along the Banbury road.

With 2,500 foot and his whole body of horse numbering nearly 5,000, the King marched via Port Meadow, Wolvercot and Yarnton, slipped across the River Evenlode at Handborough Bridge, reaching Bourton-on-the-Water on the afternoon of the 4th. It has almost invariably been accepted that the credit for this bold, swift, and successful march belongs to Charles himself. The war had now been going on for two years, during which time he had acted always as his own Generalissimo. At first, however, he had been to all intents and purposes an inexperienced civilian observer. But two years of constant campaigning, endless Councils of War, three or four general actions and a major siege, had transformed him into a general well versed in the Art of War, quite capable of holding his own against officers of the calibre of Essex and Manchester.

Charles having given his enemies the slip, arrived at Worcester on 6 June. But he was not out of the wood yet. Massey had taken Tewkesbury on 4 June, and on the 9th Waller who had followed the Oxford army captured Sudeley Castle. The King did not know which way to turn, and candour compelled Digby to confess in a letter to Rupert (8 June): 'We have now found the mischief of not following your advice; . . . Essex comes upon us one way, Waller likely to go about us on the Welsh side by Gloucester . . . Massey and the Lord Denbigh towards Kidderminster, both with considerable forces. . . .' It was a tale of woe, but the worst, had they known it, was over.

On the 6th Essex and Waller had met in council at Stow-on-the-Wold, and, incredible though it may seem, had decided to part company! The Earl was to relieve Lyme, while the Knight was to pursue the King. Thus Maurice's apparently abortive siege of Lyme had succeeded in drawing Essex away from his proper quarry – in war the right thing often happens for the wrong reason.

Essex had now determined to push down into the West, and had succeeded in convincing himself that cutting off the main source of the King's supplies would have as good an effect as victory in a pitched battle. The Committee was far from being convinced and wrote ordering him to relieve Lyme with a detachment and to move on Oxford with his main body. This letter which reached him at Blandford on 12 June Essex answered with bitter sarcasm. 'Pardon me, if I make bold to order and direct my own Major-General, for in truth I do not see how Sir William Waller can take care of all the countries along the seaside from Dover to St. Michael's Mount. If you think fit to set him at liberty and confine me, be pleased to make him General and me the Major-General of some brigade, that my soldiers may have free quarter, free plunder, and contributions besides, as his have without control.' Such insubordinate language can hardly have been pleasing in his masters' ears, but they did not remove him from his command. An early success, the relief of Lyme on 15 June, placed Essex in a stronger position, and served for a space to silence his critics in London.

One hostile army being now out of the way the King decided to return to Oxford and build up his own. By 21 June he was at Bletchingdon with 4,000 horse and 5,000 foot. Waller, who was at Kineton, intended to offer battle and Charles was resolved to accept it.

The Battle of Cropredy Bridge. 29 June 1644

On the night of 27 June Charles was at Culworth, and hearing that Waller was near Banbury he determined to march in that direction. Setting out early on the morning of the 28th the army had a rendezvous about 10 o'clock on Leigh Grounds, a mile east of Banbury. It was a misty, rainy morning, but it soon cleared up and the Royalists then spied Waller's army drawn up near Hanwell Castle nearly two miles west of the River Cherwell. Waller took up a position on Crouch Hill, the Cavaliers occupying Grimsbury Hill. There was some skirmishing during the afternoon in which the Royalists, although they got the upper hand, failed to draw Waller from his strong position. As the witty author of *Mercurius Aulicus*, the Court newspaper, puts it, 'you know his condition of old; hills, bogs, hedges, these you must grant him, he'll not fight else'.

Next day, rather than storm Waller's Crouch Hill position, Charles marched north towards Daventry, hoping for a better opportunity to give battle. This move was immediately effective. Looking across the river Cherwell westwards the Cavaliers could see Waller's men marching parallel with them up the Banbury–Southam road. The two armies were moving through rolling country in full view of each other, and at first little more than a mile apart. As they neared Cropredy the roads diverged and the distance between them widened to about two miles as Waller's soldiers climbed the hill above Bourton. Brentford, who led the van of the King's army, protected its left flank by sending dragoons to hold the ancient bridge at Cropredy.[1]

Soon news came in, probably from cavalry patrols, that 300 Roundhead horse had been seen two miles ahead, evidently attempting to join Waller. The Royalist advanced guard was ordered to intercept this body and in consequence it pushed on with such speed that there was soon a wide gap between the van and the rear of the Royalist army.

A dangerous development of this sort could easily pass unnoticed farther back down the column, but Waller two miles to the flank (telescope in hand no doubt) was not the man to miss a slip of this sort. Seizing his chance he launched two columns to the attack. Shouting their field word, 'Victory without Quarter!' the Roundheads went into the attack. Lieut.-General Middleton and 1,000 horse crossed the ford at Slat Mill one mile south of the bridge and fell on the Royalists' rear; while 1,500 horse, and 1,000 foot with 11 guns attacked Cropredy Bridge, which the Royalist dragoons abandoned without much resistance.

The next phase of the battle was mostly cavalry work, charge and counter-charge, and is no easier to sort out than usual. Middleton met with some success at first and seems to have advanced for about a mile. The young Earl of Northampton faced his brigade about, and forced the Roundheads back across the ford at Slat Mill.

Cleveland, whose brigade was at the head of the Royalist rear, drew up his brigade on rising ground facing Cropredy Bridge and seeing a great body of Parliamentary horse about to fall on his rear, realized that there was no time to wait for orders from Wilmot, and charged on his own initiative, routing the enemy and taking some prisoners. This done he rallied his men and made a little stand under a great ash tree, where, not half an hour previously the King, who was

---

[1] There had been a bridge there at least as early as 1213. Royalists troops had used it on their march to Edgehill in 1642.

himself commanding the main body of the army, had been invited to dine.[1]

When the Roundheads first advanced Charles had quickly divined Waller's plan. He made a stand beyond Hays Bridge and sent his young cousin, Lord Bernard Stuart, the commander of his Lifeguards, a troop of 100 gentlemen, which according to Walker was 'ever fullest in time of action' to return and attack two bodies of Parliamentary horse which threatened Cleveland's flank. The Lifeguards, few in number though they were, put the Roundheads to flight, thus contributing greatly to the success of the Earl's first encounter.

Cleveland now charged a second time, routing all that Roundhead column which had crossed Cropredy Bridge, and driving them beyond their cannon. Waller quaintly admits that the loss of his artillery was 'extreme wounding' to him. With it was captured James Wemyss, a turncoat whom Charles had formerly made Master Gunner of England. 'Guid faith,' said he when brought before his master, 'My heart was always with Your Majesty' – 'so is mine with the State-Committee' was *Mercurius'* malicious comment. In this charge Cleveland's losses were light, though they included two colonels killed; and Wilmot, hastening to join him was wounded and temporarily captured.

Waller had now no alternative but to fall back to the west of the Cherwell, where he posted his men on the high ground between Cropredy and Hanwell, while foot and dragoons held Cropredy Bridge and the ford at Slat Mill.

The King, not content with his success, determined to seize both crossings, but at the bridge the Kentish Regiment and the Tower Hamlets with two Drakes staved them off throughout the hot summer afternoon, but at Slat Mill the Cavaliers were successful, crossing the ford and capturing the buildings.

The main bodies of each army remained on the high ground, but towards evening the Royalists drew up below Slat Mill, and opened fire on the Roundhead cavalry on the hill near Bourton forcing them to fall back in disorder, covered by the fire of Waller's remaining guns. It was probably at this juncture that some shots were deliberately fired at the King himself by cannon planted on the heights beyond the Cherwell, the cannoneers being shown their target 'by several perspective glasses'.

[1] The 'Wardington Ash' has twice been replaced since by new plants, so this historic spot can still be exactly identified.

There was no further action. Charles, mindful that his foes were also his subjects, sent Sir Edward Walker to the Roundheads with 'a message of grace and pardon' and writing to the Queen next day described the battle as 'yesterday's good success'. Indeed it had come in good time to restore the morale of his army, which had not tasted a victory for many months. The Royalist losses were very light. Nevertheless they were unable to follow up their success, for Major-General Browne, who had left London on 24 June had arrived at Buckingham with 4,500 men.

But although the King did not immediately seek a second battle he had regained the initiative in his own theatre of operations. Even Gardiner, a most hostile critic, wrote '. . . so superior was the composition of his army to that of Waller, and so hopelessly were the councils of the Parliamentary Generals in the South divided, that, unless disastrous news arrived from the North, the Royal army could hardly fail to get the upper hand in the regions in which Charles himself was fighting'. The King had indeed shown himself a match for Waller, a general of no ordinary skill.

Waller's army, shaken by its defeat began to disintegrate. Writing on 2 July he complained of the mutinies of the City brigade who had 'come to their old song of "Home!, Home!"'. Browne's men, who had joined him, he found in 'no very good temper', the Essex soldiers were already threatening to quit him, and the Hertfordshire men were impatient of their bad quarters. 'My Lords,' he adds, 'till you have an army merely your own that you may command, it is in a manner impossible to do anything of importance,' words prophetic of the New Model which, as yet, lay in the distant future.

On 7 July the mutinous trained bands of Essex and of Hertfordshire attacked Major-General Browne and wounded him in the face: 'Such men', wrote Waller, 'are only fit for a gallows here and a hell hereafter. . . .' Essex was one of the most Puritan counties, but it is evident that Puritan enthusiasm alone was not going to win the war.

The Cavalier army had its faults too: many men were frittered away in relatively unimportant garrisons: there were far too many regiments, many of them only a few hundred strong, but even so the Royalists had welded together a far more permanent and mobile military instrument than their opponents.

CHAPTER 12

The Marston Moor Campaign

IT WAS ON 22 April 1644 that the Earl of Leven and Lord Fairfax
sat down before York. Newcastle sent away most of his cavalry,
about 2,000 in number, under Sir Charles Lucas, retaining only
a few horse and 4,000 or 5,000 foot as his garrison. Prince Rupert
knew well that he and he alone could relieve the Marquis, and he was
determined not to be diverted from this object. Summoned to the aid
of his uncle he had, as we have seen, laid down the strategy which
with some modification was successfully followed in the Cropredy
campaign. By 8 May he was back at his headquarters.

When on 16 May he set out from Shrewsbury on 'The Yorke
Marche', as the compiler of his Journal called it, he did not immediately
direct his steps towards that city. He had as yet only 2,000 horse and
6,000 foot, including the remains of Byron's Anglo-Irish army, and
such a force was not nearly enough for the work in hand. Accordingly
the Prince decided to march by way of Lancashire, picking up reinforcements as he went.

On 25 May he appeared before Stockport which was garrisoned by
some 3,000 Roundheads. The defenders marched out to confront him
but were quickly beaten back by Washington's dragoons, who drove
the Parliamentary troops back into the town in such disorder that the
Prince and his horse pressed in on their heels. Hearing of this Colonel
Rigby, who for 18 weeks had been besieging the Countess of Derby in
Lathom House, beat a retreat to Bolton which he reached on the 27th.
Here with not more than 2,500 men he intended to hold an open town
against Rupert and some 8,000 Cavaliers.

Rigby had not much time for preparation, for the Prince appeared
on the following afternoon. Repelled for half an hour, the Cavaliers
made a second and more furious assault. Led by the Earl of Derby, who
was the first man to break in, the Royalists overran the luckless
garrison giving little quarter. Sixteen hundred Roundheads fell that

day; the town was plundered and the local feud between Roman Catholic and Puritan made the struggle more than ordinarily bloody. Rigby himself learned the Royalists' field word and escaped by posing as one of their own officers.

Upon this success the Lancashire Royalists flocked to Rupert's standard. In addition Lord Goring and Lucas with 5,000 horse and 800 foot joined the Prince on 30 May. On 7 June Rupert appeared before the earthworks of Liverpool, which fell on the 11th. With Lancashire secured for the time being and his army recruited to some 14,000 men the Prince was now ready to march for York.

Far away in the south the King too was thinking of York. With Digby looking over one shoulder and Wilmot over the other he took up his pen and wrote to his nephew: 'If York be lost I shall esteem *my crown little less; * unless supported by your sudden march to me; and a miraculous conquest in the South, before the effects of their Northern power can be found here. *But if* York be relieved, and *you beat the rebels' army* of both Kingdoms, which are before it; then (*but otherwise not*)[1] I may possibly make a shift (upon the defensive) to spin out time until you come to assist me. Wherefore *I command and conjure* you, by the duty and affection which I know you bear me, that all new enterprises laid aside, you immediately march, according to your first intention, with all your force to the relief of York.' No more direct order was ever penned. The forthright Lord Culpeper, who was not present when it was written, hearing that it had been sent, said to the King: 'Why, then, before God you are undone, for upon this peremptory order he will fight, whatever comes on't.' Rupert carried this letter about him to his dying day.

Meanwhile the Earl of Manchester after storming Lincoln on 6 May had reinforced the Allies before York bringing their numbers up to about 27,000. The Allied generals, despite Rupert's conquering progress and the anxiety of the Committee of Both Kingdoms in London, were determined to continue their siege rather than to detach part of their great host to oppose the Prince. Even so they allowed Newcastle to engage them from 8 to 15 June with negotiations which were evidently designed to gain time.

On 23 June Sir Henry Vane wrote to the Committee of Both Kingdoms from the 'Leaguer before York' explaining that the generals had decided to send a body of horse and foot to join with the Parliamen-

---

[1] Words in brackets inserted by Wilmot.

tary forces in Lancashire. These, it was hoped, would be able to deal with Prince Rupert while at the same time the siege of York could go on uninterrupted. Vane's information was that Prince Rupert had about 11,000 men and was to rendezvous that night at Preston (he had actually reached that place on the previous day). Vane deduced that the Prince would move towards York, though it was thought by others in the Allied camp that he would not do so immediately. The generals were content to await further intelligence.

Rupert marched east from Preston on 23 June, and moving along the modern A59 by way of Clitheroe and Gisburn reached Skipton Castle, 36 miles from Preston, on the 26th. Here the Cavaliers halted to send messengers into York and to put their arms in order.

According to Thomas Stockdale, a reliable eyewitness, it was not until 28 June that the three generals, Leven, Lord Fairfax and Manchester received intelligence of Rupert's rapid advance. It was their wish to continue the siege and to offer battle simultaneously, but they doubted their ability to do so. Reinforcements under Meldrum and the Earl of Denbigh were expected from Cheshire, but their progress was uncertain. Rupert's numbers (accurately assessed by Vane a week earlier) were now overestimated; it was thought – quite wrongly – that he had been joined by Clavering and a contingent from the four northern counties. They cannot have appreciated that, even without Meldrum, their armies before York, outnumbered the total forces of Rupert and Newcastle by three to two.

While the Prince (at Skipton) was still 43 miles from York, the Allied commanders prepared to break up their siege, thus abandoning all the advantages they had won – for the Marquis was undoubtedly hard-pressed. Rupert's swift approach seems to have made them lose their heads for his prestige, at this time, was at its height.

On 29 June Rupert advanced again, with his usual rapidity, and on the 30th reached Knaresborough only 18 miles from York, and almost due west of that city. That evening the Allies, who had heard that Meldrum could not reach Wakefield, 29 miles south-west of York, until 3 July decided to break up their siege immediately and march with their whole army to meet the Prince. And so on the morning of 1 July the three Allied armies concentrated on Marston Moor, six miles west of York on the Knaresborough road, expecting their enemy to come that way.

It was not long before the Allied commanders discerned Cavalier squadrons approaching – evidently Rupert's advanced guard – and content that they had divined his intentions correctly they proceeded to marshal their men for battle. The hours passed but the Royalist main body failed to put in an appearance.

After quartering for the night in Galtres Forest the Prince had marched early that morning and crossing the Ure at Boroughbridge, seven miles north-east of Knaresborough, pushed on to the passage of the Swale at Thornton Bridge. Sweeping round to the south-east he headed for York, following the north bank of the Ouse. At Poppleton, three miles north-west of York, he surprised a regiment of dragoons guarding a bridge of boats, which had been constructed by the Earl of Manchester's orders, so that in the event of Rupert's approaching from the north the Allied armies could cross the river to meet him. Meanwhile a cavalry screen 'amused' the Allied army.

By nightfall the Prince, leaving his army outside, had entered York; the city had been relieved. This rapid encircling movement, involving a march of rather more than 20 miles during the day, completely deceived the Allied generals, and was probably Rupert's most brilliant manoeuvre: it put a fitting crown on his 1644 campaign.

Outwitted and outmanoeuvred the Allied generals held another consultation that night and resolved to march south-west towards Cawood and Tadcaster, so as to cover Meldrum's approach and by cutting off supplies from the East and West Ridings, to force Rupert to fight – not that he was reluctant to do so. It seems odd that the Scots should have agreed to leaving the enemy astride their line of retreat to Scotland. (According to Sir Thomas Fairfax they even proposed it.)

Meanwhile another protracted conference was taking place in York. The cautious Newcastle was opposed to a battle till the reinforcements under Clavering had arrived. Rupert, fortified by his letter from the King, was clamant for a battle. Being the senior he had his way, and next morning, 2 July, his army set forth to engage the enemy on Marston Moor.

The head of the army had almost reached Tadcaster when an urgent message was received by Leven from Fairfax[1] who was still with the rearguard covering the withdrawal, warning him that an attack appeared imminent. Thereupon Leven, rather surprisingly, reversed his whole army and returned to Marston Moor. This was a sudden change of policy. Fairfax had only seen hostile cavalry, and it

---

[1] Cromwell was also with the rearguard and the fact that Fairfax sent the message is an indication that he was rated senior to Cromwell in the army.

was only to be expected that the enemy would throw out a cavalry screen, whatever their ultimate intentions were.

Unfortunately the accounts of this episode and of Leven's reasons for his action are scanty, but it looks as if the Allies had no clear-cut plan and that Leven was overborne by the vehemence of his younger English colleagues. Yet he was a commander with a considerable reputation who had been brought up under that great soldier Sir Horace Vere and had afterwards served under Gustavus Adolphus, and had worsted the great Wallenstein. Gustavus, indeed, had made him a field-marshal. Leven was by this time 55 years of age.

Even so Fairfax had correctly sensed Rupert's intentions; perhaps he had received information from spies. Rupert also was having his troubles. Newcastle after some hesitation had acquiesced in a battle, but did not rouse himself to get his men moving quickly, having wasted time looting the abandoned camp of the Allies. Consequently his contingent arrived very late on the field. It was not until after 4 p.m. that his whole force had reached the battlefield, where Rupert's troops having crossed the bridge of boats, had been drawn up for some hours.

The Battle of Marston Moor. 2 July 1644

The flanks of the Allied line, one and a half miles in extent, rested upon villages: Long Marston on the east, Tockwith on the west. A ditch bounding the moor divided the two armies. The course of this ditch is well known, and in two places – where Atterwick Lane and Moor Lane cross it – it is still visible, and is marked by a hedge along most of its course.

On the Roundhead side the ground has not altered much since 1644: a few large fields of arable – mostly rye – slope gently down for 1,200 yards to the ditch. The flat moor beyond, which was occupied by the Royalists, has now been enclosed, but at the time of the battle it was open and partly covered with gorse. In summer a blaze of yellow buttercups on the old moorland clearly marks the dividing line between it and the arable land. The Allies had the advantage of higher ground, but the Cavaliers had the advantage – such as it was – of occupying the actual ditch.

This ditch was 'wide and deep', but how wide or how deep is nowhere recorded. There was a hedge on the south side, that is towards the enemy. This was unfortunate for the Cavaliers, for obviously they would like to line the hedge and have the ditch as an obstacle in their front. But now they had the option of putting the ditch behind them or having the hedge directly in their front, thus screening the approach of the enemy. Probably the ditch was only manned by outposts and the main line of resistance was farther back. An unspecified length on the western extremity of the ditch had however been filled in and the hedge levelled before the battle. Here, then, we must picture the Royalist army drawn up, musketeers and a few light Drakes lining the ditch, while the main line of resistance was some 100 yards behind, sufficiently close to bring the enemy under musket fire when they attempted to cross the ditch.

The Prince had been at great pains to draw up his men so as to take the best advantage of the ground, and on the arrival of Newcastle and Lord Eythin – General King had been elevated to the peerage with this title – he showed them a sketch map of his dispositions, explaining how he meant to fight his battle. Asked what he thought of it Eythin rudely replied, 'By God, sir, it is very fine on paper, but there is no such thing in the field', a remark scarcely calculated to endear him to the Prince. This was not their first meeting. There were those who thought that Rupert's capture at Lemgo in 1638[1] was due to King's failure to support him.

The Allies were drawn up in a parallel line some distance back from the ditch. Lord Leven, as commanding the largest contingent, was given the supreme command, and another experienced Scot, David Leslie, who also acted as Cromwell's second-in-command, marshalled the line of battle. Though the road between the two villages is curiously absent from all the accounts, it may be assumed that Leslie used it as a line of dressing for his front line. He could not wish for a better one. Thus it would be exactly a quarter of a mile from the ditch. This, though outside musket-shot, was well within cannon range, and it is not surprising to learn that there was a desultory cannonade by both sides in the course of the afternoon.

Leven's headquarters were by a clump of trees on the hill-top, now known as Cromwell's Plump. We hear no mention of the Allies fortifying the houses in the two villages, but this is not to be wondered at, for such a procedure on the battlefield was unusual in the Civil War.

Accounts of the Allied order of battle are hopelessly conflicting. The confusion is probably caused by the fact that whereas the Scottish foot are usually described as being in one body, they were in reality disposed all along the line, probably an intentional mixing of the two armies. The bulk of them, under Lieut.-General William Baillie,

[1] See p. 18.

were however on the right of Lord Fairfax, as shown in the sketch-map. On the right were Sir Thomas Fairfax's horse, and on the left Cromwell's horse. (Here it may be noted that in describing the engagement we shall use the terms right and left as for the Allied army, and as the reader, with the north of the map on the top, would naturally see it.)

The Allied army numbered at least 27,000 men, half of them Scots. Manchester's army was rather larger than the contingent under the Fairfaxes, his cavalry regiments being well up to strength. The Royalist army numbered about 17,000.

There is not the same doubt about the order of battle of the Royalists, for a plan of the line made by de Gomme is still in existence in the British Museum.[1] Of the infantry in the centre we need say nothing, except that Newcastle's Whitecoat regiments formed the nucleus, and better infantry did not exist on either side. On his right Rupert placed his own horse under Lord Byron, less a reserve in his own hands behind the centre. Lord Goring was in command of the horse on the left flank.

The guns on each side were placed for the most part in twos and threes in the intervals between the regiments, though a few Drakes were sited by Rupert along the ditch. Rupert had 28 guns and his opponents had 25. The artillery on both sides played an insignificant part in the ensuing battle.

As in most of the Civil War battles, neither side evinced a desire to take the offensive. There were good reasons for this hesitation at Marston Moor. Newcastle, as already noted, was reluctant to fight at all, and Rupert no doubt was influenced by him to postpone the attack till next day. Leven, on the other hand, holding the advantage of the higher ground, was not anxious to forgo it, especially as his opponents held the ditch, and that obstacle would be likely to impede and disarray his advance. Thus both sides sat narrowly eyeing one another till about 7 p.m. Prince Rupert then decided that the enemy had no immediate hostile intentions, so ordered up provisions from York for his troops and rode off to the rear to get some supper, while Newcastle repaired to his coach to have a quiet smoke.

Suddenly, without any warning, the whole Allied line advanced

[1] In his *Battles fought in Yorkshire* (p. 177) A. D. H. Leadman has cast doubts on its strict accuracy, but it does not seem to contain any errors of moment, though it probably gives the formation as ordered, and minor alterations may have been made later.

down the hill (they had previously pushed their line 200 yards forward
from the road so that only 250 yards separated the two lines). On the
left there was a small preliminary action. Some Parliamentary dragoons
advancing on the extreme left cleared the opposing musketeers from
the ditch (approaching it in a 'running march'), thus opening the way

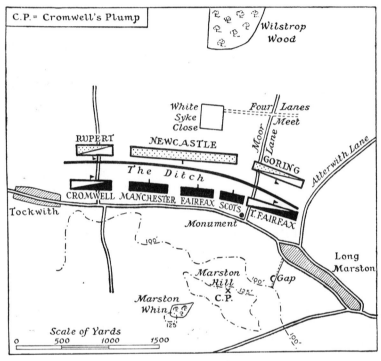

MARSTON MOOR

for the cavalry. Part of the ditch in this neighbourhood had been filled
in, which made it easier for Cromwell's cavalry to charge.

Contrary to the usual practice we will describe events on the right
flank first (though the clash was practically simultaneous all along the
line). As Fairfax's cavalry approached the ditch the musketeers lining
it fired one volley, and the Drakes one salvo, and then fell back to their
main line. Thus Fairfax got successfully across the ditch. But then his
troubles began. The ground was dotted with gorse bushes, which
split up his line and made ordered progress difficult.

Before they had gone far Fairfax's horse met the onrush of Goring's first line. Fairfax himself, at the head of 400 men, charged them successfully and pursued his immediate opponents off the field. Not so the remainder of his first line, many of whom were raw troops. Goring, ably seconded by Sir Charles Lucas, swept through them, putting them to headlong rout. Back over the ditch they hied and, not drawing rein, galloped over the hill in rear and right off the battlefield. Some of Goring's horse followed them for nearly two miles; others stopped on the hill-top to loot the baggage wagons, while the second line were kept in hand. But worse was to follow. In their mad rush to safety a portion of the defeated cavalry had galloped through and over the right of Baillie's Scottish foot. Some of these were trodden to the ground, others joined in the panic flight. For panic it was – all the chroniclers are emphatic on this point.

Panic spreads rapidly unless taken firmly in hand at the outset, and one suspects that there was some bad failure in leadership among the Scottish officers to account for this dire disaster. But the panic did not only spread from contagion; it was increased by Goring's second line which wheeling to the right, struck the open flank of Lord Fairfax's foot, who had by this time advanced some hundreds of yards beyond the ditch. These followed the example of the Scots and fled. Soon there were, on the admission of their own people, several thousand foot in mad flight from the field. The panic even spread to Manchester's division and he was himself for a time swept from the field. The Parliamentary chronicler Vicars describes his compatriots 'amazed with panick feares', and Stockdale, whose account is the most reliable of all, not excluding Chaplain Ashe's, admits that 'in all appearance the day was lost'.

Amid this hectic scene a remnant of the Scottish regiments stood firm; surrounded on three sides they kept their ranks, their pikemen forming a solid wall against which Goring's horsemen flung themselves in vain. But the pressure on them was prodigious and they were hard put to it to maintain themselves.

On the left of the line Cromwell's Ironsides deployed to charge over the ground opened up to them by the dragoons. Over the ditch they went, without losing their formation; on the flat moor beyond, here devoid of gorse, they encountered Byron's first line of horse. The events of the next hour on this part of the field have been the occasion of fierce controversy from that day onwards. For something went wrong, and Scots blamed English and English blamed Scots, while each took the credit for the final upshot of the action. Our reconstruction must therefore be taken with some reserve, though it seems possible to establish the essentials.

As Cromwell's first line neared the ditch Byron led out his men to meet them. Cromwell's onslaught swept away two Royalist brigades, but he himself was slightly wounded in the neck – perhaps by the accidental discharge of a pistol behind him – at the beginning of the action.

Prince Rupert was not present in this first clash, for he was at his supper near his reserve brigades of horse in rear of the centre of his line. Here perhaps he should have stayed to direct the battle, but that was not his nature. Moreover he had discovered from prisoners taken before the battle that Cromwell and his Ironsides were on the Allied left wing. Seeing things going wrong among his cavalry, he took at least a portion of his reserve and galloped to the rescue. *En route* he was met by some fugitive horse – men from his own regiment which formed the left of Byron's *second* line. In a towering rage he shouted 'Swounds! Do you run? Follow me!' and falling upon Cromwell's leaderless troopers drove them back. Only the arrival of David Leslie, who commanded the third line of Cromwell's horse, turned the tide.

Cromwell, though wounded, had rallied a considerable body of his cavalry, but in the confusion was uncertain how to act. Major-General Lawrence Crawford, the impulsive commander of Manchester's foot, saw these squadrons standing idle and, according to his own account, which may be accepted as substantially true, rode up to them furiously cursing them as poltroons. Cromwell explained that he was hurt, and Crawford, who had not noticed him apologized for his language and sent a man with him to Tockwith village, where the Lieut.-General's wound was dressed. Crawford himself took charge of Cromwell's cavalry for a time – at least until the arrival of David Leslie.

For almost an hour, Cromwell being off the field for most of the time, there was a prolonged and bitter fight, both sides being now practically stationary. Lord Saye, a Roundhead, paid this generous tribute to his opponents: 'The enemy's horse stood very firm and long time, coming to a close fight with the sword, and standing like an iron-wall, so that they were not easily broken.'

Eventually numbers told, Leslie's horse wrested the advantage from their opponents, and slowly at first then with gathering momentum, they pushed the Cavaliers off the battlefield.[1]

---

[1] Cromwell's own account of all this is misleading, to say the least of it. 'The left wing, which I commanded, being our own horse, saving a few Scots

While this strenuous contest was going on on the extreme left, Manchester's foot were at grips with Rupert's in the left centre. As the Allied cavalry gradually made ground, Manchester's men, recovering from their earlier panic, were able to wheel slightly to the right and take the Royalists in flank. At the end of an hour, say about 8.30 p.m., the sun being now set, the greater part of Manchester's line was facing to its right and the cavalry were starting off in pursuit. At about this juncture, Cromwell, in the saddle once more, began to exert his influence and his restraining hand. Leaving Leslie's Scots to carry out the pursuit, he rallied his own horse and formed them up, facing to the right, and in prolongation of Manchester's foot. Thus the whole line of battle had made a vast 'screw' as in a football scrum.

Meanwhile most of the leaders on each side were in flight. In Principal Baillie's memorable phrase: 'all six generals took to their heels'.[1] Rupert had had a narrow escape from capture, cut off from his Lifeguards, he broke from his enemies, cleared a fence and found himself in a beanfield. Rallying a few broken squadrons he fell slowly back towards York, lining hedges and beating off his pursuers; Newcastle had not even time to get back to his coach, which was taken with all his papers. Goring, however, at this moment was not in flight. In the other camp, Leven had got clear off the field, riding non-stop as far as Leeds. Manchester did not run far, and was soon back on the field, bringing some fugitives with him, but Lord Fairfax is reported to have fled to his own house at Cawood and to have gone to bed. Has such an extraordinary situation ever been seen elsewhere in war? Principal Baillie was guilty only of slight exaggeration. Probably the bulk of the Cavalier horse and the bulk of the Allied foot were in flight simultaneously, and all the leading generals on each side were wounded or in flight. For besides Cromwell, Sir Thomas Fairfax too was wounded. And this brings us back to that doughty warrior at one of the most dramatic moments of the Civil War.

We left Fairfax somewhere behind the Royalist front line, with his 400 troopers pursuing a body of Cavalier horse off the field. But his

---

in our rear, beat all the Prince's horse.' About a third of his 4,000 horse were Scots. However, his only account of the battle is a letter sympathizing with a friend whose son had been mortally wounded. A full description of the battle is hardly to be expected in such a document, but it naturally gave umbrage to the Scots.

[1] The six generals presumably being Leven, Lord Fairfax, Manchester, Cromwell, Rupert, and Newcastle.

M

second line was in full flight. Without attempting to rally his own party he returned to find out what had happened to the remainder of his command. But he was cut off by the triumphant cavalry of Lord Goring. Surrounded and wounded, he found himself almost alone amid a sea of enemies. Escape to his own lines seemed hopeless, and Sir Thomas took the desperate course of attempting a circuit right round the rear of the Cavalier army in the hopes of reaching Manchester's division. To do this it was essential to disguise himself. Now, in order to recognize friend from foe when the uniform of both sides was practically identical, the Allies wore white hat-bands (much as one side does in modern manoeuvres). Fairfax therefore did what an umpire at manoeuvres would have condemned; he removed his white cap-band and mingled with his enemies. By this simple ruse he passed unrecognized through the ranks of his foe, pursuing a course between Wilstrop Wood and White Syke Close (see sketch-map on p. 160). Somewhere on the modern Wilstrop Moor he encountered Oliver Cromwell in the dusk.

The latter was inactive at the moment, thereby drawing from Lawrence Crawford stinging words which have duly gone down to history. But though inactive he had got his Ironsides in hand, and was ready for any operation that might seem advisable. One would like a picture of the young Fairfax, slightly breathless and with a gash across his face, greeting his comrade in arms, seated on his horse with a bandage round his neck. Life had been hazardous for both of them personally during the last hour and still seemed hazardous for their cause now as Fairfax poured out his tale of woe. It was his first really big battle and for Oliver it was only the second. But neither of these great men faltered. While there is life there is hope; with the Ironsides intact and unshaken no one could say the battle was over! Moreover Manchester's infantry, resolutely led by Crawford, were also intact and victorious, unmoved apparently by the disaster on the rest of the field.

The two generals put their heads together and a plan was evolved. Fairfax lays no explicit claim to this plan, but it is tolerably certain that it was his. He was the senior of the two and he only was in possession of all the facts on which to base a feasible plan. If Manchester was present on the field he must have endorsed it but if he was still absent it may have been conveyed direct to Crawford.

It was a simple plan, as such should always be, especially when initiated in the gathering darkness; in the confusion of a battle a complicated plan however good has little chance of being carried out. The gist of the plan was that Cromwell with the horse should skirt round the rear guided by Fairfax who alone knew the ground, on the route he had just followed. Arriving on the right wing, they would attack Goring and go to the help of the Scottish regiments which were still holding out. Meanwhile Manchester's foot on the other flank would attack the hostile infantry that were pressing upon the Scots.

Cromwell therefore swept round the rear of the Royalist army (which by now was without a commander) and joined battle with Goring's horse. These were very scattered by this time, and no doubt in some disarray. Some were still attempting to penetrate the Scottish square as we may call it, for that is what it must have looked like. Others were trickling back from the pursuit over the hill, rather exhausted and in no trim for another fight against a formed body of Ironsides. Cromwell's horse promptly charged them and had not much difficulty in dispersing them. But note the extraordinary situation that had arisen. The two sides were exactly reversed: Cromwell was now charging from the very same spot and in the same direction as Goring had an hour before, while Goring's men were on the ground occupied by Fairfax at the opening of the battle. No wonder there was confusion in the ranks of both armies, bands of stragglers and fugitives from both armies using the same roads and tracks, dressed and armed much alike, and inextricably mixed.

The sun had set, and the armies fought on under a harvest moon. Under these conditions the first commander to make a resolute offensive has a good chance of success. What remained of Goring's gallant horse were swept away, and the pressure on the Scots' square was relieved. Not content with this, Cromwell now directed his attack against the hitherto intact Whitecoat regiments. Shortly afterwards (exact chronology is quite impossible to ascertain) Crawford, with some of Manchester's men, attacked them from the opposite flank while Baillie's foot pressed on their front. The triple pressure was too much for these hard-tried men. They fell back slowly and steadily till after some few hundred yards they entered White Syke Close, a large field, bordered with a ditch and hedge, which can still be identified. The rest of the Royalist foot had by this time disintegrated. No doubt some had joined in the pursuit of the defeated Lord Fairfax, and had not been able to regain the field; but curiously little has come down to us about their actions. Of the end of the Whitecoats, on the other hand, we have two graphic accounts. On the testimony of their enemies nothing could exceed their valour: they did not testify to it themselves; they could not, for they did not live to do so. Scorning surrender, they died almost to a man mostly from musket shots, for their opponents did not relish their pikes. Out of a few thousand men a mere thirty or forty survived that fearful but glorious night.

The battle was over; it had lasted under two hours. In a few short minutes the situation had been transformed, and to two men above all is credit due: to Sir Thomas Fairfax and to Oliver Cromwell. Marston Moor should be eternally connected with these two names.

It is significant of the degree of confusion and dismay in the Allied camp that the victors sat down on the battlefield for nearly 48 hours and did not resume the siege of York till they had been joined by their Cheshire reinforcements.

Rupert managed to collect about 6,000 of his cavalry in York next day and with them he marched out north-westwards back into Lancashire. But the infantry was completely destroyed and the Marquis of Newcastle, his spirit broken, took ship for Hamburg. Without his aid it was impossible for the Prince to rally the North to his uncle's cause. With the remnants of his army he made a wide sweep round to the north sucessfully eluding the enemy and slowly withdrew, first to Chester (25 July) where he left Byron in command, and then to Bristol which he reached a month later (26 August). York surrendered on 16 July. As a direct consequence of the battle the North was lost to King Charles: irretrievably lost.

Marston Moor was one of the hardest fought battles of the war: perhaps 4,000 men were killed and at least 1,500 were taken prisoner. The result was far from being a foregone conclusion. Rupert was well satisfied with the way his outnumbered men had behaved, and the Northern Cavaliers, particularly the Whitecoats, had gone down fighting. If Newcastle, who had charged bravely, now threw in his hand, Langdale was able to rally the cavalry and continue the struggle, but the northern spearhead of the King's trident had been shorn off. It remained to be seen whether the Cavaliers of the Centre and the West could stem the tide.

Cromwell's Ironsides won the praise of friend and foe alike. In Watson's words 'Major-Generall Lesley seeing us thus pluck a victory out of the enemies' hands, professed Europe had no better soldiers', while they owed their nickname to Rupert himself. The six Scots regiments which stood their ground on the Roundhead right had shown themselves worthy of the stubborn spearmen, their ancestors of Flodden.

COMMENTS

From almost every point of view the battle of Marston Moor was the most remarkable of the Civil War, if not of all the battles fought on English soil. It is hard to account for the excess of panic that swept through the ranks of the Allies. Whatever the various causes, we must allot the credit to Goring's magnificent troopers, and to his leadership. Unfortunately for his reputation Goring had few friends among the scribes. He was always painted as a debauchee; but a permanent drunkard could hardly have accomplished what he did, not only on this occasion. He cannot have been physically soft; he had no coach and six to convey him about with the minimum of exertion as Newcastle had. His deeds have remained unsung. But when we consider that his cavalry, practically unaided, had routed more than half the opposing army, a force more than three times as numerous as itself, and had struck such a panic into the enemy that fugitives are reported as far from the field as Hull, Lincoln, Halifax, and Wakefield, we get a fair measure of his achievement. Nor can we be surprised that in the darkness his scattered troopers were eventually driven off by the compact lines of Ironsides on fresh horses. We could well do with an account of Goring's personal motions during the battle, but a defeated army finds but few chroniclers; so we must abandon a profitless conjecture, only remembering that if Cromwell and Fairfax were the heroes of the victors, Lord Goring was the hero of the losers.

It is difficult to assess the work of Prince Rupert on this day. Once again the accounts are inadequate, and there is virtually nothing to add to what we have already related of his movements. Once he had launched his reserve – which indeed he led in person – he could do little to influence the battle. It is to be feared that he merely let the battle take its course, being personally absorbed in the cavalry mêlée almost throughout the brief engagement – nevertheless it is difficult to see what else he could have done. But his true spirit shone forth next morning. While Newcastle was making plans for his getaway, Rupert, finding his cavalry fairly intact, contemplated attacking his victorious enemies. When on the previous day someone expostulated at his wish to attack, he exclaimed: 'Nothing venture, nothing have!' His spirit also flashed out in a painful scene after the battle, when Newcastle declared that he should take ship for Holland – 'And I,' said the Prince, 'shall collect my troops and join the King.' Which he did. Nor do the eyewitnesses tell us anything material of Lord Leven, except his prolonged flight, and his natural remorse when hearing next day of the upshot of the fight. The first news to reach London and Oxford was of a Royalist victory.

From quite another point of view the battle is unique. It was the only pitched battle during the first Civil War in which English and Scots armies fought as allies. When two or more allies share in the same disaster one may be sure that there will afterwards be mutual recriminations. And even success leads to recrimination in allotting the credit. Such was the case after Marston Moor. It is worth while reflecting on this weakness which is inherent in such an army. Since, in the nature of things, the British Army fights its big battles with allies it is important to realize what hazards and pitfalls there are and to take studious care to minimize them.

APPENDIX

Cromwell's absence from the battlefield

Some biographies of Cromwell, including the most recent, pass over in silence the absence of Cromwell from the field for an appreciable period of the brief battle. Since this question has a bearing on the disputed part played by David Leslie, it is important to establish the facts. Firth in his account of the battle devotes more than two pages to an examination of the subject. The evidence for the absence can be summarized as follows.

(1) Major-General Lawrence Crawford, who served on the left wing, declared that shortly after the first charge of Cromwell's line he met Oliver on the field, wounded, and that he had him led off the field to get his wound dressed, adding that he himself took charge of Cromwell's line – an action which this bold, impulsive soldier might quite well have taken, pending the arrival of David Leslie.

(2) Lieut.-Colonel William Crawford (no relation to Lawrence) who fought on the immediate left of Cromwell's line asserted on oath that Cromwell received a little wound 'in the craige' which obliged him to retire, and that in consequence David Leslie led forward the left wing in his place.

(3) Principal Baillie asserted that 'all six generals took to their heels'. This inexact and sweeping statement, for what it is worth, must presumably have included Lieut.-General Cromwell.

(4) Local tradition declares that Cromwell sat in a cottage in Tock-with to have his wound dressed. The cottage pointed out (about the fourth from the eastern end of the village) was demolished during the second World War.

The silence on this point of Cromwell's protagonists Ashe and Watson is under the circumstances quite understandable.

The evidence seems conclusive that Oliver Cromwell was wounded early in the battle, and that his place was taken by David Leslie, but that he resumed his place in time to play his part in forging the victory.

CHAPTER 13

The Lostwithiel Campaign

O N 7 July a Royalist Council of War at Evesham advised the
King to move against Essex, who by this time was in Devon.
The advice was welcome to Charles, who was anxious for the
safety of the Queen; a week later she left Falmouth for France, her
voyage attended as usual by the salvoes of Parliamentary men-of-war.

After reinforcing Lyme Essex had occupied Weymouth and Mel-
combe Regis; then, his army somewhat diminished by the garrisons
left behind, he had pushed westwards. He reached Tavistock on
23 July while the King was still in Somerset. He wrote that day to the
Committee of Both Kingdoms announcing his intention to adhere to a
former resolution of relieving Plymouth, and expressing a hope that
Waller would 'take care of the King's army'.

Sir Richard Grenvile now abandoned the siege of Plymouth, and
assembling the small garrisons of Saltash, Mount Stamford and
Plympton, marched north to guard the passage of the Tamar at
Horsebridge.

On the very day (26 July) that the King reached Exeter Essex
decided to invade Cornwall. He was encouraged in this course by
Lord Robartes, who over-estimated his own influence in that county,
and who pointed out that the King depended on the export of Cornish
tin for the import of munitions.

Brushing Grenvile aside Essex reached Bodmin on 28 July. There
on 2 August he heard that the King was hard on his tracks and had
reached Launceston only 20 miles away. Thoroughly alarmed, he
moved to Lostwithiel so as to keep open his communications with the
sea, while a detachment was sent to hold the little port of Fowey. On
4 August Essex wrote to the Committee that three armies under the
King, Maurice, and Hopton were approaching from the east, 'and the
country rising unanimously against us, with the exception of a few
gentlemen. We must expect another army from the west.' This was a

reference to Grenvile's force, which on the previous day the King had ordered to advance to Tregony, 15 miles south-west of Lostwithiel, in order to check the Roundhead foraging parties. Already Essex's army was short of bread, and hoped for supplies from Plymouth. 'Then', says the Earl, 'we shall sell our lives at as dear a rate as may be, for I have never seen soldiers more willing to undertake anything nor to undergo wants with more patience.' The soldiers may have been resolute: their commander was badly rattled.

Essex still had an army of some 10,000 men, but the King now had not less than 16,000 horse and foot at his disposal. The Cornish peasantry, their traditional loyalty inspired by the presence of the monarch and by hatred of the 'foreigners', were whole-heartedly for the King. Provisions and intelligence, both denied to the Parliamentary army, were offered to the Cavaliers. No Roundhead straggler was safe.

On 7 August Charles called on Essex to surrender. The negotiations, a symptom of war-weariness, consumed several days, but to his credit the Earl resisted all appeals.

Though Essex was now in a difficult position, all was not well with the Cavaliers. Wilmot, the Lieut.-General of the Horse, out of pride and vanity had been talking sedition, using language which Charles considered contemptuous of his person. On the 8th the King suddenly relieved him of his command, and gave it to Goring, who had just joined his army. Wilmot's chief confederate, Henry Percy, the inefficient General of the Ordnance, was replaced by Hopton, who was obviously an excellent choice.

Goring was a less obvious selection, but he had done much to efface the evil impression caused by his conduct at Portsmouth in 1642. One of the few Cavaliers who enhanced their reputations at Marston Moor, he was at this period *persona grata* with Rupert.

The Committee of Both Kingdoms, realizing the Earl's danger, voted £20,000 for pay and provisions to be sent to Plymouth for his army and ordered Waller's Lieut.-General, Middleton, with 2,000 horse and dragoons to march to his relief. A further £10,000 was voted for Waller, but by 27 August Sir William had got no farther than his old quarters at Farnham, a place that seems to have had a fascination for him.

Meanwhile the Cavaliers were closing in. On 11 August Grenvile with 2,400 men forced his way into Bodmin. Next day he secured

Respryn Bridge three miles north of Lostwithiel, thus ensuring his communications with the King. He then occupied Lord Robartes' house at Lanhydrock, between Bodmin and Lostwithiel.

On the 13th Goring and Sir Jacob Astley reconnoitred the east bank of the river Fowey southwards to the sea and next day posted 200 foot with two or three guns, at Polruan Fort at the mouth of the river and at Hall, Lord Mohun's house by Bodinnick Ferry. Colonel Sir Charles Lloyd's regiment was posted at Cliffe opposite Golant to guard that ferry.

Essex made no attempt to hold these important positions or to re-capture them. The Royalists now overlooked and menaced Fowey harbour, and it is strange that the Roundheads did not try to dis-lodge them from Hall and Polruan by landing a party from ships' boats.

Meanwhile on 14 August Middleton's force, which had penetrated as far as Bridgwater, had been defeated by Sir Francis Doddington and had fallen back to Sherborne.

For about a week nothing of moment took place at Lostwithiel, though on the 17th the King, whose headquarters were at Boconnoc, made a personal reconnaissance from the 'fair walk' which still runs below Hall House. He came under fire, a fisherman standing near him being slain. Charles was in every respect the commander in the field.

The Battle of Beacon Hill. 21 August 1644

On 21 August the Royalists carried out a well-synchronized general advance along their whole front from Lanhydrock to Boconnoc, a distance of four miles. Such an operation was most unusual in those days and has a very modern look.

Zero hour was 7 o'clock. Grenvile on his side stormed the ruined but still formidable Castle of Restormel, which was held by some of John Weare's Devonshire regiment. The Roundheads retreated with-out orders either from Essex or their colonel.

It was a misty morning, and the forces of Maurice and the Earl of Brentford, Lord Forth's new title, took possession of Beacon Hill, overlooking Lostwithiel, and Druid's Hill without serious opposition – the mist covering them like a smoke-screen. Prince Maurice then sent a column, 1,000 strong, to take the hill north-east of Lostwithiel on the north side of the road to Liskeard.

Towards nightfall the main body of the King's foot penetrated into the fields on the hillside on both sides of the Lostwithiel–Liskeard road. Colonel Matthew Appleyard with 1,000 men held Beacon Hill, while Prince Maurice's army held the more northerly hill.

Essex was completely taken by surprise and offered little resistance. Not until the afternoon did he send a force to oppose Grenvile's further advance. It is not surprising that Charles' Secretary-at-War, Sir Edward Walker, found it difficult to understand Essex's failure to fortify Beacon Hill, for it is indeed the key to Lostwithiel. The Cavaliers worked all night raising a redoubt twenty yards square to secure this vital ground.

On the following two days the situation remained unchanged, and there was only sporadic fighting. Essex, it seemed, had accepted defeat. On the 24th so little movement could be detected that the King's entourage suspected a Roundhead withdrawal to Fowey.

The King planned a general advance for the 25th, and half the cavalry were sent across Respryn Bridge to support Grenvile on the west bank of the Fowey. During the morning reconnaissance disclosed that the Roundheads were not gone; they were merely taking cover from the Royalist battery, all ready to receive the Cavaliers if they should advance.

Seeing this the King changed his plans and postponed the projected attack. Next day, the 26th, he sent Goring to the west with 2,000 horse and 1,000 foot under Maj.-General Sir Thomas Bassett to post himself at St. Blazey so as to stop the Roundheads landing provisions at Par, four miles west of Fowey, and to prevent their foraging. On the same day supplies, including 100 barrels of powder, reached the Cavaliers from Dartmouth and from Pendennis Castle.

The Roundhead army was now in a desperate plight, bottled up in a narrow tract of land five miles long and two miles wide. With his sea communications practically severed Essex could not find subsistence for his 10,000 men. Even so, five days went by before the King had any assurance that by dividing his forces as he had done he had produced any good effect. He too had his anxieties; the weather was turning foul and provisions were growing scarcer. His 16,000 men were strung out on a 15 mile front. The country was intricate and badly roaded, and messengers were prone to lose their way. Even with wireless and the weapons of the present day he would have been taking risks. With seventeenth century means of inter-communication Charles' dispositions were of a remarkable boldness. At last on the evening of 30 August two deserters were brought to the Royal headquarters at Boconnoc and disclosed Essex's plans. During the night his horse were to break out, while his infantry were to fall back to Fowey and embark.

Instantly the King gave orders that both his own army and Prince Maurice's should stand to their arms all night. The two armies were little more than a musket shot apart and in the event of the Roundhead cavalry trying to escape they had orders to fall upon them. A cottage beside the Lostwithiel-Liskeard road half way between the two main Royalist bodies was fortified and manned by 50 musketeers. All the various detachments of the army were alerted and Sir Edward Walde-grave's regiment of horse, stationed near Saltash, was ordered to break down the bridges across the Tamar. The Lifeguards, quartered at Lanreath, received the information at about 1 a.m. and rode in to Boconnoc.

About 3 o'clock in the morning the Roundhead cavalry, led by the redoubtable Sir William Balfour, sallied out of Lostwithiel, and made their way up the Liskeard road. It was a hazardous venture and few of them can have expected to get through. But the musketeers in their cottage were presumably asleep for they did not fire a shot. However, the movement of so great a body, about 2,000 horse, could not be accomplished in complete silence. The trampling hooves, the clashing armour, the muttered orders – and oaths – roused the Cavaliers' gunners who fired a few rounds into the darkness, but they did little damage, and that probably moral rather than physical.

Except for Cleveland's brigade there were few cavalry at hand to deal with this eruption, and they could do little until daylight. Then with about 500 horse Cleveland pursued over Braddock Down and Caradon Down to Saltash, where Balfour managed to beat off Waldegrave, and to ferry his men across into Devonshire, reaching Plymouth with the loss of about 100 men.

The Royalists were mortified by Balfour's escape, and Clarendon (writing in about 1671) laid the blame on Goring, alleging that 'he was in one of his jovial excesses when the order to pursue reached him', but this is quite untrue and the accusation must be put down to malice or carelessness. Goring at St. Blazey could do nothing to stop Balfour. The Royalists by adopting a cordon system laid themselves open to an attempt of this kind, but by no other means could they prevent Essex obtaining provisions. Nevertheless it was a sparkling achievement on the part of Balfour, and is a good example of the adage 'Nothing venture, nothing gain'.

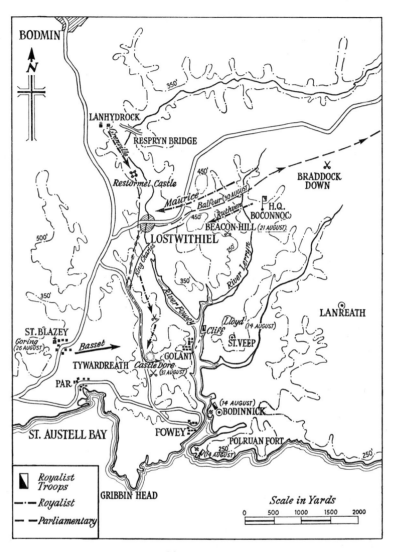

LOSTWITHIEL

The Battle of Castle Dore. 31 August 1644

Most of the Royalist foot were straggling about the countryside in search of provisions, but with what men he had at hand the King now lost no time in marching on Lostwithiel. He could see the colours of the Parliamentary rearguard on the hill south of the town, where Major-General Skippon was covering Essex's withdrawal. In his despatch the Earl reported that the narrow lane leading to Fowey was 'so extreme foul with excessive rain, and the harness for the draught horses so rotten as that in the marching off we lost three demi-culverins and a brass piece . . . thirty horses were put to each of them, but could not move them, the night was so foul and the soldiers so tired that they were hardly to be kept to their colours'.   Thus Essex explains his plight, but he does not excuse it. He had been at Lostwithiel for four weeks and he should have known the state of the roads and of the harness of his gun-teams.

While Essex was reeling backwards the King, who never showed more vigour and ability than now, was moving in for the kill. At 7 a.m. 1,000 Royalist foot entered Lostwithiel without much opposition, driving off some Roundheads who were breaking the bridge. Immediately after Charles ordered up two or three guns and planted them 'in the enemies' leaguer' to command the hill where Skippon's rearguard was posted. On this the Roundheads fell back, the Royalist infantry 'following them in chase from field to field in a great pace'.

About 8 o'clock the King at the head of his Lifeguards moved westwards from the redoubt on Beacon Hill and forded the river Fowey south of Lostwithiel finding everywhere evidence of a disorderly retreat; first a cartload of muskets broken down in the mud and then five cannon in different places, '2 of them being very long ones' (demi-Culverins).

The King was in aggressive mood, fully realizing that the enemy were on the run. 'With this small force', Symonds wrote in his diary, 'his Majesty chased them two miles, beating them from hedge to hedge. Being come near that narrow neck of ground between Trewardreth[1] Bay and St. Veepe pass,[2] the rebels made a more forcible resistance . . .' to Grenvile's foot who were now leading the vanguard.

The Cornish Cavaliers retreated hastily but rallied on a body of foot commanded by Lieut.-Colonel William Leighton of the Guards. The scene of this rearguard action, which took place between 11 and 12

[1] Tywardreath. The O.S. calls it St. Austell Bay.
[2] Golant ferry.

o'clock, can still be identified. It is the hedges and fields just west of Trebathevy Farm.

Charles now launched his Lifeguards to the attack, who inspired by his personal leadership were not to be denied. Major Brett 'led up the Queen's troop, and most gallantly in view of the King charged their foot and beat them from their hedge, killing many of them, notwithstanding their muskets made abundance of shot at his men: he received a shot in the left arm in the first field . . . yet most gallantly went on and brought his men off. . . .' As the Major was riding back to have his wound dressed 'the King called him and took his sword which was drawn in his hand, and knighted Sir Edward Brett on his horse's back', in the very forefront of the battle. One cannot recall a similar action by a King of England in our history.

A lull followed, for the foot had been far outpaced, but by about 2 o'clock the Royalist infantry, advancing fast, came up in force. Sir Thomas Basset from St. Blazey fell on the enemy's left flank, and about the same time the King's own infantry with Colonel Appleyard leading the van, made a frontal attack, gaining ground in the face of heavy musketry.

It was probably about 4 o'clock when Essex organized a counter-attack by two or three troops of horse, which he had retained, and 100 musketeers. Captain Reynolds and the Plymouth horse charged bravely, driving the Royalist foot back for two or three fields and taking a colour. Lieut.-Colonel John Boteler of Essex's own foot regiment supported Reynolds well and took a colour with his own hand. Then seeing the King's Lifeguards approaching they fell back again.

Goring with his cavalry arrived about this time and was ordered by the King to pursue the Roundhead horse towards Saltash, which he proceeded to do.

At 6 o'clock the Roundheads put in a more serious counter-attack, trying to regain the high ground north of Castle Dore, an Iron Age fort. They drove the Cavaliers back for two fields, but after an hour's fighting, during which Northampton's brigade of horse came up to support the Royalist foot, the Roundheads were beaten right back to Castle Dore. Night was falling fast as the Cavaliers charged forward, and although they could see signs of disorder in the Roundhead ranks east of the earthwork, they pursued no farther.

Castle Dore, now the centre of the Parliamentary position, is a double entrenchment and commands the roads east to Golant, west to Tywardreath and south to Fowey. Five or six regiments held this front, two to the west, and three or four to the east of the ancient earthwork. So small a force could not hope to hold this extensive position indefinitely, even under favourable circumstances. By now the morale of the Parliamentary infantry was at its lowest. Abandoned by their cavalry, tired and hungry after a hard day's fighting the regiments began to disintegrate in the dusk. Weare's regiment, which had put up so feeble a resistance at Restormel on the 21st was one of the first to go. There was now a great gap in the Roundhead line east of Castle Dore: the Cavaliers had an open road to Fowey.

To Skippon the position must have seemed hopeless indeed, but he was determined to save the situation if he could, and sent officers to seek instructions from the Lord General. His messengers did not reach Essex until about an hour before dawn, and then they received not orders, but a few words of ambiguous advice. The Earl advised Skippon to bring the train to Menabilly, and with the army to secure that place and Polkerris. If that could not be done he should draw up the foot round the train and, by threatening to blow it up, obtain the best conditions he could.

Essex had had enough. 'I thought it fit to look to myself, it being a greater terror to me to be a slave to their contempts than a thousand Deaths. . . .' Accompanied only by Robartes, the author of his downfall, he set sail for Plymouth in a fishing boat.

Skippon was made of sterner stuff. Calling a Council of War he proposed that the foot should cut its way out as the horse had done, but his officers, who, as is often the case, knew better than Skippon how exhausted and demoralized their men were, considered this impossible.

The King supped and spent the night under a hedge amid his foremost troops, with complete absence of ceremony. The night was a stormy one, but Charles was in a happy frame of mind, for the wind would make escape for the enemy by sea out of the question. There was some desultory firing during the night, one shot falling close to the King, but the next day was a quiet one; the monarch was biding his time, for he knew that the enemy were caught like rats in a trap, and he wished to avoid useless loss of life.

On 1 September, while the Cavaliers were preparing for a final effort the Roundheads, still nearly 6,000 strong, asked for a parley. Next day they surrendered, being allowed to march away with their colours; the officers with their swords, and one carriage to each regiment, but a total of 42 guns, a mortar, 100 barrels of powder and 5,000 arms, fell into the hands of the victors. Harried by the revenge-

ful Cornish peasantry the remnant of Essex's army eventually found
its way to Portsmouth.

Thus Essex's invasion of Cornwall ended in disaster. The King had
now got the better of both his opponents: Waller at Cropredy Bridge
and Essex at Lostwithiel, but Waller's defeat, though it put his army
out of action for most of the summer, was not nearly as serious as that
suffered by Essex, though the army that surrendered at Fowey was a
far more homogeneous force than that commanded by Waller. The
victory at Cropredy had been if not a soldiers', a brigadiers' battle. But
in Cornwall the King's personal intervention had been decisive in
every phase of the fighting. He had been Generalissimo in practice as
well as in name. From his headquarters at Boconnoc he controlled the
whole wideflung front. His energy and careful arrangements ensured
the harmonious co-operation of the various columns – not an easy feat
when we consider the intricate nature of the terrain, the absence of
roads and the primitive nature of his intelligence service. For example,
the co-ordinated advance on 21 August could only be achieved by a
strict adherence to a pre-arranged plan for there was no means of inter-
communication save by galloper. And yet Charles' generals managed
to carry out a well synchronized attack.

Essex exhibited none of the skill which he had shown in the relief
of Gloucester, nor of the dogged courage he had displayed at Newbury.
On the contrary, his indecision, infirmity of purpose and finally his
abrupt abandonment of his army are painful to contemplate even after
this lapse of time.

In glaring contrast, the King, who had noted the Earl's lack of
resolution on the morrow of Edgehill and had taken the measure of his
man – a mark of the good general – deliberately and rightly decided to
take risks. He conducted the campaign with cool confidence in himself, awaiting in patience the day – August the 21st – when he judged
it was time to strike. And he judged right. The more deeply one
examines this little studied campaign the clearer stands out the firm
grip on the situation that Charles possessed. In short, the campaign of
Lostwithiel was a triumph for the King of England and the biggest
success obtained by the Royalists in the whole of the war.

CHAPTER 14

The Second Newbury Campaign

WHEN ON 7 SEPTEMBER the Commons heard of the surrender in Cornwall they were far from blaming Essex. Indeed they drew up a letter thanking the Captain-General for his conduct, and making Middleton, whose small force had failed to relieve him, the scapegoat. Only Sir Arthur Hazelrig, whose loud laughter was much resented, seems to have appreciated the ridiculous nature of this document.

The Committee of Both Kingdoms expected the King to advance eastwards before Essex's army could be reorganized. To meet the threat there were still the armies of Manchester and Waller, which had already been ordered west and Middleton's detachment which was already in Dorset.

But the King did not at once return towards Oxford. On 11 September he summoned Plymouth, hoping that Essex's defeat might have demoralized the garrison, but being rebuffed, left Grenvile to blockade the town and marched to Exeter. Some days were consumed in providing for the wants of the army – pay, clothing, and shoes – and in settling garrisons to hold the West.

Despite his successes during the summer there is no hint in Sir Edward Walker's narrative, the official Royalist account, that the King ever contemplated an advance on London in the autumn of 1644. His object was to relieve the garrisons of Banbury Castle, Basing House, and Donnington Castle and then to dispose his army in winter quarters. But to his opponents another thrust at the capital seemed a very real risk. On 10 September Waller, then at Salisbury, wrote to the Committee: 'If there be not present course taken to oppose the enemy with a strong power, I know of nothing to hinder them from marching to London. . . . I hear but of 2,000 prisoners who are coming with the convoy, so that the rest, for ought I can perceive, have taken entertainment with the King. May God direct your counsels.' Black though the situation may have seemed to Waller it was not actually so grave.

When his letter was penned the King was still before Plymouth and it was not until 2 October that his army, 10,000 strong, reached Sherborne. By that time Manchester had concentrated around Reading, where he arrived on 29 September, and Waller, after reinforcing the garrisons of Weymouth, Poole, and Lyme with all his infantry, had posted himself at Shaftesbury with his cavalry (21 September). Essex and his foot were at Portsmouth. Though the Parliamentary forces were still widely scattered the danger to London was past. There remained the danger that the King would advance and destroy their armies in detail.

The Royalists were fully aware that in order to relieve their beleaguered garrisons they must risk another battle, and that being so they consulted as to how they could increase their army. Prince Rupert, who had set up his headquarters at Bristol at the end of August, came to Sherborne to take part in their deliberations. It was agreed that he should take the field with 2,000 horse, the remnants of Newcastle's army, who were moving south under Sir Marmaduke Langdale, and 2,000 foot from South Wales under General Gerard. Hopton and Rupert left for Bristol on 5 October, in order to organize these reinforcements.

Charles with 10,000 men took the offensive on 15 October and entered Salisbury.

The Parliamentary armies could put nearly 17,000 men in the field. Waller with a mounted force about 6,000 strong, drawn from his own and Essex's army, fell back eastwards before the Royalist advance. Manchester, who had 4,000 foot and 3,500 cavalry, had his head-quarters at Reading, where he was joined on the 18th by a brigade of the City Trained Bands numbering 3,000 men. Essex with the 2,000 foot that had survived the march from Cornwall was still at Portsmouth.

On the afternoon of the 18th Goring with the vanguard of the King's army caught up with Sir William Waller and drove him out of Andover.

Meanwhile Manchester, acting on Waller's advice had advanced from Reading to Basingstoke (17 October), hoping to effect a junction with Essex. Late on the night of the 18th Manchester received 'a very hot alarm' whereupon he concentrated his forces and ordered up four regiments of the London Trained Bands from Reading.

ITINERARY

Oct.	*King*	*Waller*	*Manchester*	*Essex*
15	Salisbury	Andover	Reading	Portsmouth
17	Salisbury	Andover	Basingstoke	Portsmouth
18	Andover	Andover	Basingstoke	Portsmouth
19	Whitchurch	Basingstoke	Basingstoke	Petersfield
20	Whitchurch	Basingstoke	Basingstoke	Basingstoke
22	Kingsclere	———————	Basingstoke	———————
23	Red Heath (just N. of Newbury)		Swallowfield (17 miles E. of Newbury)	
26	Newbury		Thatcham (3 miles E. of Newbury)	
27	———————	SECOND BATTLE OF NEWBURY		———————

By the 19th Waller had joined him at Basingstoke and, although Essex was still at Petersfield, Balfour with his cavalry had also reached Basingstoke. Next day (20th) Waller could write to the Committee: 'You may now look upon the forces as joined.' The King's sudden advance had obliged the Parliamentary armies to concentrate, but satisfactory though this must have been to their masters in London, one problem had greatly exercised their minds – the question of command. This the Committee had resolved at a meeting on 14 October. Instructions (17 in number) had been sent to the generals, the most significant being:

'(1) Those forces shall be ordered by his Excellency the Earl of Essex, Lord General, the Earl of Manchester, Lord Robartes [who was still in Plymouth], Sir Wm. Waller, Sir Arthur Haselrig, and Oliver Cromwell, Esq., M.P.'s, and . . . this Committee.

'(3) That designs, battles, sieges, assaults, and the disposing of the forces in whole or in part (when they have no particular direction from this Committee, or that in . . . their judgment . . . they have not convenient time to advise with this Committee), shall be ordered by the advice of the greater number of the persons before named, four of them at least being present, whereof those sent from hence to be two.'

Two civilians, Sir Archibald Johnstone and John Crewe, were the two deputies sent to represent the Committee. Though the war was now more than two years old the Parliamentary armies were still being run by remote control – from Derby House.

On the day (18 Oct.) that the King entered Andover the Round-head detachment which had been besieging Donnington Castle since 29 September, fell back on the main body at Basingstoke. There was now no Parliamentary force in a position to prevent the relief of Banbury, but the third of the beleaguered Royalist fortresses, Basing, was hemmed in by the three main Parliamentary armies. Nevertheless, the King, encouraged by his minor success at Andover, continued his eastward march, reaching Whitchurch, 7 miles to the east, on the 20th. A battle was practically inevitable for in the words of Sir Edward Walker 'now we were engaged and could not in Honour retreat. . . .' and indeed on the 21st Charles pushed on to Kingsclere (10 miles north-east) in the hope of relieving Basing. Here more prudent counsels prevailed and in view of the openness of the country and the numerical superiority of the Parliamentary horse, the Cavaliers marched next day to Newbury (8 miles north-west) and took up a strong position north of the town. This done the King despatched Northampton's brigade of horse on a 50 mile march to the relief of Banbury Castle. This left little more than 9,000 Royalists to hold the Newbury position. It was the King's intention to remain on the defensive, trusting that the rigours of a winter campaign would exhaust his opponents, and give him an opportunity later to relieve Basing. The next few days passed peacefully but on the 26th the Parliamentary armies were in contact.

The Second Battle of Newbury. 27 October 1644

The situation on the evening of 26 October was that the Roundheads, 17,500 strong were confronting the Royalists, 9,000 strong, the two armies facing respectively west and east, immediately to the north of Newbury. It looked as if the King had been out-manoeuvred; but there were certain points in his favour which appeared to justify his decision to stand his ground. The first was the natural strength of the position that he occupied. His right flank was protected by the river Kennet and the town of Newbury in which he placed a garrison; his left by a small tributary, the Lambourn, while still farther to the left rear, stood the formidable Donnington Castle, under its heroic defender, Colonel John Boys. The centre rested on a large mansion belonging to a Mr Dolman and called Shaw House. Round three sides of the garden, forming a sort of courtyard, were some ancient embankments,[1] making the house a veritable fortress.

---

[1] Incorrectly believed of old to have been thrown up for the battle.

The Royalists had another but intangible advantage, namely the divided command of their opponents. We have seen that the command was vested in a council – a notoriously bad form of command in war. Moreover, Manchester, the senior general on that council was a commander of mediocre capacity. Cromwell ranked lower in the Parliamentary hierarchy than Waller and Hazelrig, and merely commanded the cavalry of the Eastern Association. Essex's army had no overall commander for the Earl was sick and had remained at

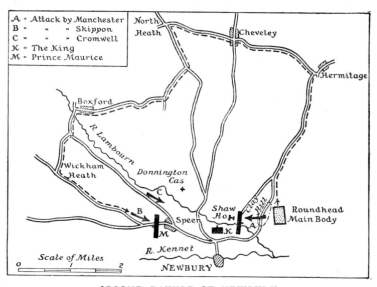

SECOND BATTLE OF NEWBURY

Reading: Balfour commanded the horse and Skippon the foot. In addition there was the City Brigade under Harrington, evidently an independent formation, answerable only to the Council of War.

But this peculiar council now nerved itself to a remarkable decision – one that gives this battle its distinctive interest. Not liking the look of the Royalist position from the front, the council decided – on whose proposition does not appear – to attack it simultaneously from front and rear. To encompass this would entail a wide *detour* by the out-flanking column owing to the position of Donnington Castle on the left rear – a site that might have been purposely selected to frustrate such a manoeuvre. The route decided on was as follows: three miles north-east nearly to Hermitage – west, via Chieveley to North Heath –

south to Winterbourne – west to Boxford – south to Wickham Heath – south-east to Speen. Total 13 miles. It was a bold decision to take, even though the Royalist army was greatly inferior. Including a period for rest and sleep the march (most of it by night) would take the best part of 24 hours, and during that time the remainder of the army risked being attacked by the whole force of the Royalists. But this decision is a good example of the profound truth that in war risks *must* be taken. In actual fact there was never much prospect of the King attacking during this period. By some means he managed to get wind of the flanking move, and in order to counter it he shifted Prince Maurice's troops to occupy a position to the west of Speen.

The reserve, consisting of two brigades of horse and the artillery train, was stationed in the open in a large field, which can still be identified, stretching from the northern outskirts of the town to the banks of the river Lambourn. Maurice took up his position on the rising ground just west of Speen village, and spent the morning of October 27th busily entrenching his position.

Meanwhile the outflanking force – Essex's army, and the London Brigade with Waller's and Cromwell's horse – was steadily plodding on its long, circuitous march. It constituted the greater part of the army – probably two-thirds of it, for though exact figures are not given it cannot have been much less than 13,000 strong out of 17,500. Waller, Cromwell, Balfour, and Skippon appear to have shared the command – a strange arrangement. Waller was no doubt the senior, but Skippon took command of all the foot. The force had set out shortly after midnight and halted to bivouac at Heath End.

The essence of an attack on exterior lines such as the Roundheads planned to make, is that both attacks should be delivered simultaneously – a difficult matter when communications were as primitive as they were in the Civil War. It is true that the King had successfully employed this strategy at Lostwithiel, and it may be that this had led Balfour and Skippon to suggest it now by way of turning the tables on him.

But in spite of the difficulties and hazards inherent in an operation of this nature in the seventeenth century, there remained one form of communication common to both ancient and modern times – sound. Manchester very sensibly arranged that Skippon should fire his cannon as a signal that he was in position and about to attack; on hearing that signal Manchester would also attack; thus co-ordination would be achieved in the simplest possible manner. It seemed almost foolproof – but nothing is foolproof in war.

The Parliamentary army formed up on the ridge to the west of Speen. The infantry under Skippon were in the centre, and the horse on the wings. Balfour on the right and Cromwell on the left.

Manchester attempted a feint attack in the early morning. The tendency of such attacks is either to be transparently feints, or to be pushed too far. The latter happened in this case and the attacking troops were only extricated with difficulty.

Skippon came into contact with Prince Maurice's detachment at about 3 p.m. The exact time is disputed; even today it is difficult to ascertain exact times of occurrences in the course of an encounter battle, and naturally it was much more difficult then. It is important though to fix this moment as precisely as possible in view of what transpired, and it cannot have been far from 3 p.m. There remained two hours of daylight (it was 6 November New Style[1]). If Manchester's attack was to prove effective against the strong Shaw House position there was no time to lose. But no sound came from that part of the field. Meanwhile the attack on Prince Maurice was being launched. In spite of their fatigue after their long march, the Roundheads attacked resolutely. The trenches to the west of Speen had not been completed, and the position was overrun, after a sanguinary struggle. The guns defending it – captured at Lostwithiel – were, by a curious coincidence, recaptured by the men who had lost them. The Royalist foot was sent reeling down the road into the village of Speen, and even farther. The situation for the Cavaliers looked critical. The King himself, with Prince Charles, was standing at the head of his reserve in the open field, when some fleeing cavalry came charging past him. The King did his best by his own personal efforts to rally them, but without marked success. At this critical moment a small reinforcement to either side would probably decide the issue, as so often happens in war.

There was an obvious quarter from where it might be reasonably expected. Hitherto we have not spoken of the redoubtable Oliver Cromwell, whose cavalry had added such lustre to his name on the field of Marston Moor, only three months before. Both Manchester and the chaplain Ashe asserted that he performed no service during the battle, and the surprising fact must be accepted. Oliver's latest biographer maintains, apparently by way of excuse, that his position was on most unfavourable ground, intersected by hedges, and that he

[1] At the date of the second battle of Newbury sunset occurred at 4.26 p.m. The moon was at its First Quarter, and set shortly after midnight.

came under artillery fire from Donnington Castle. Neither of these excuses is valid. There were hedges all over the battlefield, and we have accounts of bodies of cavalry negotiating them successfully. If all the hedges directly opposite Cromwell's command were impassable thus rendering his cavalry immobile, why did he not take steps to change position? Waller had done this at Cheriton, and at Nantwich Fairfax had caused his pioneers to make gaps in the hedges, through which his cavalry passed. But there is no record of Cromwell attempting either of these steps. As for the Donnington artillery, there appear to have been four cannon – demi-Culverins or Sakers – in the castle. Cromwell's horse would be upwards of 1,000 yards distant, and the guns of that period seldom fired at such a range, not because they could not reach, but because of their inaccuracy at long ranges. They did however fire a few rounds at Skippon's infantry in the centre but that was a stationary target. If Cromwell had executed a charge it is unlikely that these cannon would have had time to fire more than one round apiece, before he closed with his enemy and as their target would have been a moving one, passing across their front, it is most improbable that Cromwell's troops would have suffered a single casualty.

The cause of Cromwell's inactivity must remain a matter of speculation, but the suspicion intrudes that he sulked that day – just as Stonewall Jackson did when fighting under Lee at White Oak Swamp.

Whatever the cause, Cromwell failed to intervene; on the contrary it was a Royalist, the old Earl of Cleveland who seized this critical moment to charge. General Goring put himself at the head of Cleveland's brigade, only 800 strong, and went in with them.

On the southern flank Balfour had made some progress at first but was then charged by Sir Humphrey Bennet's brigade and others and put to flight. The Roundheads were hurled back to Speen, the King's personal safety was secured, and the battle on this sector of the front became stationary.

Meanwhile what was happening on the opposite side of the field? The commonly accepted theory is that Manchester refused, despite the reiterated appeals of those around him, to intervene, in spite of the engagement he had made to do so. In point of fact, his troops did attack, though it is impossible to ascertain precisely at what hour this happened. What probably occurred was that Manchester was so doubtful as to whether the attack would take place that day at all, that he did not issue any 'warning order' to his troops, preferring to wait until the moment actually arrived when he would issue the orders that seemed appropriate to the occasion.

Assuming then that he set about mounting an attack as soon as he heard the cannonade opening, it might easily take an hour before the attackers actually came to blows with the enemy. His plan was not a particularly simple one; the attack was to be delivered by two columns, one to attack Shaw House from the north-east, and the other from the south-east. If Skippon's attack started at 3 p.m. that means that Manchester's would materialize at about 4 p.m. which is probably what actually occurred. The sun set at 4.2 p.m. on that day, and the moon had not risen. The fight therefore took place in the gathering darkness, as is agreed on all hands. Our contention receives support from Ashe. According to this worthy Manchester was able to see from Clay Hill the attack on Speen (probably battle smoke over the tree-tops) and 'animated with this encouraging sight, the Earl prepared to descend to the more difficult work of forcing the strong position at Dolman's house'.

So the attack was launched, while still the action was in full swing on Speen hill. Thus were the two essential conditions of an operation on exterior lines – superior numbers, and a simultaneous attack – observed. This made it impossible for the King to turn his central position to account by concentrating against first one and then the other of his opponents, nor does it seem that Charles even attempted this. The position now looked ugly for the Royalists, but Manchester's attack, after a homeric contest in the garden of Shaw House, was decisively repulsed by Colonel George Lisle's brigade and some of his troops were chased back as far as Clay Hill. Even so, the numerical superiority of the Parliamentary army, now that it was fully engaged, would probably have won the day, had not darkness put an end to the battle.

The King, who had decided that morning that if he were attacked on both sides he would slip away to the north by night and try to regain Oxford, carried out his plan to the letter. He left his guns in Donnington Castle, and while he himself with an escort rode to join Prince Rupert at Bath, the army marched through the night, to Wallingford, reaching Oxford next day. Meanwhile the Roundheads were fast asleep, and when morning dawned were still ignorant of the departure of the royal army.

The ambitious plan of the Parliamentary commanders had failed.

Never before had they enjoyed a numerical advantage of nearly two to one, yet they had allowed the royal army to slip through their fingers.

The reasons are not far to seek.

In the first place the lack of an overall commander to co-ordinate their movements had robbed them of the advantage conferred by their numbers. Moreover an operation on exterior lines, such as this was, in essence demands resolute and bold action by the commanders of both columns, and it was lacking in each of them.

In the second place there is the timing of the afternoon attacks; that they were imperfectly synchronized we have seen. But in any case 3 p.m. was too late for 'zero-hour'. Moreover the Cavaliers were in considerable depth for after clearing the defences west of Speen, and then the village itself, there were the hedge positions bordering Speen-hamland.

Lastly the Cavaliers were allowed to escape through the 1,500 yard gap between Shaw House and Donnington Castle. During the night the whole Royalist army must have trooped across the little bridge over the river Lambourne in Donnington. A brigade of foot with some cavalry support could easily have cut this exit route, and at the same time watched Boys' garrison in Donnington Castle. The Royalists, their retreat cut off, would have run out of ammunition, and then 28 October might have seen a surrender yet more complete than the capitulation at Castle Dore. As it was Prince Maurice and Astley extricated the army – no mean feat of staff work – and got clear away.

If the Roundheads had won a victory they did little or nothing to prosecute it. The Council of War consulted at length as to their next move and Waller and Hazelrig were in favour of moving against Bath, so as to force the King to give battle or to drive him back to Bristol, while relieving Taunton. Letters passed between the generals and the Committee of Both Kingdoms, but little came of them except that it was agreed to keep the three armies together until the Cavaliers should go into winter quarters. The Roundheads lingered about Newbury, and contented themselves with summoning Donnington Castle threatening that they would not leave one stone on another, to which Sir John Boys (he had been knighted just before the battle) charac-teristically replied that 'he was not bound to repair it. . . .'

The King was far more active than his opponents, and by 2 November he was back in Oxford with 5,000 reinforcements. These with a strong detachment from the garrison of Oxford swelled his army to

15,000. At a muster on 6 November Prince Rupert was made Lieut.-General of all the King's armies in place of Brentford, who had been wounded at Newbury, and was now too old for active service.

It was now time to recover the train of artillery which had been parked under the walls of Donnington Castle at the end of the battle. Marching south on 6 November the Cavaliers reached Donnington Castle at 1 p.m. on the 9th. Some bickering followed, but the Roundheads refused battle. This bold and successful exploit by the new Royalist general made a painful impression on the Londoners.

On 19 November Sir Henry Gage with a party of 1,000 horse, each man carrying a bag of corn or other provisions on his saddle bows, relieved Basing. On the 23rd the King went into winter quarters.

The campaign of 1644 had ostensibly ended in a draw. But the King had achieved his objects: his army was intact, and indeed stronger than when it began; his three besieged garrisons were all safe. The Parliamentarians had no such cause for satisfaction and the bitterest recriminations now broke out among them. Essex's failure in Cornwall was quite forgotten; Manchester was the target for the shafts not only of Cromwell and the Independent officers whom he favoured, but by the Presbyterians Waller and Hazelrig. The unedifying details of the quarrel have been studied in detail elsewhere, and since they were as much political as military we will not discuss them here. The upshot, however, is important. The Parliament now decided to raise a New Model Army, a 'regular' army, which would never raise the cry of 'Home! Home!' but would see the war through to the end. A Self Denying Ordinance excluded Members of Parliament from holding military rank, and supreme, undivided command was given to Sir Thomas Fairfax, who despite his modesty and the fact that his battles had all been fought far from London, was recognized as the outstanding leader on the Parliament side.

CHAPTER 15

The New Model and Naseby

TWO AND A half years of war in which neither side had as yet obtained any decisive advantage had sharpened the temper of every ardent partisan, while inducing a marked degree of war-weariness in the more lukewarm. The majority of the Oxford Parliament, which met during the winter of 1644, was urgent for peace – so much so that the King, who valued the members' purses more than their opinions, ungraciously described them in a letter to the Queen as 'our mongrel Parliament. . . .'

A subtle change had been coming over Charles: always obstinate, he had in his earlier years vacillated between one policy and another, but now a fatalistic tenacity had taken hold of him. It may in part be attributed to the execution on 10 January of Archbishop Laud, long a helpless prisoner of the Parliament, for, since the execution of Strafford, his chief minister, in 1641, the King had been oppressed by a sense of guilt. He now felt that 'the hand of justice' was on his side. But even before Laud's death Charles had expressed his determination not to abandon the episcopacy 'nor that sword which God hath given into my hands'. The 1644 campaigns had proved to him that his sword was a sharper weapon than any wielded by his enemies.

It was *his* sword, for in 1644 Rupert, victorious at Newark, had met with disaster at Marston Moor, while Brentford, the compliant old professional on whose advice Charles had so long depended, had failed at Cheriton: only where Charles himself had commanded, at Cropredy Bridge and at Lostwithiel, had victory rewarded his Cavaliers. In 1644 Charles had twice been willing to offer pardon to his enemies, but now his private opinion (as delivered to Secretary Nicholas) was that his enemies 'were arrant rebels, and that their end must be damnation, ruin, and infamy. . . .' The King had hardened his heart.

On the Parliament side the English war-party had no more faith in negotiation than the King himself and while, during the winter, a treaty was in progress at Uxbridge pressed on with its plans for military reorganization.

It is time to look at the military situation on the eve of the campaign of 1645.

In the West Goring now commanded the Royalist field army. With it he laid siege to Taunton on 11 March. Plymouth, Gloucester, Weymouth, Wareham, and Poole were still held by Parliamentary garrisons, and since the Parliament still had command of the sea there was little danger to any of these save Gloucester.

In the North the Cavaliers still held Carlisle and a number of castles, but Newcastle had fallen to the Scots on 20 October 1644, and on 22 February 1645 Colonel Thomas Mytton had shaken the Royalists' hold on the upper Severn by surprising Shrewsbury.

In the Midlands the situation was practically unchanged, though Rupert's attempt to recapture Abingdon and restore the circle of garrisons round Oxford, was repulsed on 10 January.

The winter saw a slight improvement in the position of the Parliamentary armies, but they also had their difficulties – chiefly want of pay which had led to several mutinies and much plundering. In February even Cromwell's troops showed signs of disaffection. But at the beginning of April the New Model Army began to form at Windsor, and since, at long last, bitter experience had taught the Parliament that 'constant pay' is the sovereign means of ensuring discipline, the City of London had been persuaded to advance £80,000. By this stage in the war the Parliamentary cavalry had greatly improved and many regiments, besides Cromwell's, could hold their own with the Cavaliers. Their tactics too had improved. It was no longer the custom to advance slowly, firing pistols. Both sides had become accustomed to charge home.

The New Model was to consist of 11 regiments of horse, each 600 strong; one regiment of 1,000 dragoons; and 12 regiments of foot of 1,200 men each. The total was to be 22,000.

The army was formed out of those of Manchester, Essex, and Waller, who all gave up their commands, but there were not sufficient old soldiers to form the new regiments and compulsory enlistment had to be resorted to. The Committee of Both Kingdoms ordered the county committees only to press men 'of able bodies, and of years meet for their employment' and to see that they were well clothed. According to the French Ambassador young men were seized in the streets and carried off forcibly. In Kent men raised by such means mutinied, and had to be repressed by force of arms. The State was determined to have discipline in return for regular pay, and in Fairfax it had a general who could enforce it. There were enough old soldiers to teach the new men their trade, and the officers had been carefully selected from Puritans of the Independent persuasion.

As for the Royalist army, Monck when he was still serving the King once called it 'a rabble of gentility' and there was some truth in his taunt. By 1645 many regiments only consisted of 80 or 100 men, a high proportion being officers. There were also many commanders without troops, 'reformadoes' as they were called. Innumerable small garrisons held down the areas controlled by the Royalists, living off the country, guarding places of varying strategic importance, but contributing nothing positive to the winning of the war.

Pay was a thing seldom heard of; free quarters and plundering were becoming ever more common. Goring was proving less of a disciplinarian than Wilmot had been; even the dour Langdale was unable to prevent the excesses of his Northern troopers; pillage and rape marked their path when they passed through the West Riding on the way to relieve Pontefract in March. The King needed a New Model as much as his opponents did.

A new factor to be taken into account was the victorious career of Montrose. There is no room in these pages for the details of operations in Scotland. In the spring of 1644 James Graham, Marquis of Montrose, failed in an attempt upon the Lowlands. Making his way to York he met Rupert on the day after Marston Moor. It is scarcely surprising that he found no help in that quarter.

The true Cavalier spirit breathes in the Marquis' own verse:

> *He either fears his fate too much,*
> *Or his deserts are small,*
> *That puts it not unto the touch,*
> *To win or lose it all.*

– and that is precisely what Montrose did. Leaving Carlisle in August armed with a commission as Lieut.-General and accompanied by only two companions he 'invaded' Scotland, and joined forces with Alastair Macdonald, who had come over from Ireland in July with 1,600 of his clan.

Montrose defeated three armies in turn and on 2 February 1645 cut up Clan Campbell at Inverlochy under the eyes of its chief, Argyle. Next day Montrose wrote to the King: 'I doubt not before the end of this summer I shall be able to come to your Majesty's assistance with a brave army, which . . . will make the rebels in England as well as in Scotland feel just rewards of rebellion.' This dispatch arrived while the futile Treaty of Uxbridge was still dragging on, and encouraged Charles in his obduracy.

Fortified by his new-found belief in his own generalship the King now proceeded to deprive himself of the presence of most of his principal officers and advisers. Those who disagreed with his Irish policy, Hopton, Capel, Culpeper, and Hyde, were sent with Prince Charles to Bristol to act as a Council for the West; Astley went to winter with his infantry in Gloucestershire; Maurice to relieve Chester and Langdale to relieve Pontefract. In March Prince Rupert, although he was now General of all the Royalist armies, was sent to Ludlow to support his brother's operations and to prepare the way for an advance northwards, which was to be the summer campaign. During the early months of 1645 Charles' chief adviser was that gifted intriguer Lord Digby who, it will be recalled, had become Secretary of State on the death of Falkland. Digby was determined to ruin Prince Rupert and the latter, who had no illusions on that point, was quite unable to conceal his distrust of the unscrupulous courtier who now had his uncle's ear.

Prince Rupert's plan was that the King should bring the train of artillery from Oxford to Worcester, prior to a thrust northwards to relieve Chester. Recruits could then be raised in Lancashire and Yorkshire, and it might even be possible to stretch out a hand to Montrose, whose victory at Inverlochy had necessitated the return of many of Leven's soldiers to Scotland.

The King lingered at Oxford, and although Maurice temporarily relieved Chester on 19 February, little could be achieved without the King's central army.

Meanwhile in the Severn Valley, Rupert was engaged with the enterprising Massey who with 900 horse and foot had occupied Ledbury, 17 miles north-west of Gloucester.

From his headquarters at Hereford Rupert marched under cover of night, capturing the Parliamentary scouts on the way, and surprised Massey at daybreak (22 April). The latter, as at Ripple Field, fought stoutly in adversity, covering the retreat of his foot with his cavalry, but after half an hour's fighting the Cavaliers drove him out of Ledbury, and caught up with his infantry who suffered severely.

After some petty operations in the West under Waller Cromwell had at last received his first independent command – and he found it very much to his taste. He was about to lay down his commission in consequence of the terms of the Self-denying Ordinance, when Parliament ordered him to take his brigade into the Oxford area in order to frustrate the Royalist plan to transfer their artillery into the Severn Valley.

Although he failed to surprise Northampton's regiment at Islip on 23 April, Cromwell found means to ferry his force across the Cherwell, and when next day the Earl fell upon him with three regiments of horse he routed them, killing 40 and taking 200 prisoners and 400 horses.

On 24 April Cromwell who had no infantry with him, and but few dragoons, bluffed the unfortunate Governor of Bletchingdon House into surrender. Colonel Francis Windebank, son of Charles' former Secretary of State, though he had fought bravely at Cheriton, was unnerved by the presence of his young wife. He was condemned to death at Oxford and even Rupert's intervention could not persuade the King to reprieve him – though Charles, with a characteristic twinge of conscience, later granted the widow a pension, which he had little enough money to pay.

Cromwell then moved westwards, and after a stout resistance captured 200 Royalist foot at Bampton in the Bush (18 miles west of Oxford) on 27 April. Things were going so well that he now decided to try his luck at Faringdon Castle (29 April). Summoned to surrender, Lieut.-Colonel Roger Burges replied briefly: 'You are not now at Bletchingdon', and when Cromwell attempted to storm the place beat him off with loss. *Mercurius Aulicus'* claim that 200 Roundheads were killed is probably too high, but there is in existence a letter, unusually subdued in tone, which Oliver wrote to the Royalist Governor: 'Sir, There shall be no interruption of your viewing and gathering together the dead bodies, and I do acknowledge it as a favour, your willingness to let me dispose of them'; he goes on to thank Burges for his civility to the prisoners he had taken and to discuss their exchange. But if his raid had ended in a bloody repulse, it had achieved a great deal. There were no longer enough draught horses left around Oxford for the King to move his artillery even had he wished to.

o

Cromwell showed by the vigour of these operations that the 'winter of his discontent' was passed. With Manchester gone, the mood in which he had fought at second Newbury was dispelled. The New Model was to know a new Cromwell.

Meanwhile the New Model was putting the finishing touches to its training, and by the end of April the Committee of Both Kingdoms adjudged that it was ready to take the field.

Fairfax was accordingly ordered to relieve Taunton, and on 30 April, he set out with 11,000 men. By 7 May he had reached Blandford.

On that day Charles left Oxford, despite the efforts of Cromwell to prevent it, joining Prince Rupert's army next day at Stow-on-the-Wold. On the same day Goring, who had also been summoned to join the King, captured 40 of Cromwell's horse near Burford. This success served to magnify his reputation at a time when his independent command was in danger. Altogether the King had about 5,000 foot and 6,000 horse.

The Royalist Council of War now debated whether to pursue their march north or to fall on Fairfax. Rupert, Langdale, and the Northern Horse were for the former plan; the Prince being eager to avenge Marston Moor, and Langdale's men anxious to deliver their home country from Lord Fairfax and the Scots. On the other hand Goring, Digby, and others were equally eager to try conclusions with the New Model and it may well be that they were right. But by this time the rivalry in the Royalist camp was so bitter that instead of agreeing on one plan or the other the King weakly decided to allow Goring to return into the West: the remainder, reinforced by various garrisons, were to pursue the northern project.

While Charles' strategy was bedevilled by the quarrels of his generals, that of Fairfax was still dictated by the Committee of Both Kingdoms. This arrangement was unlikely to work well. The Committee had to weigh its intelligence, make a decision, and then, as often as not, get it passed by the Houses. Only then could it send its orders to the New Model – which was getting farther and farther away with every day's march. By the time a plan reached Fairfax it was liable to be out of date. When Taunton was relieved on 11 May the Committee made Oxford the next objective. While Fairfax was besieging that City Leven was to march south to combat the King. But meanwhile Montrose had defeated Sir John Urry (now a Covenanter!) at Auldearn on 9 May and consequently Leven abandoned all intention of coming south. Marching into Westmorland he posted his army so as to prevent the possibility of Charles joining Montrose.

It was on 21 May that Fairfax appeared before Oxford and next day Secretary Nicholas wrote to the King that the City was not well provisioned. Ignoring this warning the Royalists marched on Leicester in order to relieve the pressure on Oxford. The town was not strongly fortified, and the garrison was weak; nevertheless a summons was rejected. Rupert's batteries soon made a breach through which the Cavaliers stormed on the night of the 30th, pillaging the shops and houses, but sparing all save about 100 of the defenders who fell in the fighting.

The fall of Leicester caused consternation in the Parliamentary ranks. The horrors of the storm were exaggerated – one officer compared it with the sack of Magdeburg in the Thirty Years' War when thousands were done to death.

In this crisis the Committee of Both Kingdoms displayed great resolution. After their routine meeting on 1 June messengers set out from Derby House, carrying their commands in every direction. Sir Samuel Luke at Newport Pagnell was authorized to call in the country to defend the place, and to fetch in provisions. Sir Thomas Fairfax was to be in readiness to march, but meanwhile was to continue with his siege at Oxford.

Charles had galvanized his foes into activity, but he himself now displayed a lamentable irresolution.

It was the old story of divided councils, Rupert adhering to his original plan while Digby still advocated an attack on the New Model which was to be followed by the invasion of the Eastern Association, whence Parliament derived so much of its support. In consequence the King lingered about Daventry, while collecting supplies for the relief of Oxford.

On 5 June Fairfax broke up from before Oxford and marched north-east to Newport Pagnell. From this time forth the Roundheads out-manoeuvred the King. This change was due to three events that followed in three successive days. On 8 June, Fairfax's council of war resolved to make the Royalist army their fixed objective. On the 9th, Parliament gave their general a completely free hand in conducting his operations; and on the 10th Oliver Cromwell was definitely appointed to the New Model army as Fairfax's lieutenant-general or second-in-command. A new spirit of enterprise and clear-cut policy was thenceforth visible in the Parliamentary ranks.

The Battle of Naseby, 14 June 1645

On 12 June, Fairfax, pursuant to his new plan, advanced by the south of Northampton to Kislingbury, eight miles east of Daventry, driving in the royal picquets. The King was at that moment not prepared to fight in the open, and breaking up his camp, he retreated hurriedly by night 18 miles north-east to Market Harborough, *en route* for Newark. Fairfax spotted the move betimes and set off in pursuit next day, the 13th. By nightfall he had reached Guilsborough, four miles south of Naseby, while his vanguard entered Naseby and captured some Cavalier patrols feasting at a long table in the inn.[1]

This startling news was brought to the King in the middle of the night. He rose and called a council which met in the early hours of June 14th. It was decided that the enemy was too close upon their heels to avoid a fight, so it was resolved to hold the high ground two miles to the south of the town as a defensive position. This position ran from East Farndon to Oxendon, extending for two miles. As it covered the road from Naseby it formed a very strong position, just made for the purpose. Here the Cavalier army was drawn up well before 8 a.m. From it the view to the south was not impeded by the tall hedges and numerous trees that now abound, and the ridge immediately to the north of Naseby was in full view. So also must have been a number of hostile horsemen on the ridge at about that time. But either because they were only a few in number or because the light was bad, Rupert sent his scoutmaster to report on the disposition of the enemy. This feeble individual came back shortly afterwards declaring that he had been two or three miles forward and could see no enemy. Rupert disbelieved this report, and did the obvious thing a young, energetic commander would do under such circumstances – he went forward himself, taking with him a body of horse.

Fairfax broke up camp shortly after 3 a.m. and at the moment when the Royalists were ascending the East Farndon ridge he was ascending the Naseby ridge, four miles to the south. Each army discerned the motions of the other, though dimly.

It was now evident to Fairfax that the King, contrary to expectation, had arrested his retreat; but it was not yet clear whether he was merely awaiting attack on the East Farndon ridge, or whether he intended himself to attack. As a preliminary precaution Fairfax decided to occupy a position covering Naseby, and rode forward,

---

[1] This table is now kept in the north aisle of the church.

accompanied by his lieutenant-general to reconnoitre for such a position. Crossing the ridge-top he dropped down into the valley. The
ground was boggy and a little stream crossed the road, about a mile
south of Clipston. Fairfax was contemplating occupying this position,
covered by the stream and the boggy ground, when Cromwell inter-
vened. The enemy seemed to be strong in cavalry, he observed, but
this was no cavalry ground. Rupert, he sensed, would either turn the
position or else remain on the defensive on the high ground to the
north, declining battle. This would not fit in with the Parliamentary
plans; it would be better to occupy the ridge in rear, he urged; this
would tempt Rupert across the valley and he would be obliged to
charge uphill at them.

Fairfax saw the force of the contention, and agreed to it. At this
moment his army was strung out on the line of march, the rear portion
being still in column of route, gradually closing up to the rendezvous
near the village. Here the head of the army had halted.

Thus it came about that, at the moment when Rupert with his
escort of horse was approaching Clipston, Fairfax with his escort was
withdrawing up the hill to the Naseby ridge. Rupert, seeing this
retrograde movement, imagined quite naturally that the enemy were
going to occupy the ridge. At the same time he took note of the boggy
ground beyond Clipston in front of the hostile position, and decided,
as Cromwell had foreseen, that it would not do to commit his cavalry
to such ground. From the ridge to the north of Clipston, however, he
could see what looked more promising terrain away to the right, by
which his horse might ascend the Naseby ridge. It would be in the
nature of a flanking movement, and would give him the windward
position, no mean advantage in the days of black powder. Sending back
an urgent message to the army to follow in his tracks, Prince Rupert
therefore struck off to his right, and hit the Sibbertoft–Naseby road
probably near point 571, one mile south of the village.

Rupert's flanking move was spotted from the Naseby ridge and
Fairfax divined his intention. In order to forestall him he decided to
side-step to the same flank. The result of this decision was that both
armies were by 9 o'clock moving westwards on almost parallel lines –
a curious and almost unique manoeuvre for two armies on the eve of
battle. This move involved a side-step of about one mile for the leading
troops. This brought them to an open valley between the two ridges,
where the valley was at its shallowest and the slope at its most gentle.
At this point, now called Broadmoor, there is no stream, for it is on

the great 'divide' of England. Here both armies decided at the same
moment to stand and take up position.

It forms a fine site for a battle,[1] with two parallel ridges, now joined
by the modern Sibbertoft–Naseby road along the invisible 'divide', the
Avon having its sources just to the west of the road, and the Ise
(flowing into the Wash) to the east.

Midway down the slope on which the Parliamentary army formed

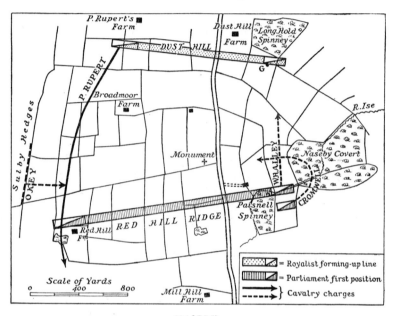

NASEBY

up there was a ledge of level ground. Except that the ground on the
eastern portion of the field was pitted with rabbit warrens and furze
bushes, the ground there was much the same in appearance as it is
today.

It was just in front of this ledge that the Parliamentary army was at

[1] Until quite recently no monument indicated to the traveller that he was
passing over a famous field (for the so-called Naseby Obelisk, erected in 1825,
is a good mile from the site of the battle). The Cromwell Association have now
erected a memorial to commemorate the charge of Oliver Cromwell, but this,
though useful to attract the attention of the passer-by, is some 500 yards west
of the correct site.

first arrayed by Skippon (see sketch-map on p. 200). Fairfax, however, came up and decided to withdraw the line behind the ledge, whilst it was being marshalled, in order not to proclaim his dispositions to the enemy.

This incident is of significance as it shows (what some of the sources seem to deny) that the Roundheads started to take up their position before the Cavaliers. If it had been the other way, Fairfax's withdrawal behind the ledge would have been pointless, for it would have been too late.

This brings us to the Royalist army. We have seen how Rupert sent a messenger back from Clipston, calling the whole army forward. It followed pretty closely in his own footsteps and was seen by the enemy at intervals as it crossed the crests. On reaching the Sibbertoft road, where Rupert had been waiting for it for an hour, it turned south and found itself on the Dust Hill ridge. From here the advanced troops of the hostile army could be seen straight across the valley. If Rupert had had hopes of turning the hostile flank and coming upon them from the west along the top of the ridge, he must have been disappointed, for he had been forestalled. A frontal attack, straight across Broadmoor Valley, was the only course left to him. Still, this terrain was a great improvement on the Clipston position, the ground being firmer and the slope up which his horse would probably have to charge being much more gentle. In short, Prince Rupert was justified in being satisfied with the position.

As soon as the Royalist army reached Dust Hill, Lord Astley proceeded to deploy the foot in line of battle whilst Prince Rupert marshalled the horse. Rupert himself took the right wing cavalry, Lord Astley commanded the infantry in the centre, while the cavalry on the left were under Sir Marmaduke Langdale. Owing to the sudden move from East Farndon most of the guns had been left behind; a few light pieces (Sakers) however, did manage to join in the battle.

The extreme right flank was about 200 yards west of the present Prince Rupert's Farm, i.e. 1,000 yards to the right of the road. The left flank probably rested on the southern tip of Long Hold Spinney, 600 yards from the road. Thus the total front was nearly one mile. For an army of slightly over 9,000 (5,000 horse and 4,000 foot) this was quite as wide as desirable, and did not allow of a strong reserve. For reserve the King mustered about 900 horse and 700 foot. The King's own post would be near Dust Hill Farm, whence he could get a good general view of the field.

The Parliamentary army was drawn up in the same formation and on the same frontage, except for one detail on the western flank. The ground falls away rather sharply to the right, and is what the French call *accidenté*. Cromwell, who commanded the cavalry on this side, probably formed up his horse in consequence slightly behind the infantry line in order to keep to the higher ground. The infantry in the centre, under Major-General Skippon, were (when drawn back) just behind Red Hill ridge. The cavalry on the left were under Ireton, the Commissary-General. Their left rested just short of the Sulby hedges. Behind Sulby hedges Cromwell placed 1,000 dragoons under Colonel Okey. This was a striking disposition since they were in front of the general line of battle, and perpendicular to it. Their object was to enfilade Rupert's horse when they charged. Very nice, but very risky; for if Rupert 'fetched a compass' the dragoons might find themselves enfiladed, or even taken in reverse. Not only were Okey's dragoons perpendicular to the line, and out on an exposed flank, but they were well in advance of the line. It is clear from Okey's own account that they were not fully deployed when the battle commenced, and in addition some dragoons were necessarily employed as horse-holders.

Fairfax had all his guns up, but, remembering the small effect they had at Marston Moor, he did not rely on them, and they played an insignificant part in the battle.

By 10 a.m. both armies were ranged in battle order, over half a mile apart, the Broadmoor Valley separating them. Which would make the first move? At Edgehill the Royalists had deliberately forsaken their commanding position and had attacked; at Marston Moor their opponents had done the same thing. Considering that the King's army was so weak in numbers it would have been natural for him to stand on the defensive, and probably Lord Astley desired this course. But the impulsive Rupert once again decided the issue. With or without the concurrence of Astley he prevailed upon the King to order a general attack. It is more difficult to determine what Fairfax's real intention was. He must have seen the hostile advance from its start, and might have stood his ground on the 'ledge'. But he did in fact advance his line down the hill below the ledge. Was this in order to meet the enemy on the move, or merely to reoccupy his original line just in front of the ledge? It is impossible to say, but the latter seems the more likely, for his cavalry on both flanks made no sign of attacking at first. We must conclude that the battle was in essence an attack by the Cavaliers on the Roundheads. The chronology of this, as of all battles, is vague, and most writers assume that the first episode was the charge of Rupert's horse. It is more likely that Rupert on this occasion allowed the foot to come to 'push of pike' at the same time as, if not before, he himself obtained contact. Seated on his horse near the present Prince Rupert Farm, he could see perfectly the progress of the infantry across the valley and up the gentle slopes to the hedge where the new memorial now stands. A few seconds later he would see the Roundheads streaming forward over the crest beyond it. The two lines of foot were almost at grips. The moment for action had come!

Sinking the hill and trotting across the valley in two lines, his cavalry would be abreast of their infantry in a very few minutes. At the foot of the slope Rupert momentarily drew rein, either to give his horses a breather before charging up hill, or to allow the infantry on his left to get farther forward. Opposed to him were Ireton's horse, almost twice the strength of his own. Rupert's charge went a bit wide of the infantry line, however it kept inside the Sulby hedges, from whence it received a ragged fire which did not impede or divert the charge. Sweeping up the gentle slope at an increased pace, his first line crashed into the left of Ireton's line about Redhill Farm. Rupert, accompanied by his brother, led the first line, the Earl of Northampton the second, and the clash with Ireton's troops occurred half way up the hill. The Roundheads seemed undecided as to their course of action; some advanced to meet the enemy head-on; others preferred to halt and give battle in a stationary position. Whichever they did the result was the same – a static sword-fight – for this was no Edgehill charge; these were no raw troops but trained men, and Marston Moor had lowered the reputation of Rupert's troopers. How long the mêlée lasted no man can say, but eventually the swordsmanship of the Cavaliers prevailed, the opposition dwindled, individuals began to slip away, the rot set in and Prince Rupert gathering up his men, resumed his victorious advance, sweeping the remnants of the enemy before them. After covering a good mile in this way Rupert suddenly saw the Parliamentary wagon-laager in a hollow depression to the west of Naseby village.

The camp guard, however, put up a sturdy resistance, and valuable time was lost by the Cavalier horsemen in attempting to capture it. Mindful of his experience at Edgehill under similar circumstances, Rupert drew rein and exerted himself to collect his troopers and lead them back to the battle. This, as always, was a difficult and lengthy task, and the best part of an hour elapsed before he reappeared on the field, at the head of his victorious horse.

In this short space of time two crises had been witnessed elsewhere. The first was in the centre. In spite of the fact that they had the slope of the hill against them, the Royalist foot managed to push their opponents back over the crest in a retreat which soon began to have the aspect of flight. Skippon himself was wounded and the position had suddenly become critical. Fairfax saw his left wing dispersed and now his centre was giving way. In such a critical situation in the heat of battle Fairfax was at his best. Flinging forward his reserves, and entering the turmoil himself 'Fiery Tom' managed to bring the Royalist onset to a halt.

But this was not all. The weight of Rupert's attack had struck the left or centre of Ireton's command; only the fringe of it took in his extreme right, and when the charge swept on, this remnant was left fairly intact; and Ireton himself was with it. At some moment, probably as the mêlée was nearing its end, an episode occurred that may have had some influence on the issue.

We have seen how Astley's foot had gradually pushed back their opponents, fighting their way up the hill. As they did so their extreme right flank began to pass Ireton's extreme right. The youthful Commissary-General, seeing Skippon's infantry hard pressed, wheeled his troopers to the right and charged straight into the open flank of Astley's veterans.

The latter, momentarily taken aback, quickly recovered themselves and facing to the right beat off their mounted assailants with musket-stock and pike. Ireton, dashing into the midst of his enemies, was wounded, unhorsed, and taken prisoner. Leaderless, the Roundhead horse drew back defeated.

Of this exploit Gardiner coldly remarks that Ireton was 'distracted from his proper work'. Was he? One cannot be positive without much more knowledge than we possess of the situation and of the precise moment when this occurred, for we have to rely for the details on a single chronicler, the chaplain Sprigge, who was a mile away in the wagon-laager.

It is certainly possible that Ireton's sudden intervention turned the scales and helped to win the battle, for the Parliamentary centre was passing through a critical stage. Skippon as we have seen had been wounded and Fairfax was feverishly throwing in his reserves to stabilize the situation. Ireton's diversion may well have been 'the last straw' that brought the Royalist attack to a standstill.

However that may be, Ireton's initiative shows that he possessed the qualities of a leader – quickness of perception, instant decision, personal gallantry and the ability to convey totally unexpected orders to his men whose attention, heretofore, had been fixed on an entirely different foe.

Another sparkling episode followed close on top of Ireton's. When Rupert's horsemen had swept past them Okey's dragoons 'gave up ourselves for lost men', for an isolated body of Royalist horse was also attacking their rear. However, Rupert had disappeared, and now Okey perceived the action of Ireton's horse against the Royalist foot, and recovering his head and showing a like initiative, he mounted his dragoons and charged the enemy – an interesting and early example of the gradual merging of dragoons (mounted infantry) into cavalry.

Even now the cup of the Royalist infantry was not full. On the other side of the field Cromwell, as we have seen, had drawn up his horse somewhere to the rear and well up the hill. From this vantage point he calmly watched an attack developing. Langdale's troopers were threading their way through furze bushes and rabbit warrens at the bottom of the hill. As they began to breast the rather steep rise Cromwell gave the signal, at exactly the right moment, and Whalley's horse thundered down the hill in greatly superior numbers and in an irresistible charge. No mounted troops alive could withstand a mounted attack over such ground if it was pushed with resolution. Langdale's horse were swept off the field, with the leading three of Cromwell's regiments in hot pursuit. Now came the dramatic moment of the battle. We have seen twice in the case of Rupert's horse how they disappeared from the field despite what the Prince could do to stop them. But Cromwell did stop the bulk of his horse and retained them on the field. How are we to account for the difference? The usual course is to dismiss the matter with the observation that Cromwell's men were better disciplined. But quite another explanation can be advanced.

It seems, then (though the details of the charge are, as always, obscure) that whilst the left of the line under Whalley drove back Langdale's, the right of Cromwell's front line (under Rossiter), outflanked the Royalists and wheeled to their left, thus facing the exposed left flank of the Royalist foot. Meanwhile Cromwell's second and third lines remained halted behind their general, for Oliver outnumbered Langdale by nearly two to one; and his first line alone had sufficed to defeat Langdale.

Cromwell therefore sat stationary at the head of his second lines until he saw the upshot of Whalley's charge. This would be a matter of minutes and as the victorious horse galloped off the field in much the same manner as had Rupert's only a few moments previously on the opposite flank, Cromwell seeing his opportunity, wheeled his second, followed by his third line, to their left, appreciably without advancing. This would bring their left flank on to the spot now marked by the northern edge of Paisnell Spinney, whence they would be in prolongation of the line of Royalist infantry. Hence an advance to their new front would take them straight into the Cavaliers' exposed flank, albeit charging slightly uphill. During this operation Rossiter's men would, of course, be on their right flank.

It was at this point, no doubt, that Cromwell's personal part in the battle was played. He launched his second and third lines to the attack in a series of waves.[1] In a curiously unnoticed passage, 'A gentleman of Publicke Employment' (probably Rushworth) explains the reason for this success. 'That which made our horses so terrible to them was the thickness of our reserves, and their orderly and timely coming on, and not one failing to come on in time.'

The devoted Royalist infantry, who up to date had given such a good account of themselves against odds, and against the ground, were now beset on three sides. They began to give way and soon found themselves back in the valley.

Only one thing could now save them – intervention by the King's reserve. Charles realized this himself and started to lead them forward towards the left flank. One can easily imagine this movement, starting from near Dust Hill Farm and passing along the front edge of Longhold Spinney. When the head had reached the eastern end of the spinney, the Earl of Carnwarth seized the bridle of the King's horse, exclaiming: 'Will you go upon your death?' Charles was quite ready, if need be, to go upon his death, but at that moment some unknown person shouted: 'March to the right' (in other words, in the reverse

---

[1] We have accorded the credit for initiating the great charge to Cromwell, but it is possible, if not probable, that the order or inspiration originated with Fairfax. 'Fiery Tom' seems to have been everywhere he was wanted during the battle (like the Duke of Wellington at Waterloo); he must have been in the vicinity as he himself took part in the charge, and must therefore have approved of the movement. Like Granby at Warburg, he galloped about the field so fast that his hat blew off and he finished the battle bare-headed.

direction). The cry was passed down the ranks and the whole body of horse turned files about and rode off at a rapid pace. Now, as we have frequently noticed, it is a difficult matter to halt or control a body of cavalry from the rear. The King was now in the rear, and it speaks well for his control of the reserve that in a space of 400 yards he managed to pull them up. By this time they were back nearly where they had started from, and it was still perfectly feasible to return to the charge. But for some unrecorded reason Charles did not do so. The presumption is that his councillors overbore him; but it is useless to speculate. What, however, should be noted is the unfair way history has treated the Royal reserve. Gardiner, for example, asserts without a particle of evidence that they 'rode hurriedly' to the rear in what he calls a 'flight'. They did no such thing, they merely returned to the centre of the line. A recent account goes so far as to assert that they 'fled from the field'.

A curious lull now set in over the field. The Royalist infantry were by this time practically surrounded, for some of Cromwell's surplus horsemen had swept round their rear. The King witnessed, as an impotent spectator, the tragedy that was now enacted in the valley some 600 yards in front of him. It was the end of his infantry – and for all practical purposes the end of his reign. Surrounded and left to their fate by their cavalry the remnant of the regiments of foot one by one laid down their arms. Their ammunition had doubtless all been expended and their case was quite hopeless. All fought it out to the end, extracting the reluctant admiration of their opponents thereby.

It must have been during this sad episode that Rupert led back to the field the greater part of his cavalry. He would have liked to put all to the touch with one final desperate charge. Desperate it would have been, and the upshot not in doubt; for by now his horse were wearied and not in a condition to sustain a rapid gallop. Occasions when the same cavalry charge twice within a short period are few in number. Rupert's horse were not equal to this supreme test and the Prince was constrained, like his uncle, to gaze upon the tragedy, a hopeless eyewitness, powerless to intervene.

After the last regiment had laid down its arms, and Fairfax, having methodically marshalled his infantry, began to move forward once more, the King recognizing that the end was come, turned his horse and rode from the field.

Oliver Cromwell conducted a pursuit of 18 miles to the gates of Leicester.

The Royalists lost their 4,000 foot almost to a man, and their 12 guns. The cavalry too suffered heavily. Many of the infantry were taken prisoner, but several regiments, notably Rupert's Bluecoats, fought to the end like Newcastle's Whitecoats at Marston Moor.

The Parliamentary losses are not known, but Ireton's men and Skippon's too must have suffered severely, the two commanders themselves being numbered among the casualties.

The defeat may be attributed, at least in part to the disastrous decision, to detach Goring's 3,000 horse, a decision comparable to the parting of Essex and Waller in 1644 – and taken curiously enough, as Gardiner has pointed out, at the same place: Stow-on-the-Wold.

As a consequence of this detachment of Goring the disparity in numbers was greater than at any other major battle of the War. Thus the popular belief that the Roundhead victory was primarily due to the creation of the New Model is as ill-founded as the equally popular belief that Cromwell was its creator. The fact is, its Parliamentary foot (the majority of whom were conscripts) were out-fought by the King's veteran infantry. Nevertheless the victory set the New Model on its feet and was of good augury for the future.

CHAPTER 16

After Naseby

NASEBY HAD SHOWN that in the New Model Fairfax had the makings of a formidable army. Moreover, Parliament still had two other armies in the field. These smaller local armies were those of the Western Association, formed under Major-General Massey, and of the seven associated northern counties under Colonel-General Sydenham Poyntz – a professional soldier who had recently returned to England after serving in Holland and Germany.

Besides the three English armies the Committee of Both Kingdoms still had the Scots at their disposal. Leven, realizing that Charles no longer threatened to invade Scotland, had marched back from Westmorland and moving through Yorkshire had by 20 June got as far south as Mansfield in Nottinghamshire.

Although the King still had about 4,000 cavalry it was only with the utmost difficulty that he scraped together 3,000 foot, and these naturally were not to be compared with the homogeneous body destroyed at Naseby. It is true that in South Wales General Gerard still commanded a force some 3,000 strong, but that was more than counterbalanced by Massey's army. Byron at Chester was hemmed in by Sir Thomas Middleton and Sir William Brereton, the one commanding in North Wales, the other in Cheshire. Both – like Cromwell – had been allowed to continue in arms despite the Self-denying Ordinance.

It is not an exaggeration to say that the Royalists had now only one army left to pit against the New Model – namely the Western army under Goring.

There can be little question that the best course still open to the King was to march into Somerset and build up his field army by combining Goring's men with his own. Only by such a concentration of his remaining strength could he achieve any considerable success. There was little to prevent such a move, for Fairfax, instead of pursuing his beaten foe, sat down before Leicester, which fell to him on 18 June. Next day Charles entered Hereford.

There was now nothing to prevent the King either marching to Goring's assistance, or at the least holding Massey in check. Goring was still held up before Taunton, but it was thought that once that place was captured he could advance to join the King, who would then have an army of 6,000 horse and perhaps 8,000 foot. However, this was to reckon without Robert Blake, who had stubbornly held Lyme against Prince Maurice in 1644 and was now putting up a heroic resistance at Taunton. Goring in fact had his hands full.

In London there was popular clamour for the relief of Taunton, and Fairfax now resolved to make the attempt. He had already got as far south as Marlborough when this decision was made. The date was 28 June, and he had done the 113 miles from Leicester in a week.

Fairfax could not be sure how long Taunton would hold out and he decided to take no risks, but to march to its relief with the maximum speed. This was all the more necessary inasmuch as the direct route was barred by several Royalist garrisons – Devizes, Bath, Bristol, Bridgwater. Fairfax therefore elected to approach from the south, at the same time changing his base for supplies to the ports of Lyme and Weymouth.

On Monday, 30 June, the forced march began. Twenty miles were covered the first day and the army billeted in Amesbury that night. Next day the army marched out to Stonehenge and then south-west to Bower Chalk (seven miles west of Salisbury). On Wednesday Blandford was reached. On Friday the army was at Beaminster (seven miles south of Crewkerne), having come via Dorchester. This represented a five days' march at 17 miles per day – in hot weather too. Here totally unexpected news reached it: Goring had suddenly abandoned the siege of Taunton and marched towards Yeovil.

Unfortunately nearly all the eyewitnesses' accounts of this campaign come from the Parliamentary side, and the brilliant but unpredictable Goring has not left us his own account. We are thus reduced to guessing what was in his mind at any given moment, and his movements were on the surface so curious that we are left very much to conjecture. It is, however, fairly safe to presume that the reason for abandoning the siege was the news of the approach of Fairfax, for the Roundhead could muster 14,000 men, when General Massey's army in the west had joined it, whilst the Cavaliers were slightly less than half this number. But why, having abandoned the siege, did he march right across the front of the pursuing army and occupy a line that laid Bridgwater open to the enemy's attack? For the line he took up was that of the river Yeo from Langport to Yeovil, a wide front of 12 miles in a straight line, but much more measured along the windings of the river. True the Yeo was only fordable in places and there were only three bridges in this sector, those of Load Bridge (opposite Long Sutton), Ilchester, and Yeovil. But a long river line is a difficult thing to hold, as military history abundantly shows.

Fairfax on 5 July concentrated his infantry at Crewkerne, opposite the centre of this line and distant 10 miles from it, while he sent his cavalry forward to gain touch with the enemy. Following them himself, and taking Cromwell with him, the Roundhead leader made a personal reconnaissance of the hostile position along the river Yeo. Finding all the bridges down, he decided that the line could not be rushed, and that a concerted plan must be made.

Next day, Sunday, the main army rested (Fairfax always rested on the Sabbath whenever possible). Meanwhile outlying contingents were continuing to come in. On Monday the 7th Sir Thomas made another reconnaissance, after which he assembled a council of war. It was decided that the infantry should force the crossing of the river on the right, at Yeovil, while the cavalry watched the remainder of the front. This was done, the weak Royalist detachment in Yeovil fell back without fighting and the river line was gained without firing a shot. Again we cannot say what was Goring's intention, and whether Yeovil was given up by his orders or not. Ilchester also was abandoned, the Royalist army concentrating on Langport.

That night Goring, upset no doubt by a disaster to some of his best troops, decided to fall back on Bridgwater. But it was to be done in an orderly manner and in his own time. The slowest moving units must start first — the baggage and the guns. He estimated that he could, if necessary, hold out in his strong position on the eastern outskirts of the town during daylight without the support of artillery, except for two small pieces that he ordered to stay behind. The artillery departed early on the morning of 10 July, and the remainder of the army took up position to defend themselves. This position must now be described.

The Battle of Langport. 10 July 1645

Goring by a clever piece of deception had made as if to march on Taunton. Thereby he induced Fairfax to detach a force of 4,000, which wandered down the road towards Taunton with the result that

P

when on 10 July battle was joined the Parliamentary commander only had 10,000 of his 14,000 men, while Goring was at full strength, nearly 7,000.

The little town of Langport lies on slightly rising ground on the north bank of the rivers Parrett and Yeo at their point of junction.

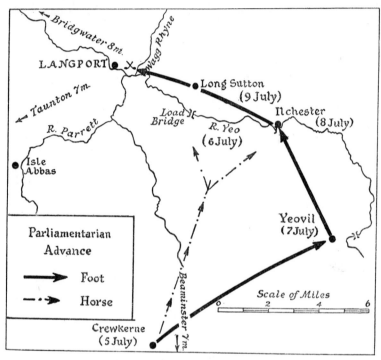

THE LANGPORT CAMPAIGN

One thousand yards east of the town is the church of Huish Episcopi with its beautiful lofty tower. From its summit a splendid view can be obtained of the battlefield. The Royalist position ran along the west side of a little brook sometimes called the Wagg Rhyne that runs through Pibsbury Bottom and crosses the Long Sutton road about 700 yards east of the church. The slope down to the brook is very gentle and is equally so up the far (east) side. But farther to the left, or north, it is steeper and the watercourse runs through a slight ravine, thus making it a fair obstacle to mounted troops. On the day of the battle a good deal of water was coming down, and the ford by which the road crossed the brook was exaggeratedly described as 'up to the horses' girths'.

The country beyond the brook was open, but on the near side it was enclosed, and the road was lined with hedges. Royalist musketeers occupied these hedges and others along the line of Pibsbury Bottom, while cavalry were posted on the slight ridge in rear, and the two guns were brought into action at the top of the slope covering the ford (or 'pass' as it was called in all contemporary accounts). The right flank was covered by the deep river Yeo. Thus the position was a fairly strong one. Lord Goring placed himself at the head of the horse overlooking the 'pass', and awaited events with apparent confidence.

In the other camp a council of war had been held in the early morning, the problem being how to bring the Cavaliers to battle. Whilst the council was in session, however, news was brought that they were evidently intending to hold their ground, so the problem was solved. All that remained was to decide on the plan of attack.

The rival commanders were agreed in one thing – the key to the position was the pass. We may wonder why this should be so, for the infantry at least could have crossed the Pibsbury Bottom anywhere, and there does not seem any reason why the Royalist position could not have been turned from the north. But when both commanders are agreed there must be some compelling reason, hidden from the modern historian, that ruled out these two expedients. Everything therefore centred on the pass. Goring's measures to defend it seemed adequate; Fairfax's measures to attack it were equally thorough. His first step was to silence the two cannons that commanded the pass. This was a comparatively easy matter; the Roundhead guns were deployed in a line along the ridge that runs parallel to the Wagg Rhyne and a few hundred yards from it. The position is quite obvious. From here the range to the two lone guns was about 700 yards. An overwhelming fire was concentrated upon these unfortunate pieces, 'the cannon playing their part as gallantly as ever I saw gunners in my life', declared the enthusiastic Colonel Lilburne, though it was a one-sided duel. By noon the Royalist artillery was silent and the next step was put in hand. This was an infantry attack on the hostile musketeers lining the hedges and the pass itself. A hot and stubborn contest developed, lasting a good hour before the Roundheads effected a crossing of the stream and a firm lodgment on the far side to the north of the road.

Now was the time for the decisive operation of the day, one which everything else had led up to. It was no less than a cavalry charge on a frontage of four yards, the width of the narrow lane leading to and from the pass. It was indeed a 'pass'; there was just room for four horses abreast, their riders knee to knee, and no more – unless all the eye-witnesses have exaggerated. The horsemen were called 'the forlorn hope' and such they must have seemed. Fairfax gave the order direct to Cromwell, and the latter detailed the three troops of Major Bethell of his old regiment. Down the hill they galloped, the gallant squadron, Bethell at their head; through the ford they splashed, and up the gentle slope on the far side. They received a ragged fire from some musketeers in the hedges on the upper part of the slope but this did not check their progress. Without drawing rein, or even deploying (as far as one can tell) the leading troop crashed straight into the front ranks of the waiting Cavaliers and broke them. The second troop meanwhile managed to deploy out of the lane, and having done so charged in its turn, and overthrew the second line of Royalist horse. But Goring had more behind; the three Parliamentary troops were in fact in the heart of the enemy's position and once the momentum of the charge was spent there was no hope of further progress. Gradually by weight of numbers they were overborne, and began to fall back.

But not for long. Three more troops under Major Desborough were coming up the hill to their support. On reaching the top Desborough swung his squadron round to the north, and then, wheeling to the left he fell upon the open left flank of the Cavalier horse, who recoiled from the shock. But this was not the last shot in Fairfax's locker. His musketeers were also co-operating in a beautiful manner and added their fire to the combined assault. It proved too much for the Cavaliers; after a fierce and fairly prolonged hand-to-hand contest they gave way, split up into small parties and dissolved in flight. The bulk of them retreated over the river-bridge and took the road to Bridgwater; Goring himself, accompanied by the faithful Bulstrode, made off to the north and reached Bridgwater late that night, 'overjoyed' to find that the greater part of his army had already arrived there.

But the defeat though not complete broke the morale of the Royalist army of the West, which was no longer capable of making a stand against the all-conquering Roundheads, and the First Civil War was virtually over.

COMMENTS

The leadership of the two commanders in this, the last pitched battle of the First Civil War, was in marked contrast. Sir Thomas had shown himself a sound tactician; but his strategy had not been impressive. Of Lord Goring on the other hand it can be said that his handling of his troops in the battle was not impressive but his strategy before the battle was masterly. He found himself confronted by an army of 14,000 while he could only muster a little over half that number. Yet he had brought on to the battlefield nearly 7,000 to his opponents' 10,000. He had achieved this by his feigned threat to Taunton. The upshot of this was that he misled his opponent, threw him off his balance and induced him to divide his army, with three rivers – the Isle, the Parrett, and the Yeo – separating them at the critical moment of battle; for Massey had not rejoined and his troops had no influence on the decision. Nor does it appear that Fairfax gave any specific orders to co-operate. This might have been done by approaching Langport from the south-west, and thus threatening the enemy's retreat. But in the event Massey's 4,000 men were totally wasted.

Fairfax had taken the bait offered him. In fact he appears to have been a little bit 'rattled' by the surprise move of his opponent. A Roundhead eyewitness writes of Goring 'dancing from side to side of the river'. A good simile; Goring led his opponent 'a song and a dance'.

But tactically we can have nothing but admiration for Fairfax's handling of the battle. His action in launching a cavalry force four abreast through a defile commanded by the enemy's fire may appear almost foolhardy; but it succeeded, and that is the acid test. Fairfax had guessed correctly what was on 'the other side of the hill', and that after all is the supreme gift in a general. To put it in another way, he calculated correctly the relative forces and values of the two sides; his experience and judgment of war had served him in good stead, and he reaped his reward by a sterling victory. On paper it might look that the cavalry attack was bound to be defeated and such a manoeuvre in a peace-time war game would have been stigmatized by the umpires as 'impossible in war', but 'Fiery Tom' judged aright the effect of relative morale just as he had done at Nantwich; and above all it was superior morale in the Parliamentary army that won the victory.

To some extent Goring's defeat may be attributed to the King's inactivity, for while the Langport campaign was going on he had remained at Hereford (19–30 June) and at Raglan (3–15 July). Massey on the other hand had co-operated with Fairfax with a considerable portion of his army.

The war had still more than a year to run, but after Naseby and

Langport, it was a hopeless struggle. It is scarcely surprising that the Royalists everywhere, with few exceptions, were losing heart. Those of them who were professional soldiers saw all too clearly that all was lost: those who came from the landed gentry began to think of saving something from the wreck. The stream of Cavaliers making their way to Westminster to pay their fines and compound for their estates was now becoming a flood. The Parliamentarians did not demand unconditional surrender: few Royalists were exempted from pardon, and these were denounced by name.

At Naseby the Parliamentarians had captured much of the King's correspondence. The revelations published in *The King's Cabinet Opened* were damaging indeed. Many a Cavalier now learned for the first time that the King had been negotiating for the landing of an Irish army in England, and was prepared to abolish the laws against the Roman Catholics. Charles had indeed attempted to bring the Duke of Lorraine's mercenaries to England: few of the Royalist gentry would have welcomed allies such as these.

The number of Cavaliers who actually changed sides was comparatively small. Even so defeat, privations, lack of pay, and desertion were daily diminishing the remaining Royalist forces. Few but the King and Digby could persuade themselves that it was worth struggling on. Digby, clinging desperately to power, could conjure up illusions of future triumphs from the slenderest successes and even from his fertile imagination. The King's attitude though less optimistic, was no more practical.

'His Majesty', Rupert wrote to the Duke of Richmond on 28 July, 'hath now no way left to preserve his posterity, Kingdom, and nobility but by treaty. I believe it a more prudent way to retain something than to lose all.' This letter was shown to the King, who himself replied. 'As for your opinion of my business, and your counsel thereupon, if I had any other quarrel but the defence of my religion, crown and friends, you had full reason for your advice; for I confess that, speaking as a mere soldier or statesman, I must say there is no probability but of my ruin: yet, as a Christian, I must tell you that God will not suffer rebels and traitors to prosper, nor this cause to be overthrown; and whatever personal punishment it shall please Him to inflict upon me, must not make me repine, much less give over this quarrel; . . .' It was in this mood of fatalistic but heroic resignation that the King nerved himself to continue the unequal war.

Even after Langport something might perhaps have been achieved if Charles had placed himself at the head of the Western Cavaliers. Demoralized by defeat, as they and their commander were, they needed the stimulus of the King's presence to rouse them from their apathy. The King, however, was thinking not of his English troops, but of Montrose, who had added two more to his series of victories – Alford (2 July) and Kilsyth (15 August).

It was no longer safe to linger in South Wales, chiefly because Leven at last bestirring himself had laid siege to Hereford on 30 July. On 5 August the King, who had been trying unsuccessfully to recruit his forces around Cardiff, marched north with the intention of joining Montrose.

After Langport Fairfax had set himself in the most methodical manner to subdue the West. Bridgwater fell, after a stubborn resistance, on 23 July thus giving the Roundheads the line of the Parrett. They struck next at Bristol where Prince Rupert with a garrison only 1,500 strong was endeavouring to hold a line four miles long, with a plague-striken City at his back. In his summons Fairfax struck a shrewd blow at the Prince's morale, referring to the efforts made by Englishmen in the Palatine cause: 'Let all England judge, whether the burning of its towns, ruining of its cities, and destroying of its people, be a good requital from a person of your family, which had the prayers, tears, purses, and blood of its Parliament and people.' None can tell what effect these words may have had upon the Prince; but at any rate the summons was rejected and Fairfax decided – as Rupert had done two years earlier – to storm. His success was no less marked. Fairfax had a far more powerful artillery than Rupert had employed in 1643, and a breach was soon made. On the south the Royalists resisted successfully, but the defenders of the eastern part of the line – not more than five feet high in places – were soon driven back, and the Parliamentary horse broke in. Rupert launched a cavalry counter-attack but it was defeated. Priors Hill Fort in the northern angle of the defences held out for two hours, but then it was stormed and the garrison massacred. Faced by the collapse of his outer line, the Prince, with the concurrence of his Council of War, capitulated.

The Parliamentary Colonel, Butler, testified that Rupert could not have held Bristol 'unless it had been better manned', but his enemies in the Royalist party condemned him for not holding out in the castle. As soon as the news of the surrender reached the King he deprived the Prince of his rank of Lieutenant-General. Colonel Will. Legge, now Governor of Oxford, who had been one of the Prince's chief supporters throughout the war was placed under arrest, and Sir Thomas Glemham, the resolute defender of Carlisle, which had held out until July 1645, was given command of the Royalist capital.

The Battle of Rowton Heath. 24 September 1645

Charles' plan was to make for Scotland and, marching through Lancashire and Cumberland, to join hands with Montrose, and he therefore responded readily to a call for assistance from Chester, which had been besieged, on and off, since July 1643, and was now hard pressed. For this enterprise the King could not assemble more than 4,000 men, mostly cavalry.

Chester is built on the east bank of the river Dee, which at this point flows from south to north. The Roundheads had been able to invest it only on the east or English side, and it was still open on the west or Welsh side. The King therefore was able, after a rapid and tiring march, to enter the City by the Dee Bridge. He had with him a handful of infantry under Lord Astley, his Lifeguards under the Earl of Lichfield (formerly Lord Bernard Stuart) and some cavalry under Lord Charles Gerard, perhaps 1,000 in all. Langdale with the bulk of the cavalry some 3,000 strong, was sent to cross the Dee by a bridge of boats at Holt, eight miles to the south, with orders to swing left-handed and fall upon the besiegers from the rear. It was an admirable plan.

Meanwhile Colonel-General Poyntz, who had failed to engage the King near Worcester, had pursued him from the south with some 3,000 horse and by dint of a night march he came up with the Cavaliers at about 6 a.m. on 24 September. Langdale, however, had learned of his approach from an intercepted letter. About 9 a.m. he charged Poyntz and drove him back with loss, but the Parliamentarians were not routed. Thus the situation was one of stalemate. Langdale could not march on Chester with Poyntz just behind him, while Poyntz could not join the besiegers while Langdale was on Rowton Heath. Both sides required reinforcements, but while Langdale somehow failed to get news of his predicament to the Royalists in Chester, Poyntz did manage to get in touch with the besiegers and his appeal was promptly answered. About noon 500 horse under Colonel Jones and 300 foot under Adjutant-General Lothian marched to meet Poyntz, going round the flank of the Royalists and making contact with Poyntz, who was drawn up on Hatton Heath, two miles south of Rowton.

During the morning the Royalists in Chester had been making preparations for a sally, the citizens clearing away the dung that barricaded the East gate, but it was past 3 p.m. before the King sent orders for a sortie. Then Gerard and Lichfield led their horse out of Chester and drew them up under the walls.

Meanwhile, attacked by Poyntz in front and by Colonel Jones on the flank, Langdale's outnumbered men were after a short resistance overpowered; they broke and fled, some making for Farndon bridge and Wales, but the majority galloping towards Chester. Here beneath the City walls they met the rest of the Roundhead besieging force and also their own reinforcements. A terrible mêlée ensued, friend and foe inextricably mixed and both fired upon from the walls. Gerard's horse at one time looked like stemming the tide, but a fresh wave of fugitives swept them away, and the unhappy King from his seat in the Phoenix Tower on the north-east corner of the city wall had the mortification of seeing his troops driven away from the city in a northerly direction and hunted down in the narrow and boggy lanes of Hoole Heath. The young Earl of Lichfield was among the slain.

Though the numbers engaged were small the victory was of some importance for it prevented the King from proceeding to Scotland, but since Montrose also had met with disaster at Philiphaugh on 13 September, little good could have come of that enterprise. The Cavaliers lost 600 killed and 800 prisoners from their small force. These cavalry were in the main the survivors of Marston Moor and Naseby. The disaster of Rowton Heath was the final blow to their morale.

The fate of Chester was now sealed, for although Byron hung on with dogged courage until 3 February 1646, there was no longer any possibility of relief. With Chester and Bristol in the hands of the Parliamentarians there was no hope of further reinforcements from Ireland.

In the West Fairfax kept up the pressure. Garrisons fell before him like ninepins though several, notably Sherborne (which fell on 15 August), resisted stoutly. Devizes Castle yielded on 23 September and Berkeley Castle was stormed on the 25th. Goring did nothing to impede the conquering progress of the New Model, perhaps because he was sick. In November he decided to give up his command, and wrote to the King to say so. Then without awaiting a reply, he departed to France, stating – untruly – that he would return in two months.

Since his operations were unhampered by any activity on the part of Goring, Fairfax was able to send Cromwell to reduce the Royalist garrisons in Hampshire. Oliver marched first on Winchester, which surrendered on 8 October. Next he laid siege to Basing House, so long a thorn in the side of the Roundheads. The Marquis of Winchester underestimated the power of his assailant's battering train, and refused to yield. On the 14th the Puritans carried the fortress by storm. In the heat of action the exultant soldiery massacred many of the Papist garrison, including six priests. The daughter of one clergyman who attempted to protect her father from ill-treatment was struck dead before his eyes. Massacre as usual was accompanied by pillage, but the old Marquis when reviled for fighting in a hopeless cause, still had the courage to reply: 'If the King had no more ground in England but Basing, I would adventure as I did. . . . Basing is called Loyalty,' adding, 'I hope that the King may have a day again.'

Cromwell, justifying the slaughter by the laws of war, and his own interpretation of the politics of the Almighty, wrote grimly to the Commons saying: 'I thank God, I can give you a good account of Basing. . . .' – a letter that might have come from Lord Byron or Sir Richard Grenvile. By this time the country gentleman had taken upon himself some of the less attractive characteristics of the professional soldier of his day.

In the West Goring had handed over his command to Lord Wentworth, who shared the former's liking for the bottle, while possessing none of his military talent. Outside Devon and Cornwall only Dunster Castle, near Minehead, now held a Cavalier garrison. Exeter itself was threatened. Wentworth was not the man to restore so desperate a situation.

By the end of December Fairfax had occupied Crediton. On 9 January 1646 Cromwell, who had returned to the West, surprised Wentworth's cavalry at Bovey Tracey, 14 miles south-west of Exeter, and in the panic that ensued the Cavaliers fell back into Cornwall.

The Prince of Wales and his Council now gave the command in the South-west to Hopton. Wentworth was to be General of the Horse and Sir Richard Grenvile Lieut.-General of the Foot. It was indeed a thankless task that fell to the victor of Stratton and Lansdown; only his loyalty could induce him to accept it. He caused a great banner to be made bearing the motto: 'I Will Strive To Serve My Soveraigne King.'

Troubles began at once, but Hopton faced them with resolution. When on the day after he assumed the command he found Grenvile disobedient he promptly placed him under arrest – much to the latter's astonishment. This was a step towards restoring discipline, and the Cornishmen who liked Grenvile as their fellow countryman would doubtless have recovered from the shock if given time. Wentworth's cavalry, however, seem to have been past hope by this time: Hyde wittily but truly described them as 'horse whom only their friends feared and their enemies laughed at, being only terrible in plunder and resolute in running away'. Only the Prince's Regiment of Lifeguards could be thoroughly depended upon. Nevertheless Hopton took the offensive in the hope of relieving Exeter. He had less than 2,000 foot and only a little more than 3,000 horse when on 10 February 1646 he occupied Torrington.

Fairfax had not been idle in January for after relieving Plymouth he had stormed Dartmouth on the 19th. On 14 February the New Model advanced from Crediton to Chulmleigh (12 miles south-east of Torrington), but was delayed there by foul weather. At 4 a.m. on the 16th the drums beat in the Roundhead camp, and Fairfax pushed on through Ring Ash with the intention of bringing on a battle.

Hopton, as at Devizes in 1643, had thrown up barricades at the entrances to Torrington and had placed a party of dragoons at Stevenstone Park, a mile to the east. By 5 p.m. the advancing Roundheads had driven in this outpost. A body of Royalist horse and foot covered the withdrawal of their dragoons, and there was bickering on the high ground which overlooks Torrington from the east. By nightfall the Cavaliers had withdrawn into the town.

Fairfax, with the advice of his council of war, decided to attack next day so as to have an opportunity of reconnoitring the Royalist defences in daylight. It was dark by this time and Cromwell was sent to inspect the Roundhead outposts. In so doing he deduced from the noise coming from the town that Hopton was on the point of retirement. The Lieut.-General to test the defences sent forward a patrol of dragoons who drew the fire of the Cornish infantry. In consequence a general fire fight broke out and the upshot was that the Roundheads decided to attack without waiting for daylight.

For two hours a savage fight raged at the barricades, 'The dispute continued long at push of pike and with butt-ends of muskets', wrote Fairfax, but in the end the Cornish broke and fled panic-stricken through the town. The Cavalier horse under Major-General John Digby counter-attacked and there was a general mêlée in the town. In the confusion, the Royalists' magazine, which was situated in the church, blew up, Fairfax himself narrowly escaping with his life. Hopton was wounded in the face by a Roundhead pikeman, and his horse was killed under him; nevertheless he and Lord Capel fought it out with their rearguard, and the beaten army escaped with the loss of only 60 killed and more than 400 prisoners. The victory cost the Parliamentarians 400 killed, including 200 prisoners who had been secured in the church.

Torrington was virtually the end of the war in the West and on 14 March Hopton, persuaded by his officers, surrendered and his army was disbanded.

Strange though it may seem the King had still not given up all hope of forming a fresh army. Lord Astley still had 3,000 men in Worcestershire and Charles, who had wintered at Oxford, ordered him to cut his way through to the Royalist capital and join him.

Astley got no farther than Stow-on-the-Wold where early on 21 March he was overwhelmed by Brereton, Birch, and Colonel Morgan. The silver-haired old general – he was 67 – sat himself upon a drum in the midst of his captors. 'You have done your work', said he, 'and may go play, unless you will fall out amongst yourselves.'

The news of Astley's defeat quickly reached Oxford and obliged the King to try once more to obtain terms from the Parliament. There was to be an Act of Oblivion and all sequestrations were to be taken off the property of his supporters. This overture only served to put his enemies on their guard and after a month of fruitless negotiation both with Parliament and the Scots, who were besieging Newark, the King decided to trust his fortunes to the latter. On 27 April he left Oxford in disguise and accompanied by only two followers. After a devious journey through enemy country he reached Southwell near Newark on 5 May. In the words of Dr Gardiner, 'He fancied himself to be a guest, but the days of his captivity had in fact begun'.

There can be little doubt that by 1646 most Englishmen were heartily sick of the war and shocked by its depredations. The great majority had been reluctant to take part on either side. The poet Andrew Marvell, a native of Hull whose resistance had done more than most to ruin the King's plans, expressed the general war-weariness in his poem *A Garden. Written after the Civil Wars:*

Shall we never more
That sweet militia restore
When gardens only had their towers,
And all the garrisons were flowers;
When roses only arms might bear,
And men did rosy garlands wear?

The Civil War was over, though Glemham did not surrender Oxford until 24 June, and at Raglan the Marquis of Worcester held out until 19 August. The New Model had done its work well.

CHAPTER 17

In Conclusion

IN CONCLUSION, LET us take a bird's eye view of the war and see if we can descry the fundamental factors that combined to decide the issue.

Battles and wars, like all human activities, are decided not by a single factor but by the resultant of several. War is a tug-of-war; in it we are concerned, not with absolutes but with comparatives. We must measure the pull, or factor, of each member of the team, and then compare the sum total developed by each side. Now some of the factors are unknown owing to lack of eyewitnesses, some are imponderable – such as morale – and some are unpredictable – such as freaks of the weather, or good and bad luck – like the explosion that put Hopton out of action on the day after Lansdown. However in a war of long duration factors of this sort tend to cancel out, so we can safely ignore them in this very general assessment.

In this matter there appear to be four main factors – Strands of war, as we like to call them for convenience. The Strands are: the Leaders, the Led, Morale, and Resources. Let us examine these four Strands in turn.

The Leaders. Here we see a glaring contrast throughout the greater part of the war. Whereas on the Royalist side there was unity of command, under one supreme and unquestioned head, on the side of Parliament the war was conducted by a Committee, consisting mainly of civilians who naturally were ignorant of military strategy. As a consequence Parliament could not put to effective use its preponderance in numbers until it handed over the control of operations to a single general of proved capacity. Furthermore, the Royalist commander was the Sovereign, respected and implicitly obeyed. On the side of Parliament scant respect was paid to the Committee, or indeed to its military representative in the field, the Captain-General the Earl of Essex.

The army commanders on both sides had for the most part seen service on the Continent. Men like Manchester and Newcastle, who had no previous military experience, were the exception in the higher ranks, and they usually had professional soldiers such as Lawrence Crawford and General King to assist them. At the regimental level the Royalists had a far greater proportion of 'regular' officers, a fact which must have given them a great advantage in training and disciplining the rank and file. The lack of experienced junior officers accounts for many of the shortcomings of the Parliamentary armies during the earlier campaigns of the war.

The Led. Under this second Strand we do not find an appreciable difference for the Led were all of the same blood, frequently of the same kith and kin, so that the raw material of each side was fairly similar. Moreover in military knowledge and training both sides were practically equal. This generalization is only partly qualified by the Parliament's possession of the London Trained Bands, whose prowess seems to have been somewhat exaggerated. It is difficult to point to any Roundhead infantry whose exploits compare with those of Hopton's Cornishmen, or who showed the devotion of Newcastle's Whitecoats at Marston Moor. The broad distinction between the two armies was that the Cavaliers were for the most part countrymen and the Round-heads townsmen. This gave some advantage to the former as country-men are naturally hardier than townsmen. The return march from Gloucester of the Trained Bands showed up this weakness of the towns-men. The Cavaliers also included a bigger proportion of horsemen, which was a decided advantage, and one which Rupert and Goring exploited to the full. On the Parliamentarian side Hazelrig and Cromwell appreciated the value of well-organized cavalry; the 'Lobsters' and the 'Ironsides' set the standard for the rest, so that by the end of the war the Roundhead cavalry were a match for the best of the Royalist regiments.

Morale. Morale fluctuates in a puzzling manner and is difficult to assess. No man can see into the heart and read the motives of another with any degree of certainty, but broadly speaking both protagonists began the war with equal morale, which at that time amounted to self-esteem and self-confidence. The Royalists possessed a greater propor-tion of the nobility and the gentry, who naturally enjoyed a strong *esprit de grade,* which was bound to assert itself on the battlefield. Years after, in 1657, Cromwell described how, talking to Hampden, he had compared the cavalry of both sides, as they were in 1642. ' "Your troopers", said I, "are most of them old decayed servingmen and tapsters and such kind of fellows" and, said I, "their troopers are gentlemens' sons, younger sons and persons of quality; do you think that the spirits of such base and mean fellows will be ever able to encounter gentlemen that have honour and courage and resolution in them?"' The morale of the Roundheads Cromwell described in this famous passage was not of a high order, and was not proof against the onrush of horses and the flash of drawn swords at Edgehill. Later in the war – at any rate by 1645 – their morale was raised by various means, but mainly by their religious zeal and fanaticism. Though there are plenty of instances of religious zeal in the Royalist ranks, on balance the Parliamentarians doubtless had the advantage in this respect. Moreover the adage 'nothing succeeds like success' is nowhere truer than in the field. As the proportion of victories to defeats on the Parliamentary side gradually rose so did the morale of the soldiers, and, *per contra*, so did the morale of the Cavaliers fall. Thus by the end of the war the Roundheads had a perceptible advantage under this heading.

Resources. The Resources have been reviewed in the opening chapter. Here we will only summarize and compare them. Owing to the possession of the fleet, command of the sea, the chief ports and arsenals, the clothing towns, the industrial areas of the Home Counties, the capital – and with it the adherence of the merchants and financiers of London – Parliament enjoyed as great a preponderance in resources as the North in the American Civil War (one of the many parallels between the two wars). This superiority enabled Parliament to put a greater number of troops into the field, to clothe, equip, feed and pay them better than their opponents and to keep them better supplied with ammunition, the lack of which had cost the King at least one battle. Indeed this fourth Strand had greater effect than the other three Strands combined, and by the autumn of 1644 made the issue of the war as nearly a foregone conclusion as anything in the realm of war can be. In this connection it is surprising that the Royalists contrived to keep their armies in the field as long as they did.

THE LEADERS

Let us now compare in greater detail the army commanders on the two sides, in order to assess their contributions to their respective causes. Bearing in mind that we are dealing in comparatives, not in absolutes, we will pit them in pairs against one another. They fall conveniently into four pairs, the King and the Earl of

Essex; Prince Rupert and Sir Thomas Fairfax; Lord Hopton and Sir William Waller; the Earl of Newcastle and Lord Fairfax.

The King and Essex

King Charles had twice taken the field against the Scots, and although he did not see a shot fired he gained valuable experience in the realm of logistics. Otherwise he was completely ignorant of war. Essex had, on the other hand, as we have seen, served on the Continent, but did not reflect that experience when in command of an army. It was probably his rank in the Nobility as much as his previous service that gained him the post of Captain-General. His complete inability to grasp the elements of strategy was shown in the opening campaign of the war, when he allowed the King to get between himself and his base – the capital: he committed the same error in the Newbury campaign. In each case it does not seem to have occurred to him to manoeuvre his army into a sounder strategical position before engaging his opponents. His parting with Waller when almost in the presence of the enemy, just before Cropredy Bridge when their combined armies might have crushed the King, was the act of an imbecile – only paralleled by the act of the Committee of Both Kingdoms in sending the New Model Army to relieve a small town in the distant West (Taunton) thus leaving the capital exposed to attack by the Royalist main army at Oxford. Finally, and worst of all, having eventually reached Cornwall Essex allowed his army to be outmanoeuvred by the King into a hopeless strategical position where he abandoned it to its fate. Thereafter he went sick and quietly faded out of the story. The least damning adjective we can apply as a summing up, is that he was *ineffective.* His finest achievement was his relief of Gloucester.[1]

We turn with relief to the King, whose military development was in one respect strikingly similar to that of Charles VII of France in the closing stages of the Hundred Years' War. That is to say both monarchs hated the very idea of war, but both found themselves drawn into it willy-nilly. The French King, a shrewd man, watched the career of the English army and reformed his own on the same lines, becoming personally involved in the struggle more and more until eventually he became quite a good organiser and strategist. The English Charles also started from scratch, and gradually acquired practical knowledge which enabled him to discuss operations on equal

---

[1] The authors beg to state that neither of them would like to have served under this officer!

Q

terms with his generals. He made a serious error in not attempting a *coup de main* at Gloucester, but was at his best in 1644, the third year of the war, with victories at Cropredy Bridge and Lostwithiel. Thereafter he began to exhibit a curious wavering, occasioned by over-much listening to the views of others some of which were really bad. It is to this cause that we must attribute his fatal faltering in the 1645 campaign, culminating in his allowing himself to be deterred from leading his reserve into battle at Naseby. How he must have regretted that in after years! The failure of the King's wide-flung strategic plan for 1644 cannot be laid at his door. It sprang directly from the defeat of his southern army at Cheriton and the intervention of the Scots which detained the Northern army. But until that happened the King's strategy, or rather method of carrying on the war was in complete contrast to that of Parliament whose only gleam of strategical perception was their recognition of the value of Newark, as shown by their repeated efforts to capture it. The main result of their strategy was to fritter away their superior forces in scattered garrisons and in sporadic attempts on Royalist towns and strongholds such as Donnington Castle and Basing House.

A good deal of dispersion on the Royalist side was unavoidable and justifiable, especially in view of the fact that they possessed few ports, and were obliged to fight for Hull and Plymouth, besides maintaining such strategical places as Oxford, Bristol, Chester, York, and Newark. Nevertheless Charles kept steadily before his eyes the primary principle of war that the essential target is the enemy's main field army. Instances of this are plentiful: the concentration at Edgehill, the stand at First Newbury, the junction of Rupert with Newcastle to engage the Allies at York, the pursuit of Essex and the concentration against him in Cornwall.

To sum up the royal strategy, in 1643 it was a concerted attack on the capital based on the possession of exterior lines; a continuation of it in 1644 till it was wrecked by the defeat at Cheriton and the Scottish invasion: thereafter a consistent effort to confront the enemy's main armies in battle with concentrated forces; in 1645, the breakdown of all plans as a result of conflicting counsels and the defeat at Naseby.

The King exhibited some other military qualities, notably his resolution and determination, as exampled by the tenacity he showed on the evening of Edgehill, when, like R. E. Lee on the evening of Sharpsburg, he wrung victory from a less resolute opposing general.

Charles never abandoned hope; his optimism was unquenchable, and often unjustifiable. It probably originated in his profound belief in the justice of his cause, and the feeling (shared by his enemy) that God was on his side. It was also encouraged by Lord Digby who even after Rowton Heath was writing letters full of confidence and hope.

Prince Rupert and Sir Thomas Fairfax

What a splendid pair these two would have made fighting on the same side! Fairfax was never very far from being a Royalist, and had he fought for his King instead of against him it is an interesting speculation as to what the result of the war would have been.

The similarity in the military make-up of this pair leaps to the eye, quickness of thought, decision in action, combined with boldness and resolution distinguishes both generals. Fairfax was so uniformly successful in his operations that little display of resolution was required of him. That he possessed a store of it was however shown by his conduct after the defeat at Adwalton Moor; when by sheer strength of will power and driving force he kept his command together and brought them many weary miles into the Parliamentary camp at Bradford. Rupert's surrender of Bristol has been held against him for lack of resolution, though without adequate grounds, for the war was palpably decided and to hold out longer would have achieved nothing. His ardent spirit blazed forth on the morrow of Marston Moor. Newcastle was utterly cast down. When asked what he intended to do he replied that he would make for Scarborough and take ship to the Continent – and he did. Young Rupert, on the contrary, replied simply and sturdily, 'As for me I shall rally my forces and rejoin the King'. And he was as good as his word. He and his uncle shared at least one military virtue.

On the strategical plane one cannot be positive for Rupert never had a completely free hand, but his advice to the King was usually sound while the strategy by which he relieved York was the most brilliant operation of its kind in the war. Fairfax was never really his own master till the eve of Naseby, but when given a free hand the result was dramatic. Thrusting first at his nearest opponent, the King, he struck him a fatal blow; then swinging round to face the only other army in the field he lunged at Goring. It was swift and decisive. To all intents and purposes he had won the war in six weeks.

It was only in personal qualities that these two generals differed to any degree. Prince Rupert was proud and domineering, hot-tempered and rude. He did not suffer fools gladly and made no effort to conceal his contempt. Thus he was unpopular with older generals who grudged him his seniority. He was known as 'The German', and the favourite of the King his uncle. As the war proceeded this feeling seems to have abated somewhat, and there is no evidence that he failed to obtain loyal co-operation of them and obedience from those under him, while the rank and file placed implicit confidence in their youthful and dashing commander.

Sir Thomas, on the other hand, was quiet, modest, serious, and deeply religious. He was popular with all ranks and evidently worshipped by his troops. In short he possessed an impressive stock of military qualities, and it is not surprising that he was selected to form, train, and command the New Model Army and that with it he brought the war to a successful end. Though normally inarticulate, with tongue and pen, he was one of those men who is inspired on the day of action.

Lord Hopton and Sir William Waller

These two generals fall naturally into the same pair, for before the war they were close friends, and in it they fought repeatedly against each other. Hopton's military development was an interesting one. Like Waller he had some slight experience of war, and like the Roundhead he worked by trial and error. But speedily he found his feet and obtained the confidence and obedience of the Cornishmen. It was as much these qualities as purely military aptitude that brought him to the top, and kept him there. We have watched his career from Braddock Down to Cheriton, and there is no need to go over the ground again. Perhaps the most revealing episode was the brief siege of Devizes, Hopton, partially blinded and paralysed, refused to give up the command; his active brain continued to function, and his firm spirit to burn. With ammunition and powder running low, and match exhausted, he yet was able to devise the necessary means to meet the crisis, and later to drive his reluctant colonels to march to the sound of the guns in support of Wilmot.

Of his old friend and new opponent Sir William Waller it is difficult to speak with confidence. Waller was prominent throughout the war in command of armies, yet we know singularly little about the man. His autobiographical notes tell us nothing material. In the course of the war he must have acquired more practical experience than almost any other commander on his side except Sir Thomas Fairfax. As a strategist he was inclined to paint things blacker than they were. The Royalists respected him as a tactician, but it is hard to see any solid basis for their good opinion. Early in the war he obtained a reputation for ability to select a good position, what we call 'an eye for country' but on what it was based it is hard to say. It can hardly have been Lansdown, for that position was proved to have a fatal weakness, and his position at Roundway Down was imposed upon him. Gardiner allots him great merit at Cheriton for pushing his horse forward down the slope to get clear of the small enclosures, but can that be considered anything more than elementary commonsense? At least we can assert that he was a good trainer of troops, a good organizer, and apart from Ripple Field and Roundway Down that he made no obvious mistakes. To sum up he was colourless and somewhat lacking in resolution.

The Earl of Newcastle and Lord Fairfax

Our fourth pair were engaged in a prolonged duel lasting for the first two years of the war, and thus make a natural pair to examine. But the examination will not be very fruitful, for like Waller both are somewhat colourless and uninspiring. Newcastle was a loyal subject who spent a vast fortune in the royal cause, and raised and trained a fine army, which he endeavoured to place on a sound administrative footing. With this army he achieved some solid successes, notably the victory at Adwalton Moor. If he failed to do more in the first year of the war, when he outnumbered his enemies, he was handicapped by the presence in his area of the Queen, for whose safety he was responsible. His failure before Hull was offset by his dogged resistance to the advance of the Scots in 1644, and his stubborn defence of York. Opinions may vary as to his departure to the Continent after Marston Moor but in general his operations were too methodical, and he seems to have been somewhat lacking in that element of robustness which Lord Wavell has declared is so essential a quality in a general.

Lord Fairfax seems to have been an example of what is called 'skipping a generation'. His father the 'Old Lord Fairfax' was known as 'a tiger'; Tom was initiated into the mysteries of the military art by his grandfather, and imbibed them, but they passed by his father. At Hull he seems to have done well, but at Adwalton Moor he abandoned his own son and at Marston Moor he abandoned his army. Can any other general equal that record?

Lord Goring

It is probable that this extraordinary man was as impossible to pair in his lifetime as he is today. In fact he declines to be paired with anyone – even by antithesis. He was a bit of an enigma. He is commonly described, and dismissed, as a debauchee, but we cannot lightly dismiss a man who put to flight half the immense Allied army at Marston Moor. That Goring was fond of the bottle may be conceded, but that this taste effected his physical fitness when military operations were in train there is not much evidence – or probability. A successful and vigorous cavalry leader in wartime could not last long were he a mere debauchee. There were however certain features in his character that told against him. He was unreliable, unpredictable, independent, self-seeking and quarrelsome. When the New Model Army was evidently about to take the field and the King had concentrated north of Oxford an adequate army with which to confront it, Goring, oblivious of the considerations of sound strategy clamoured loudly to be allowed to resume his independent command in the West. Charles, in order to avoid friction between his generals, acceded to his request. Goring was to pay for this a few weeks later on the field of Langport.

On the credit side of the account Lord Goring seems to have trained his men well, and to have inspired confidence and loyalty in the rank and file; on the other hand he was a lax disciplinarian. He undoubtedly had a strong element of toughness. Another quality of the successful general is to outwit and deceive your opponent, a quality that Goring possessed, judging by the manner in which he outwitted General Fairfax on the eve of Langport. He had a forceful personality and the makings of a great leader of men, and as a supreme commander with a free hand, he would probably have made a great name for himself.

The reader will have noted the absence from this gallery of one well-known name – that of Oliver Cromwell. The explanation of this omission is simple: Cromwell was never an army commander in the First Civil War. This fact is a surprising one and has never been satisfactorily explained. Parliament evidently had complete confidence in him, both as a commander in the field and as a military adviser at Westminster. As early as the spring of 1643 he was a member of the Committee and throughout the war he was constantly consulted; it is likely that Pym preferred to keep his old colleague within call, rather than letting him be swallowed up in distant operations. Yet Parliament also had early formed a high opinion of his military capacity as witness his nomination as second in command to the Earl of Manchester in the newly formed army of East Anglia before the Winceby campaign. Nevertheless it remains a matter of astonishment that right up to the eve of Naseby he was kept in a lowly military role, the intention being that he should eke out the weeks pending the expiry of his service under the Self-denying Ordinance side-tracked in Ely. And there was opposition in Parliament even to allowing him this modest command.

In the foregoing pages we have traced his military education from his first harrowing but fruitful experience of panic, ill discipline, and disaster at Edgehill, through his patient application of the lesson there burnt into his mind that you cannot win battles with 'old decayed servingmen and tapsters' but 'must have men of a spirit'. The fruits of his careful personnel selection and training were to be seen at Grantham (where his men 'agreed to charge') and Gainsborough (where Oliver, with mounting self-confidence *ordered* them to charge). His foot was already firmly on the first rung of the ladder of fame, and even his upset at Winceby could not arrest his ascent – the suspicion is here insistent that his Westminster connections assisted him to ride this setback. He had the ear of Parliament (in modern parlance he enjoyed a good publicity service) whilst the real victor of Winceby passed by unrecognized.

Meanwhile his example as a trainer of troops was becoming infectious, and spreading through the army of the Eastern Association – and even farther – so much so that Oliver Cromwell may claim to be known as the Sir John Moore of the Parliamentary army.

Second Newbury, that might have finished most generals after the Earl of Manchester's open and damaging charges, failed to shake his reputation, so that his arrival at Naseby was greeted with cheers by the horse (though not necessarily by the rest of the army). On that field he showed in the most striking degree the advantage of retaining in hand in a formed body at least a portion of your mounted troops till the last possible moment. Naseby put the crown on Cromwell's reputation as a cavalry leader.

Thereafter in the concluding operations Cromwell was the right hand man of Sir Thomas Fairfax. Thus he ended the war in the tantalizing position of being an untried army commander, an impeccable tactician, a great trainer and leader of men but as a strategist quite unknown. It would require another war to test him in that capacity.

On the day the war ended Oliver Cromwell was back in his old seat at St. Stephens.

We have confined our remarks to generals of high rank, who commanded independent armies in one or more of the major battles of the war. Both sides were well served by generals of less exalted rank. In the Parliamentary armies Skippon and Balfour spring to mind – the former tough and resolute in adversity, a man who knew well how to inspire the devotion of the Puritan soldiery; the latter pre-eminent for his tactical skill. Ireton too deserves a word for his vigorous and dashing leadership at Naseby, and Massey for his enterprise and initiative in the West.

The Cavaliers numbered scores of good officers in their ranks. Ruthven, despite his defeat at Cheriton, was a valuable 'Chief of Staff' during the first three years of the war. The veteran Astley commanded the King's infantry from Edgehill to Naseby, and turned an armed mob into a formidable fighting force. Wilmot, whose reputation was greatly enhanced by Roundway Down, was a better disciplinarian than his successor, Goring, but lacked the latter's courage and resource.

We are told by Clarendon that Prince Maurice 'understood very little more of the war than to fight very stoutly when there was occasion', but his achievements at Ripple Field, Lansdown, and perhaps Roundway Down seem to belie this judgment.

To sum up in the broadest possible terms. The general trend of the war is illustrated by the tally of battles. Of the sixteen main battles fought, seven were Royalist victories, eight Parliamentary, and one was a draw. But all seven Royalist victories were won in the first half of the war whereas half the Parliamentary victories were won after that period. The pendulum was swinging slowly but inexorably; the implacable pressure exerted by superiority of resources, backed by a steadily mounting morale – two of the four Strands of war – had told its tale and decided the issue.

The four years' struggle did nothing to advance the military art, nor did it alter permanently the English constitution, but it showed that Englishmen could still fight bravely for causes which they had at heart.

Select Bibliography

Abbreviations:

A.H.R.   The Journal of the Society for Army Historical Research.

B.M.   The British Museum.

C.S.P.   Calendar of State Papers, Domestic Series.

E.H.R.   The English Historical Review.

J.P.R.M.   The Journal of Prince Rupert's Marches.

T.T.   Thomason Tracts.

It is not our intention to attempt an exhaustive bibliography, but merely to indicate the chief sources and authorities.

Godfrey DAVIES: *Bibliography of British History, Stuart Period, 1603–1714.* Oxford. 1928.

G. K. FORTESCUE: *Catalogue of the pamphlets . . . relating to the civil war . . . collected by George Thomason, 1640–1661.* (In the British Museum.) London. 1908. Thomason was a London bookseller who collected tracts as they came out.

GENERAL

Professor Wilbur Cortez ABBOTT: *Writings and Speeches of Oliver Cromwell.* 4 Vols. 1937–1947.

Maurice ASHLEY: *The Greatness of Oliver Cromwell.* London. 1957. The most recent biography. As the title suggests the work puts the most favourable interpretation on all Cromwell's actions. The present writers do not, generally speaking, concur with Mr. Ashley's views on Cromwell's military career in the period 1642–1646.

Lieut.-Colonel T. S. BALDOCK: *Cromwell as a Soldier.* London. 1899. The only life of Cromwell by a soldier. Much fresh material has come to light since Baldock wrote, but his judgments are shrewd.

Lieut.-Colonel A. H. Burne: *Battlefields of England*. London. 1950. Has chapters on Edgehill, First Newbury, Marston Moor, Second Newbury, and Naseby.

Lieut.-Colonel A. H. Burne: *More Battlefields of England*. London. 1952. Has chapters on Lansdown, Roundway Down, Cheriton, and Langport.

C.S.P.: Chiefly of value for the despatches of Parliamentarian generals and the movements of their armies.

Earl of Clarendon: *The History of the Rebellion and Civil War in England*. (Ed. W. D. Macray.) Oxford. 1888. Clarendon was not particularly interested in military affairs, but his work is of great value for an understanding of the various factors influencing the major decisions of the Royalist High Command, and the characters of the King's chief counsellors, both civil and military.

Thomas Lord Fairfax: 'A Short Memorial of the Northern Actions in which I was engaged (1642–44).' Reprinted in *A.H.R.*, Vol. V, 1926, pp. 119–25 and 160–74. The best contemporary authority for most of the fighting in the North.

Sir Charles Firth: *Cromwell's Army*. 3rd Edition. London. 1921. Extremely useful for sources and for the tactics, organization, and administration of the period.

C. H. Firth: 'The Journal of Prince Rupert's Marches, 5 Sept., 1642 to 4 July, 1646.' *E.H.R.* 1898. Gives the Prince's day to day movements, with very few omissions, for the whole period of the war.

C. H. Firth: *Oliver Cromwell*. Heroes of the Nations Series. 1900. The scheme of the series did not permit any discussion of sources or bibliography but this is nevertheless an excellent life of Cromwell.

S. R. Gardiner: *History of the Great Civil War, 1642–9*. London. 1893. This is the best general history of the war, but the military operations are submerged in the political and religious aspects of the struggle.

Lord Hopton: 'Bellum Civile'. Somerset Record Society. 1902. (Ed. Charles E. H. Chadwyck Healey, K.C., F.S.A.) Invaluable for the campaigns in the West down to and including Cheriton.

Sir C. R. Markham: *Life of the great Lord Fairfax* . . . London. 1870. Still the standard life of the commander of the New Model.

Duchess of Newcastle: *The Life of . . . William Cavendish, Duke of Newcastle*. London. 1886. (Ed. Sir C. H. Firth.) Useful for the campaigns in the North (but should be used with some caution). 1642–1646.

John RUSHWORTH: *Historical Collections . . . 1618–1649.* 7 Vols. London. 1659–1701. Besides his narrative of events, Rushworth gives many despatches and accounts of operations.

Joshua SPRIGGE, M.A.: *Anglia Rediviva; England's recovery: being the history of the motions, actions, and successes of the army under . . . Sir Thomas Fairfax.* London. 1647. This may be described as the Official History of the offensive of the New Model Army (1645–1646).

Richard SYMONDS: *The Diary of . . .* Camden Society. Vol. 74. 1859. (Ed. by C. E. Long.) Symonds served in King Charles I's Life-guard. His diary is most useful for the campaigns of 1644 and 1645. He fought at Cropredy Bridge, Lostwithiel, Second Newbury, Naseby, and Rowton Heath.

Sir Edward WALKER: *Historical Discourses.* London. 1705. Walker was Charles' Secretary-at-War and this may be called the King's Official Account of the operations of his main army in 1644 and 1645. The account of the 1645 campaign displays a considerable bias against Prince Rupert.

Eliot WARBURTON: *Memoirs of Prince Rupert and the Cavaliers.* London. 1849. Still the best biography of Prince Rupert, it includes many of the most important letters he received during the war. Most of the originals are in the British Museum (Add. MSS), while Sir Charles Firth's transcripts are in the Bodleian Library at Oxford. More recent lives by Eva Scott and Brigadier Bernard Fergusson are also useful.

CHAPTER 1

D. BRUNTON and D. H. PENNINGTON: *Members of the Long Parliament.* London. 1954. Analyses the sympathies of the Members.

Sir Charles FIRTH: *Cromwell's Army.*

P. GEYL: 'Frederick Henry of Orange and King Charles I.' *E.H.R.*, Vol. 38. Shows clearly how much support the Royalists received from Holland.

Basil N. RECKITT: *Charles the First and Hull. 1639–1645.* London. 1952. Illustrates, with a map, the distribution of the adherents in the East Riding.

CHAPTER 2

Sir Richard BULSTRODE: *Memoirs . . .* London. 1721. Sir Charles

Firth has shown (*E.H.R.*, Vol. 10, 1895) that these are genuine memoirs padded out with extracts from Clarendon and Warwick. Bulstrode fought in Prince Charles' Regiment of Horse at Powick Bridge and Edgehill, and is particularly valuable for his account of the latter.

Godfrey DAVIES: 'The Battle of Edgehill.' *E.H.R.*, Vol. 36, 1921. Particularly valuable for the bibliography, which supplements that compiled by Colonel W. G. Ross, R.E. *E.H.R.*, Vol. 2, 1887.

King JAMES II: *Life of James II . . . collected out of memoirs writ of his own hand . . .* (Ed. J. S. Clarke.) London. 1816.

Edmund LUDLOW: *Memoirs of Edmund Ludlow*. Oxford. 1894. (Ed. by Sir C. H. Firth.)

Rev. G. MILLER: *Rambles Round the Edgehills*. 1900. Contains useful topographical material.

T.T.: E.126 (39). Account of Powick Bridge by a trooper in Capt. Nathaniel Fiennes' troop. This is by far the best and fullest account of the whole operation.

T.T.: E.124, E.126, and E.128.

Edward WALSINGHAM: 'Brittannicae Virtutis Imago or . . . the life . . . of . . . Major-General Smith.' Oxford. 1644. (*T.T.* E.53 (10).) Walsingham, who served under Smith, is useful for events on the Royalist left wing, and the rescue of the Banner Royal.

Sir Philip WARWICK: *Memoires of the Reign of King Charles I. . . .* London. 1702.

Lieut.-Colonel P. YOUNG: 'The Royalist Army at Edgehill.' *A.H.R.*, 1955, p. 56. Gives Sir Bernard de Gomme's contemporary plan, the only addition to the sources since Godfrey Davies' article was written.

CHAPTER 3

Mary COATE: *Cornwall in the Great Civil War and Interregnum, 1642–1660*. Oxford. 1933. By far the best of the regional studies of the war.

Colonel Sir Bevil GRENVILE: Letters in South Kensington Museum. One describes Braddock Down.

Lord HOPTON: 'Bellum Civile.'

CHAPTER 4

Professor ABBOTT: Writings and Speeches of Oliver Cromwell.

R. BELL (Editor): 'Memorials of the Civil War.' *The Fairfax Correspondence*. Vols. III and IV. London, 1849.

Sir J. BERKENHEAD: *Mercurius Aulicus*. The Royalist newspaper.

Sir Thomas FAIRFAX: Short Memorial.

George W. JOHNSON (Editor): 'Memoirs of the Reign of Charles the First.' *The Fairfax Correspondence*. Vols. I and II. London. 1848.

Duchess of NEWCASTLE: *The Life of . . . William Cavendish, Duke of Newcastle*.

Bulstrode WHITELOCKE: *Memorials of the English Affairs*. London, 1682 and Oxford, 1853.

CHAPTER 5

Sir J. BERKENHEAD: *Mercurius Aulicus*. Gives some information about Ripple Field, taken apparently from the letters of Cavaliers present.

S. A. H. BURNE (Editor): 'The Battle of Hopton Heath, 1643.' Transcribed from Sutherland Papers, Vol. 2, fol. 69, preserved in Dunrobin Castle Library. The Staffordshire Record Society. 1936.

ANON. (?Sir Bernard DE GOMME): 'His Highness Prince Rupert's late beating up the Rebels' quarters at Postcomb and Chinnor.' Leonard Lichfield. Oxford. 1643. The best account of Chalgrove Field.

Sir Samuel LUKE (I. G. Philip, .M.A, Editor): *Journal of Sir Samuel Luke*. Luke was Scoutmaster-General to the Earl of Essex, and carried out his intelligence duties with considerable efficiency. These reports of his spies cover the period 9 Feb., 1643 to 29 March, 1644. The Oxfordshire Record Society, 1947, 1950, and 1952–1953. The originals are in the Bodleian.

(H. G. Tibbutt, Editor): *Calendar of the Five Civil War letter Books of Sir Samuel Luke,* for future publication by the Bedfordshire Historical Record Society is complementary to those edited by Mr. Philip. The originals are in the B.M.

J. WASHBOURNE: *Bibliotheca Gloucestrensis: a collection of . . . tracts relating to the county and city of Gloucester during the civil war*. Gloucester. 1825. Gives one of the two contemporary accounts of Ripple Field.

Lieut.-Colonel P. YOUNG: 'The Battle of Hopton Heath. 19 March, 1643.' *A.H.R.*, 1955, p. 35. Gives the sources and details of the Royalist units present.

CHAPTER 6

Richard ATKYNS: *The Vindication of . . .* London. 1669. The military parts of this work have been edited by Lieut.-Colonel P. Young in *A.H.R.*, Vol. XXV, 1957, under the title of 'The Praying Captain – a Cavalier's Memoirs'. Atkyns fought at Lansdown, Roundway Down and elsewhere.

Sir Bernard DE GOMME: 'Bristoll taken by Prince Rupert: Julye 26, 1643.' Transcribed in *A.H.R.*, Vol. IV, p. 180 (1925), with an Introduction by Professor Sir Charles Firth, and notes by Lieut.-Colonel J. H. Leslie (Maps and Plans). De Gomme was one of the foremost military engineers of his day. His account, which is detailed, is a thoroughly business-like and professional piece of work – in glaring contrast with most contemporary descriptions of operations in the civil war.

Lord HOPTON: 'Bellum Civile.' This work includes accounts of Lansdown and Roundway Down by Colonel Walter Slingsby, which are every bit as valuable as Hopton's accounts.

T.T.: E.60 (12) and E.61 (6).

Sir William WALLER: 'Recollections.' Scattered anecdotes of little value.

Lieut.-Colonel P. YOUNG: 'The Royalist Army at the Battle of Roundway Down, 13th July, 1643.' Map. *A.H.R.*, 1953, p. 127. Prints Sir John Byron's account from B.M.1103.d.77(5).

CHAPTER 7

Walter MONEY, F.S.A.: *The Battles of Newbury.* London. 1881. Money had great local knowledge, and reprints several eye-witness accounts, including narratives by Sir John Byron and the anonymous officer who commanded the Royalist outposts on the night before the battle. The dispositions shown on his maps are largely imaginary. An antiquarian rather than a military book.

T.T.: E.69 (2 and 10).

John WASHBOURNE: *Bibliotheca Gloucestrensis.* A valuable collection of seventeenth-century tracts. Two volumes. Gloucester. 1823. Besides accounts of the siege of Gloucester, this work reprints 'A True Relation of the late Expedition . . . for the Relief of Gloucester with the Description of the Fight at Newbury' and Serjeant Henry Foster's 'True and Exact Relation' which describes the adventures of the London Trained Bands.

CHAPTER 8

Professor ABBOTT: Prints the Parliamentarian accounts of Gainsborough.

Sir Thomas FAIRFAX: Short Memorial.

Earl of MANCHESTER: Letter describing Winceby. *Lords Journals*, vi, 255.

Sir C. R. MARKHAM: *Life of the Great Lord Fairfax.*

Basil N. RECKITT: *Charles the First and Hull, 1639–1645.* London. 1952.

T.T.: E.71 (5; 22; 24 ('The Scottish Dove') and 25 ('The Parliament Scout.' No. 18)). 'An Exact Relation' Printed in Memorials of the Civil War; *Correspondence of the Fairfax family* . . . (Ed. R. Bell.) London. 1849.

Sir William WIDDRINGTON: 'Letter to Newcastle.' Printed by Rushworth. This brief account is the only Royalist authority for the battle of Winceby.

CHAPTER 9

Rev. G. N. GODWIN: *The Civil War in Hampshire.* Revised Edition. London. 1904. Useful for Hopton's winter campaign against Waller, but rather badly put together.

Lord HOPTON: 'Bellum Civile.'

T.T.: E.40 (9 and 13).

Edward WALSINGHAM: *Brittanicae Virtutis Imago.*

Rev. J. WEBB and Rev. T. W. WEBB (Editors): 'Military Memoir of Colonel John Birch,' Camden Society, 1873. The Colonel, an energetic officer, played a prominent part at Alton, Arundel and Cheriton.

CHAPTER 10

? Sir Bernard DE GOMME: *His Highnesse Prince Rupert's raising of the siege at Newarke.* Oxford. 1644. A detailed Royalist account, by one of Prince Rupert's staff.

Life of Newcastle: Sir Charles Firth's edition gives what little information there is about the battle of Hilton.

J. R. PHILLIPS: *Memoirs of the Civil War in Wales and the Marches.* Vol. II (Documents) prints Sir Thomas Fairfax's letter to Essex, which may be considered the official despatch; Lord Byron's account, sent to Ormonde – a disingenuous document – and a clear narrative by Colonel Sir Robert Byron. See also Fairfax's 'Short Memorial'.

G. Ormerod: *History of the County Palatine.* 1882. Contains nearly all the sources for Nantwich.

T.T.: E.38 (10).

R. Thoroton: *Antiquities of Nottinghamshire.* London. 1677. Gives Lieut.-Colonel Bury's account of Newark, the best narrative from the Parliamentarian side.

A. C. Wood: *Nottinghamshire in the Civil War.* Oxford. 1937. Maps. Useful for sources.

Major P. Young: 'The Royalist Army at the Relief of Newark.' *A.H.R.*, Vol. XXX, 1952. Analyses the composition of the armies and the reasons for Prince Rupert's success.

CHAPTER 11

C.S.P.

Symond's Diary. In Oxoniensia. Vol. III, 1938.

Miss M. R. Toynbee, m.a. and J. J. Leeming: *Cropredy Bridge.*

Sir Edward Walker: *Historical Discourses.*

CHAPTER 12

E. Broxap: *The Great Civil War in Lancashire, 1642–51.* Manchester. 1910.

Carte MSS: X.664: (Bodleian Library.) Account of Prince Rupert's March into Lancashire.

C.S.P.: Useful for the campaign, but has little about the actual battle.

Sir Thomas Fairfax: Short Memorial.

C. H. Firth: 'Marston Moor.' *Transactions of the Royal Historical Society.* New Series. Vol. XII, 1898. This article is indispensable. Firth discusses the numbers and the composition of each army; the order in which they were drawn up; the authorities. He gives de Gomme's plan of the Royalist order of battle, and an appendix of contemporary documents: and shows that Clarendon's account, written in about 1670, is worthless.

J.P.R.M.: Particularly useful for the Marston Moor campaign.

Rushworth: Prints the official – if disingenuous – despatch from the three Parliamentarian generals to the Committee of Both Kingdoms.

T.T.: E.2 (14); E.3 (17); E.54 (7, 8, 11, and 19).

John Vicars: *Parliamentary Chronicle.* (Part III, 268.) Based on the narrative of Simeon Ashe, one of Manchester's chaplains – a man of known integrity.

Leonard WATSON: 'More Exact Relation of the late Battaile neere Yorke'. Watson was Scoutmaster-General to Manchester's army.

CHAPTER 13

C.S.P.:

COATE: *Cornwall in the Great Civil War.*

John RUSHWORTH: *Historical Collections.* Rushworth is particularly useful for the Parliamentary accounts of Lostwithiel.

Symond's Diary:

Sir Edward WALKER: *Historical Discourses.*

CHAPTER 14

Simeon ASHE: 'A True Relation . . .' (*T.T.*, E.22 (10)).

C.S.P.: Particularly useful for the movements of the Parliamentarian armies prior to the battle.

Camden Society: New Series. No. 12. 'Quarrel between the Earl of Manchester and Cromwell.'

Sir C. H. FIRTH (Editor): *Memoirs of Edmund Ludlow.* Ludlow's cavalry regiment was on Manchester's wing.

Walter MONEY: *The First and Second Battles of Newbury.*

John RUSHWORTH: *Historical Collections.* Prints several Parliamentarian despatches describing Second Newbury.

Symond's Diary: Fills out Walker's narrative.

T.T.: E.14 (16).

Sir Edward WALKER: *Historical Discourses.* The Royalist official account.

CHAPTER 15

C.S.P.

Sir Bernard DE GOMME: Map in the British Museum. Add. MS. 16370. De Gomme had evidently seen Sprigge's map, and, while accepting his version of the Parliamentarian order of battle, set out to give a more correct version of the Royalist dispositions. This map has never been published, though Warburton used it.

D. PARSONS (Editor): *The Diary of Sir Henry Slingsby.* London. 1836. Slingsby was one of Newcastle's colonels who continued the struggle after the disaster at Marston Moor.

Joshua SPRIGGE: *Anglia Rediviva.* Includes an interesting picture map of Naseby.

T.T.: E.288 (15, 20, 22, 25, 27, 28, and 38).

Sir Edward WALKER: *Historical Discourses.*

R

CHAPTER 16

J. J. ALEXANDER, M.A. and W. R. HOOPER: *The History of Great Torrington in the County of Devon*. Sutton, Surrey. 1948.

Bulstrode's Memoirs: Bulstrode served on Goring's staff at Langport.

Canon R. H. MORRIS, D.D., F.S.A.: *The Siege of Chester, 1643–1646*. Chester. 1924. Gives full details of the battle of Rowton Heath, including sources.

D. M. ROSS, M.A.: *Langport and its Church*. Langport. 1911. Useful for local knowledge, and also indicates the various authorities.

Joshua SPRIGGE: *Anglia Rediviva*.

T.T.: E.261 (4); E.292 (28 and 30); E.293 (3); E.293 (8 and 17).

Indexes

(a) GENERAL INDEX

Abbreviations: H—Horse, F—Foot, D—Dragoons, *—Persons who changed sides.

(b) INDEX OF PERSONS AND UNITS TAKING PART IN THE WAR

(i) ROYALISTS

ROYALIST BRIGADES, REGIMENTS AND TROOPS

(ii) PARLIAMENTARIANS

PARLIAMENTARIAN REGIMENTS, UNITS AND FORMATIONS

(c) INDEX OF PLACES